DICTIONARY OF SATANISM

DICTIONARY OF SATANISM

by

WADE BASKIN

PHILOSOPHICAL LIBRARY

New York

517106167
Copyright © MCMLXXII by Philosophical Library, Inc.
Library of Congress Catalog Card Number: 75-155971
All rights reserved. No part of this book may be reproduced
or utilized in any form or by any means, electronic or mechanical,
including photocopying, recording, or by any information storage
and retrieval system, without permission in writing from the
publisher. Inquiries should be addressed to: BONANZA BOOKS,
a division of Crown Publishers, Inc., 419 Park Avenue South,
New York, New York, 10016.
This edition is published by BONANZA BOOKS.
a division of Crown Publishers, Inc.
by arrangement with Philosophical Library, Inc.
   b c d e f g h
Manufactured in the United States of America.

ISBN 978-0-8065-2977-6

Printed in the United States of America

PREFACE

Since paleolithic times the ever-imminent enslavement of man by the powers of Evil has been a part of the human predicament. The words of one song now in vogue among the devotees of acid rock are all too revealing: 'My name is Lucifer. . . . Please take my hand. . . . The sun, the moon, the stars all bear my seal. . . . Your love for me has just got to be real.' In the song Lucifer promises to share his love until the end of time, assuring the listener that whoever follows him will have no regrets. It is obvious that the pursuit of sensual pleasures, resistance to restraints in any form, the triumph of egoism over altruism, of materialism over spiritualism — all are responses to tendencies deeply rooted in man's psyche.

The tremendous current interest in occult phenomena is widespread and embraces all levels of society and sophistication. Popular novels, films, music, magazines, and newspapers, particularly those of the underground type, produce a constant stream of Satanic encounters, first-hand accounts of presumably inexplicable situations involving spirits, witchcraft, and other Satanic phenomena in their widest applications. Dark beliefs that have haunted men for millennia have sprung into new life. Everywhere there is a passionate eagerness to discover and test, to probe the outer fringes of knowledge, to draw new assurances from superstitions, esoteric cults, and Cabalistic teachings that lack scientific verification. From the gruesome murder of Sharon Tate to the pay-as-you-join Church of Satan administered by Anton Lavey, the omnipresence of the cult of Evil is undeniable.

The present work is intended to serve as a concise but comprehensive reference for the casual reader. It embraces concepts, issues, people, places, and events associated through the ages with Satan in his multifaceted but continuous manifestations. I am fully aware that it cannot provide answers to all the questions in the mind of the reader, yet I hope that it will provide him with reliable information in many areas and with a basis for further explorations in others.

For his help in preparing this book, I am indebted to my son, Wade.

W. B.

Satan Presiding at the Sabbath
(From Paul Christian, *Histoire de la magie*)

The Garden of Delights
Detail of Satan's Throne
Hieronymus Bosch

A

A. .A.˙. Symbol of the secret society founded by Aleister Crowley and known as the Argentinum Astrum.

AAHLA In Egyptian religion, one division of the Amenti, or lower regions.

AAMON One of the three demons in the service of Satanachia, commander of the first legion of Hell.

AARON Byzantine magician reputed to have possessed the *Key of Solomon*. He is said to have been an adept in the black arts, commanding legions of demons.

AARON One of the earliest sketches of a medieval Jew (1277) is labeled *Aaron fil diaboli*. 'Aaron, son of the Devil.'

AARON'S ROD A magic wand embellished by a serpent. When cast before the Egyptian Pharaoh, it turned into a serpent.

AATS In Egyptian religion, the domain of the dead was divided into fourteen or fifteen divisions, each called an aat and presided over by a different deity.

ABADDON The leader of the demon locusts described in the ninth chapter of the Book of Revelation. This is the Hebrew name of the Angel of the Bottomless Pit. The meaning of the Hebrew word is 'the destroyer.' In Greek he is identified as Apollyon, the name by which he is called in *Pilgrim's Progress.*

ABADIR A title bestowed by the Carthaginians on their principal deities. In the Punic language, the name means 'mighty father.'

ABARIS A priest of Apollo renowned for his prophetic gifts.

ABASTOR One of the horses of Pluto, god of the underworld in classical mythology.

ABATHAKATHI An African enchanter. See Zulus.

ABATUR In Gnosticism, the father of the Demiurgus, the creator of the world. In occult teachings, he is the third Logos.

ABBA AMONA In the Cabala, the occult names of the two higher sephiroth of the upper triad.

ABBEY OF THELEME Society founded in Sicily, in 1920, by Aleister Crowley. The licentious behavior of its members discredited the society.

ABELLION In Celtic mythology, an important deity. He was identified with the Olympian god Apollo.

ABERDEEN WITCHES A witch-hunting craze that swept over Aberdeen following publication of King James' *Demonology* in 1957 resulted in the burning of twenty-four persons.

ABGURVADEL The magic blade of Icelandic wizardry was used in occult operations.

ABHAMSI In mysticism, the four orders of being: gods, demons, pitris, men.

ABIGOR Demon who commands sixty infernal legions. He appears as a handsome cavalier on a winged horse. He knows the future and all the secrets of war.

AB-I-HAYAT In mysticism, the water of immortality.

ABLANATHANALBA In Gnosticism, a term similar to 'Abracadabra.' It reads the same from either end and was used as a charm in Egypt. It may mean 'Thou art a father to us.'

ABRACADABRA A magic word of unknown origin. It is widely supposed to ward off evil, sickness, and death. Quintus Serenus Sammonicus, who accompanied the Emperor Severus to Britain in the year 208, mentions it in a poem as a cure against tertian fever. Dejae mentions it in his *Journal of the Plague Year*. Eliphas Levi discusses the 'magic triangle' at length and connects it with other occult concepts, including the symbolism of the Taro. For best results, the word should be arranged in the shape of a triangle and worn around the neck. The word is commonly written:

  A B R A C A D A B R A
   A B R A C A D A B R
    A B R A C A D A B
     A B R A C A D A
      A B R A C A D
       A B R A C A
        A B R A C
         A B R A
          A B R
           A B
            A

The word is supposed to be a corruption of the sacred Gnostic term 'Abraxas,' a magic formula meaning 'Hurt me not.'

ABRAHAM THE JEW A German Jew who was at once an alchemist, magician, and philosopher. Born in Mayence in 1362, he is supposed to have learned by word of mouth secrets transmitted by the Egyptian occultists, particularly Abramelin.

ABRAMELIN A sorcerer known through Samuel Mathers' translation of a manuscript written in French in the eighteenth century but purporting to be a French translation of a Hebrew document, completed in 1458. The central doctrine of *The Sacred Magic of Abramelin the Mage* is that the cosmos is populated by hosts of angels and demons. The demons work under the direction of the angels. Man stands between the angelic and the demonic forces. To him are attached a guardian angel and a wicked demon. Initiates can control the demons.

ABRASAX In demonology, the word designates a demon with the head of a cock, a huge belly, and a knotted tail. Also, Abraxas.

ABRAXAS A mystic term in vogue among the Gnostics. It can be traced to Basilides of Alexandria, who used it in the second century as a title for the divinity. In Greek numeration, the seven letters of the word denote the number 365, the days of the solar year, representing a cycle of divine action. Moreover, 365 was supposed to be the sum total of the spirits who emanated from God. Occultists believe that the word has magical powers when engraved on stones or gems and worn as a charm.

ABRED In Celtic cosmogony, the force opposing Cythrawl, the power of evil.

ABSTINENCE Ritual magic requires careful preparation. To summon a demon, the magician first prepares himself by abstinence or by some other means which will heighten his powers. Eliphas Levi recommends thorough cleansing before undertaking a magical operation, a minimum of sleep, and abstinence from sex, intoxicating drink, and meat.

ABYDOS The ancient holy city of Osiris, god of the dead. It lies two hundred miles north of Luxor and was the sanctuary of an even older mortuary god before Osiris came to dwell there. Kings delighted to honor the place, and people came from all over Egypt to lay their bones in its sanctified ground, hoping thereby to win greater glory in the next world. The exact location of the tomb of Osiris was known to the devout.

ABYSS In Egyptian religion, a descriptive name for the abode of the dead. In Babylonian thought, it was the primeval chaos from which the universe evolved.

ABZU (ABSU) In Sumerian religion, the watery abyss, abode of the god Enki. In Chaldean mysticism, Absu is the dwelling place of Ab, father of the source of the waters of knowledge.

ACCUSER (THE) One of the names of Satan.

ACERSECOMUS A term denoting the uncut hair on the head of the god Apollo.

ACHELOUS In Greek religion, a river god. The Etruscans used masks of Achelous to protect buildings against the powers of evil.

ACHERON In classical mythology, one of the rivers of Hades. It was called the River of Woe.

ACMON In Greek mythology, a god who existed before the creation of Heaven.

ACONITE A cardiac and respiratory sedative. It is a common ingredient of flying ointment used by medieval witches.

ACRATOPOTES A name applied to Bacchus. In Greek, the expression means 'a drinker of wine.'

ADAD A Babylonian god of wind and storm. Also known as Rammon and, earlier in Palestine and Syria, as Hadad.

ADAMITES In 1925, a group of Adamites were discovered near Oroville, California. Anna Rhodes was the priestess of the cult. She believed that she and her husband were Eve and Adam. They held naked orgies in a farmyard renamed the Garden of Eden.

ADAM KADMON A Hebraic expression associated with the Aramaic expression Adam Kadmaah. Of mystical significance, it denotes the prototype of mankind.

ADAMUS EXUL A tragedy written by Hugo Grotius. See: Temptation of Adam.

ADEPTUS EXEMPTUS One of the ten grades in Alesteir Crowley's cabalistic system. It corresponds to sephira 4, or Jupiter, and completes the student's training in practical magic.

ADEPTUS MAJOR One of the ten grades established by Aleister Crowley in his cabalistic system. It corresponds to sephira 5, or Mars. Here the adept obtains a general mastery of magic.

ADEPTUS MINOR One of the grades or ranks established in Alesteir Crowley's cabalistic system. It corresponds to sephira 6, the sun, and involves the attainment of 'the Knowledge and Conversation of the Holy Guardian Angel,' a rite of sex-magic.

ADONIS In Greek legend, a youth loved by Aphrodite, who lamented his death each year. Although he was required to descend to the kingdom of the dead, he was allowed to return to the upper earth to live with Aphrodite during spring and summer. His death and rebirth symbolize the vegetation cycle and have their counterparts in the myths of other cultures.

ADRAMELECH Mathers lists Adramelech as one of the ten evil sephiroth, commanded by Sammael, the angel of poison. Children were sacrificed to Adramelech in ancient times. His cult probably originated in Syria and later was introduced into Samaria.
In demonology, he is regarded as the grand chancellor of Hell, superintendent of the Devil's wardrobe, and president of the high council. He reveals himself in the shape of a mule or a peacock.

ADY, THOMAS Author of one of the most rational protests against witch-hunters, entitled *A Candle in the Dark, or a Treatise concerning the nature of witches and witchcraft: being advice to the judges, sheriffs, justices of the peace and grandjurymen what to do before they pass sentence on such as are arraigned for their lives as witches* (1656).

AEACUS In Greek mythology, one of the three judges in Hades.

AEGIPAN The god Pan, represented as having the feet of a goat.

AELLO One of the three dire Harpies of Greek mythology.

AELURUS In Egyptian religion, the cat-god. He is represented as a human figure with a cat's head.

AERIAL DEMONS One of six classes of demons identified by medieval theologians. They roam through the air but remain close to human beings. They can fashion bodies for themselves from thin air. Moved by passion like men, they can cause natural disturbances. They can be invoked by sorcerers and often change their shape.

AEROLITE A story meteorite presumed to be of divine origin and worthy of veneration. Aerolites were worshiped in Phoenicia, Syria and elsewhere in the ancient world.

AERUSCUTORES The Phrygian designation for the priests of Cybele. In Rome, they were called Galli.

AESCHYLUS Greek playwright (525-456 B.C.) whose *Eumenides* is permeated with allusions to demonical powers. The ghost of Clytemnestra, slain by Orestes, invokes the powers of Hell:
Awake, ye powers of Hell!
The wandering ghost
That once was Clytemnestra calls — Arise!

AESIR The Nordic pantheon, including the supreme god Odin.

AESMA In Zoroastrianism, the evil spirit of anger that inspires vengeance.

AESYMNETES An epithet of Bacchus, god of revelry.

AFRASIAB A serpent identified by the Scythians with the archfiend Ahriman.

AFRICAN BUILDERS' ARCHITECTS A mystical association founded by C. F. Koffen (1734-1797). Its purpose was to supply Egyptian, Christian, and Templar mysteries to its initiates.

AFTERLIFE In the earliest Greek records, the dead are thought to have their abode in a dark and grim realm. In mystery cults, the concept of metempsychosis was generally maintained.

AGALIAREPT Grand general of the infernal spirits. He commands Buer, Gusoyn, and Botis. He has the power to discover all secrets and unveil the greatest mysteries. He commands the second legion of spirits.

AGAMEDE A witch mentioned in Homer's *Iliad*.

AGARES One of the three demons who serve Lucifuge, Prime minister of Lucifer.

AGARTHA Vast underground realm ruled by the King of the World.

AGATHODEMON A Greek term designating a beneficent demon that accompanies a person throughout his life. Socrates had such a demon.

AGAURES Grand duke of the eastern region of Hell. He commands thirty-one legions, teaches languages, causes terrestrial spirits to dance, and routs enemies.

AGDISTIS An aspect of Cybele, primarily androgynous.

AGE OF AQUARIUS A term that has become almost synonymous with cults that glorify evil and the supernatural. It was popularized in the late sixties by the play *Hair*. See: Aquarius.

AGELASTUS Epithet of Pluto, god of the underworld. In Greek, the name means 'not laughing.'

AGE OF DEMONS According to Hesiod, demons live ten times as long as the phoenix which, in turn, lives ten times as long as a man, or 680,000 years. Plutarch notes that demons are also subject to disease and sickness, and reduces their age to 9,720.

AGLA A mystic term used for invoking demons. It is formed from the initial Hebrew letters in the expression meaning 'God will be great forever': *Aieth Gadol Leolam Adonai*.

AGLAOPHOTIS A herb growing in the deserts of Arabia and used to invoke demons.

AGLAUROS A mystery cult that flourished in ancient Athens. Aglauros was the principal deity of the cult.

AGNES First person accused of witchcraft in England. She was exonerated in 1209, after she had passed the test by red-hot iron.

AGNI HOTRI In the religion of the ancient Aryans, these were the priests of the god of fire, associated with the swastika.

AGONACES An ancient sorcerer reputed to have lived 7,000 B.C. and taught witchcraft to Zoroaster.

AGRAMAINIO The great spirit of Evil praised by Giosue Carducci in his hymn to Satan ('Inno a Satana,' 1863).

AGRICULTURAL RITES In pagan religions, agricultural rites were performed in order to win the favor of the gods. The basic need was to secure abundant harvests. The rituals included dancing around the fields and sprinkling the ground with sacrificial blood, sometimes human blood. Cattle were also offered to the deities who presided over the productivity of the earth. Phallic ceremonies were in vogue, as symbolic of fertility. Incantations, invocations to the chthonic deities were regular features of the vegetation cults. In addition, suppliants marched in procession through the fields while prayers were offered to the divinities in charge of the growing, ripening and mature crops. Rain ceremonies especially were elaborate. They included magic formulas, thunderous music, and, ultimately, joyful dancing and feasting.

All such vegetation cults, despite ethnic and geographical variations, were fundamentally identical. They sought the beneficent cooperation of the powerful, unseen forces of nature.

AGRIPPA A grimoire shaped like a man and written in black on purple pages. It should be hidden in a special room. Initially it was the property of priests alone, but its owners were easily identified since they reeked of sulphur and smoke.

AGRIPPA VON NETTESHEIM Henry Cornelius von Nettesheim (1486-1535) was a German diplomat, physician, philosopher, and author. He made religion an amalgam of Cabalistic mysticism, neo-Platonism, and Christianity. He traveled widely, lectured in Italy on Hermes Trismegistus, and wrote *De occulta philosophia* (1510), a defense of magic and a synthesis of occultism and science. In his book he explains how to summon spirits:

If you would call any evil spirit to the circle, it first behooveth us to consider and to know his nature, to which of the planets he agreeth, and what offices are distributed to him from the planet.

This being known, let there be sought out a place fit and proper for his invocation, according to the nature of the planet, and the quality of the offices of the same spirit, as near as the same may be done.

For example, if his power be over the sea, rivers or floods, then let a place be chosen on the shore, and so of the rest. . . .

These things being considered, let there be a circle framed at the place elected, as well for the defense of the invocant as for the confirmation of the spirit. In the circle itself there are to be written the general divine names, and those things which do yield defense unto us; the divine names which do rule the said planet, with the offices of the spirit himself; and the names, finally of the spirits which bear rule and are able to bind and constrain the spirit which we intend to call.

AGRUSADAPARIKSAY Ancient Hindu treatise on occultism.

AGUERRE, PIERRE D' Sorcerer who, during the time of Henri IV, used witchcraft to kill several persons. Witnesses testified that he had used a golden baton to conduct the Sabbat.

AHASUERUS The Wandering Jew.

AHHARU In Assyrian demonology, these are evil vampires.

AHRIMAN In the dualistic doctrine of Zoroaster, Ahriman (Angra Mainyu, the 'Destructive One') is the principle of evil. As the Evil Spirit, the great destroyer, and the source of all evil, he is the arch enemy of Ahura Mazda, the 'Wise Lord.' Eventually, a great world catastrophe will signal the defeat and disappearance of Ahriman. According to Zoroaster, Angra Mainyu and his twin Spenta Mainyu are the eternal antagonists. In the Avesta, Ahura Mazda is identified with the beneficent spirit.

AIGUILLETTE The French word for ligature.

AITA In Etruscan religion, the underworld.

AIWASS The spirit who dictated Aleister Crowley's first important work on magic, the *Book of the Law* (1904).

AIX-EN-PROVENCE NUNS Sister Madeleine de Demandolx was bewitched by Father Louis Gaufridi and later underwent exorcism under the direction of the Grand Inquisitor Sébastien Michaélis. Some time after she entered a convent in 1607, she began having convulsions. Her symptoms spread to other nuns, culminating in one of the most notorious investigations of the seventeenth century.

AIX-EN-PROVENCE French city, scene of a famous outbreak of diabolical possession during the first part of the seventeenth century. Madeleine de Demandolx de la Palud stated that her ex-confessor, Father Louis Gaufridi, had been her lover at the Ursuline convent at Marseille. Transferred to Aix in 1609, she suffered convulsions and diabolical attacks. Father J. B. Momillon tried in vain to exorcise the 'green demon' Gaufridi had imposed upon her. She contaminated five other nuns.
After Sébastien Michaélis, the Grand Inquisitor, failed in his attempts at exorcism, François Domptius took charge. One of the nuns, Louise Capeau, acknowledged that she was under the control of three demons: Verrine, Grésil, and Sonnillon. Madeleine was possessed by 6,666

demons led by Belzebuth. Gaufridi finally confessed under torture that he had signed a pact with the Devil. Though he later recanted, he was burned alive on April 30, 1611.

AKAR In Egyptian religion, the proper name of that division of the infernal regions corresponding to Hell.

AKIKEL One of the leaders of the angels who, according to the Book of Enoch, swore allegiance to Samiaza.

AKO MANA In Zoroastrian religion, the collective evil mind of men who are under the influence of the Druj.

AL-AIT Phoenician god of fire. Al-Ait is a mystical figure in Koptic occultism.

ALAL In Assyrian demonology, evil spirits. They are demons of destruction.

ALASTOR Chief executor of the decrees of the infernal court presided over by Lucifer.

ALBERT THE GREAT Dominican scholar (1193-1280) whose interests extended to the realm of the occult. Tradition credits him with summoning up the dead and writing occult treatises. Also known as Albertus Magnus.

ALBIGENSES A sect that arose in Italy and southern France in the eleventh century. Also called New Manicheans and Chatari, they taught the transmigration of the souls of the unperfected. They were almost exterminated by the Inquisition.

ALCHEMY The forerunner of chemistry seems to have originated in Alexandria during the first century A.D. when the practical art of metallurgy developed by the Egyptians was fused with the philosophical speculations of Greek philosophy and the mysticism of the Middle Eastern religions. Hermes Trismegistus was credited with originating the art of alchemy.

Although in the beginning alchemy was a practical series of chemical operations based on the accepted theory of nature and matter, the mystically minded soon developed alchemical ideas and stressed divine revelation, the search for the divine elixir, and the secret of immortality. The pseudo-science reached its zenith in the Middle Ages, when learned men like Roger Bacon believed in the transmutation of base metals into gold. History records that more than one imposter was put to death for failing to produce the philosopher's stone.

ALCHIDAEL Name assumed by Mme. Thibault, High Priestess of Carmel Church at Lyon, France.

ALDOVRANDI, ULYSSES Physician and naturalist (1522-1605). In his *Monstrorum Historia* (1642), the Italian scholar expressed the opinion that monsters are born of the union of women and incubi.

ALEURANTHROPY Transformation into a cat.

ALEXANDER III King of Scotland. A specter is supposed to have appeared at his nuptial ball in 1285 and to have announced his impending death. He died in a hunting accident the same year.

ALIGAR One of three demons serving Fleuretty, lieutenant general of the legions of Hell.

ALI ILLAHIJA An Asiatic sect that practices the orgiastic rites associated with the ancient cult of Anahita.

ALKAHEST In alchemy, the universal solvent.

ALLATU In Sumero-Akkadian religion, one of the names of the evil demon, Death. He is the offspring and servant of Ereshkigal. His more familiar name is Namtar (Namtary). In Assyro-Babylonian religion, Allatu is the goddess of the underworld, consort of Bel, and later the consort of Nergal.

ALLEGIANCE TO SATAN A witches' Sabbat opened with a ritual of allegiance to Satan. Guazzo's *Compendium Maleficarum* (1626) describes the ritual:
When these members of the devil have met together, they light a foul and horrid fire. . . . They approach him to adore him, but not always in the same manner. Sometimes they bend their knees as suppliants, and sometimes they stand with their backs turned. . . . Going backwards like crabs, they put out their hands behind them to touch him in supplication.

ALL FOOLS' DAY April 1, when practical jokes are played on credulous victims. All Fools' Day originated in the Celtic cult of Arianrhod.

ALL HALLOW'S EVE (HALLOWEEN) A festival of Druidic origin, celebrated on October 31, on the evening before All Saints' Day. The Druids believed that Saman, the lord of death, on this occasion summoned the souls of evil men condemned to inhabit animal bodies. Witches, demons, and the spirits of the dead assemble on this night.

ALLIER, ELISABETH Demoniac successfully exorcised in 1639 by François Faconnet. The two demons who had possessed her for twenty years admitted that they had entered her body by means of a crust of bread which they had put into her mouth when she was seven. They fled from her body in the presence of the Holy Sacrament. The demons were named Orgeuil and Bonifarce.

ALOCER Grand duke of Hell, depicted as a horned horseman with the head of a lion. He commands thirty-six legions. His dragon-footed horse is enormous. He teaches the secrets of Heaven and the liberal arts.

ALOE A plant used by the ancient Semites to ward off evil spirits. Its flowers were hung from the door-lintel.

ALP See Mare.

ALPHONSUS DE SPINA Author of the first book ever printed on witchcraft: *Fortalicium Fidei* (Fortress of the Faith), printed in 1467.

ALRAUNE In Teutonic mythology, a female demon.

ALU A Mesopotamian demon with canine features. Some artists depicted him without legs, ears, or mouth. He preferred silence and darkness.

ALUQA A female demon who is at once a succubus and a vampire. She depletes men and causes them to commit suicide.

AMAM In Egyptian religion, the devourer of the dead.

AMAN One of the demons who possessed Sister Jeanne des Anges. Aman was among the first of the demons whom she managed to expel.

AMANE According to the Book of Enoch, one of the leaders of the two hundred angels who rebelled against God and swore allegiance to Samiaza.

AMBRONAY French village where St. Bernard chained the Devil. The ring used by St. Bernard is preserved in the local church.

AMBROSIUS CATHARINUS Initiator of the idea that Satan aspired to the office of Jesus Christ. See Lancelot Politi.

AMDUSCIAS Grand duke of Hell. He commands twenty-nine legions. He has the head of a unicorn but also appears in human form. He gives invisible concerts. Trees sway to the sound of his voice.

AMENTI In Egyptian religion, the land of the dead, conceived as a dark region resounding with lamentation, where the souls of the wicked remained forever. The Roman view of the underworld as depicted by the Poet Vergil is remarkably similar to it. According to the Egyptians, the soul enters the underworld, is conducted by Anubis to the hall of Osiris, is judged by 42 judges, and passes on to Aaru or is condemned to torment.

AMERS According to the Book of Enoch, one of the leaders of the two hundred angels who rebelled against God.

AMIANTHUS Fine silky asbestos, said to absorb maleficent influences.

AMINADAR One of the names of the Devil, according to St. John of the Cross.

AMMIT In Egyptian religion, the Eater of the Dead. Depicted as part crocodile, part hippopotamus, and part lion, he eats men's hearts after they have been weighed in the hall of judgment and found wanting.

AMMONIUS SACCAS Alexandrian philosopher who lived between the second and third centuries A.D. He rejected Christianity because he could not find in it anything superior to the older religions.

AMON (AAMON) Supreme divinity of the Egyptians, became a marquis of Hell in the Satanic tradition. The wolf-headed demon with a serpent's tail vomits flame and commands forty legions. Sometimes he takes the shape of a human with an owl's head. He knows both the past and the future.

A. M. S. G. Counterfeit of the motto of the Jesuit order. The first letters of the words *Ad majorem Satanae gloriam* ('to the greater glory of Satan') are used by Satanists in their rites. These letters are inscribed in intersecting triangles encompassing the head of a goat.

AMULETS Objects worn by a person to ward off evil influences. Examples include rings, scarabs, stones, the teeth of animals, ivory phalli, and plants.

AN An aspect of Re, the Egyptian sun god.

ANACHITIS A stone used for conjuring water spirits.

ANAHITA Persian goddess, identified with Cybele and Artemis, and known under this aspect as Mater Artemis or Artemis Anahita. Her cult was marked by the sacrifice of bulls (the taurobolium) and by sacred prostitution, performed by her attendants known as hierodouloi. The name of the goddess means 'the unsullied.'

ANANCITHIDUS A stone used for invoking demons.

ANANIA, JOHANNES LAURENTIUS Sixteenth-century demonographer. Author of *De Natura Daemonum* (On the Nature of Demons), published in Venice in 1581.

ANCIENT ONE The officiating priestess at a Black Mass generally was known as 'The Ancient One' even though she was usually young.

ANCIENT SERPENT The Devil.

ANDATE (ANDRASTE) A British goddess of victory to whom captured warriors were sacrificed.

ANDRAS Marquis of Hell. The owl-headed demon with the naked body of a winged angel rides a black wolf and brandishes a sword. He commands thirty legions.

ANDROID A human-shaped automaton. Among the most famous androids, some of which were said to be animated by the Devil, were Descartes' Francine and Hoffmann's Coppelia.

ANGEL OF AUGSBURG Agnes Bernauer, a beautiful woman, was born in Biberach about 1410. She was drowned as a witch in 1435. She worked as a servant in Augsburg before Albrecht, Duke of Bavaria, fell in love with her and, against the wishes of his father, recognized her as his wife. At the father's insistence, and in the absence of her husband, she was pronounced guilty of having bewitched Albrecht. German poets have immortalized her name.

ANGEL OF DEATH According to rabbinical commentaries on the Pentateuch, the Angel of Death (Sammael), in the form of the ancient serpent, tempted Eve to commit adultery, and became the father of Cain.

ANGEL OF LIGHT One of the names of Satan, based on Paul's second letter to the Corinthians (11:14): 'Satan himself is transformed into an angel of light.'

ANGEL-PEACOCK A name given to Satan by the Moslem sect of Sunnite-Saafites who worship him under the name of Iblis. The name recalls the belief that the Fallen Angel recovered his spiritual colors because his motives were lofty.

ANGERBODA In Norse mythology, a giant ogress. She is the wife of Loki and mother of Fenrir, Hel, and Ioermungandr.

ANGES, JEANNE DES See Loudun, Nuns of.

ANGITIA Italic goddess of serpents.

ANGRA MAINYU The spirit of Evil, identified in the Avesta as the son of the prophet Zoroaster. He transformed the Daeva of primitive Iranian paganism into a legion of wicked spirits. Angra mainyu, the 'Destructive One,' allies himself with destruction, deceit, darkness, and death. The struggle between him and Ahura Mazda makes up the history of the world. At the end of the twelve millenniums accorded to the world, another son of Zoroaster, Saoshyant, will usher in an era of eternal peace. See Ahriman.

ANIGUEL One of the grand dukes of hell.

ANIMAL SACRIFICES In ancient Greece, horses were sacrificed to Poseidon, swine to Demeter, goats to Dionysus and Apollo, and dogs to Hecate.

ANIMISM Worship of the spirit that animates all things. The primitive form of worship is based on the belief that all things possess a natural life or are endowed with souls.

ANITO Among the Bontoc Igorot, the maleficent spirit of a dead person. The anito causes sickness and death.

ANIZEL One of the grand dukes of Hell.

ANKH In Egyptian religion, a T-shaped cross surmounted by a loop. It symbolized life.

ANNUNAKI In Babylonian religion, the underworld judges of the dead.

ANOLIST Anciently, a diviner who conjured demons at an altar.

ANSUPEROMIN French sorcerer, notorious during the reign of Henri IV for his participation in witches' Sabbats.

ANTHROPOMANCY Divination by inspection of human entrails. Gilles de Rays (Rais) is supposed to have engaged in the practice of anthropomancy.

ANTHROPOPHAGY The practice of eating human flesh. Witches were supposed to engage in anthropophagy at the Sabbat. Marie de Sains testified at the trial of Gaufridi that she had slaughtered several children and eaten their hearts. De Lancre states that the bones of victims were preserved for as long as a year and cooked with herbs that softened them.

ANTICHRIST Christ's great adversary. The Catholic Church teaches that he will be an individual human personality whose activity will be directly linked with apostasy throughout the world before the second coming of Christ ends his dominion. Scriptural authority (I John 2; 18, 22; 4:3; II John 7; 2 Thes.) supports the view that he will rule the earth for some time before its destruction. St. Jerome states that he will be a man sired by a demon. Medieval scholastics such as Albertus Magnus and Thomas Aquinas held that the Antichrist will be born of the tribe of Dan in Babylon, will be circumcised in Jerusalem, and will be accepted as the long-awaited Messiah. He then will rebuild the temple and proclaim himself God. After three and a half years God will send Enoch and Elijah against the Antichrist, who will defeat their hosts. Christ will dispatch the archangel Michael to destroy the Antichrist on the Mount of Olives. Early Christians identified the Antichrist as Nero. Later Christians identified him variously as Mahomet, the Pope, Attila, Napoleon, Hitler, Stalin, etc. One prophecy fixed his arrival in 1524. Albert Dürer, Jean Duvet, and others were strongly influenced by the prediction. Tertullian and others refer to him as the 'Ape of God.' See Belial, Number of the Beast.

ANUBIS The jackal-headed Egyptian god of the dead. In the judgment hall of the gods, he presides over the weighing of human souls. Among the Greeks and Romans, he was identified with Cerberus, the three-headed dog.

ANUNNAKI Children of the Sumerian god An. In the realm of the dead they acted as judges.

ANWYL The Celtic world of the dead, corresponding to Greek Hades.

APAP The serpent of evil, as described in the Egyptian Book of the Dead. See Apep.

APE OF GOD Title used by Tertullian and others in referring to the antichrist. The disparaging name was also bestowed on Satan after he organized his own kingdom and began to imitate the divine institutions and organizations.

APEP In Egyptian religion, a monster serpent, servant to the evil god Set. Apep and other monsters daily obstructed the passage of Re. Crushed and destroyed, it revived daily, having been endowed with immortality. Also Apap, Apophis, Apepi.

APIS In Egyptian religion, a sacred bull, symbol of fertility. He was credited with oracular powers.

APOCALYPSE The last book of the New Testament, also called Revelation. Its obscure but poetic symbolism is the work of St. John. It comprises seven visions revealing the future of Christianity. The Beast of the Apocalypse figures prominently in the book. Albert Dürer produced fifteen remarkable engravings on the subject. See Satan's Fall, Number of the Beast.

APOCATASTASIS The great return of universal reconciliation which, according to Origen, will entail the ultimate salvation of the Devil.

APOCRYPHON IOHANNIS The *Secret Book of John*. This is a treatise, recently discovered, that belongs in the corpus of the Gnostic writings of Egypt.

APOLLONIUS OF TYANA A Pythagorean philosopher who flourished in the first century A.D. He traveled widely, lecturing on occultism, and gained a reputation throughout Asia Minor, where temples were dedicated to him. During the Middle Ages his reputation became legendary. His ghost is supposed to have been evoked by Eliphas Levi, in London, in 1854.

APOLLYON The Greek equivalent of the Hebrew name Abaddon, meaning 'the destroyer.' The Angel of the Bottomless Pit is mentioned in the fifth chapter of the Book of Revelation as the chief of the demon locusts. He is also called Apollyon in *Pilgrim's Progress*.

APOTROPAIC CEREMONIES In pagan religions, these ceremonies, involving incantations, spells, and sacrifices, were intended to divert or drive away malefic gods or spirits that might prove harmful to human life and activities.

APOTROPAION A charm that protects one against evil spirits or the Evil Eye.

APOTROPAISM A defensive or protective form of magic. By means of incantations, spells, rituals, and amulets apotropaic magic aims to ward off malefic forces.

APPARITIONS Hallucinatory images of persons, living or dead. They are most likely to appear on Friday night. See Phantom, Poltergeist, Specter.

APPELLATION OF BACCHUS When an initiate in the Orphic mystery cult performed all the rites and ate the living raw flesh of an animal, thus absorbing Dionysus himself, the god of life, he became a Bacchus. After that, the Orphic votary abstained from meat.

APSARAS In Vedic writings, an undine or waternymph. Gautama Buddha was tempted by legions of these big-breasted nymphs. In occultism, an apsara is a sleep-producing plant or an inferior force of nature.

APULEIUS Platonic philosopher of the second century. His book, *The Golden Ass,* relates the adventures of a man changed into a donkey and reveals much concerning the mysteries of Isis. Medieval demonographers turned him into a great enchanter.

AQHAT A Canaanite myth known through texts discovered in Ras Shamra. In the myth, dying and reviving gods of fertility are symbolized by the disappearance and return of rainfall.

AQUARIUS The approaching Age of Aquarius, beginning about the year 2,000 is supposed to be marked by international harmony. The modern astrologer's Great Year lasts approximately 26,000 years. Its twelve sections correspond to the signs of the zodiac. It is generally agreed that the Age of Leo, when sun worship predominated, ended about the year 8,000 B.C.; the Age of Cancer, marked by moon cults, around 6,000 B.C.; the Age of Gemini, marked by the influence of Mercury and the invention of writing, in 4,000 B.C.; the Age of Taurus, which brought in the worship of the bull or the Golden Calf, in 2,000 B.C.; the Age of Aries, conspicuous for ram worship, about the time of Christ's birth; and that the Age of Pisces, marked by the growth of Christianity, is now drawing to a close. Aquarius, the celestial Water Carrier, symbolizes service to others. See Age of Aquarius.

AQUATICS One of six classes of demons identified by medieval theologians, following the suggestions of John Wierus. They wreak havoc at sea. When they take on bodies, they often appear as females, and as nereids, nymphs, or naiads.

AQUINAS, THOMAS The great Italian scholastic teacher (1225-1274), called 'The Angelic Doctor,' stated in his *Sententiae*: 'Magicians perform miracles through personal contracts made with demons.'

ARALLU The underworld of the Semitic tribes inhabiting ancient Mesopotamia. It was a great city shrouded in darkness and dust. The souls of the dead passed through the tomb and descended into Arallu, where they drank dirty water and ate dust.

ARANI A disc-like wooden vehicle in which the Brahmins generated fire by friction, using a pramantha, a stick which symbolized the male generator. The esoteric 'womb of the world' is a swastika used in a mystic ceremony replete with secret meanings.

ARBATEL A sixteenth-century handbook of magic. It deals with the nature and functions of the spirits that pervade the cosmos.

ARCADIAN RITUALS Human beings were frequently sacrificed to the gods in Arcadian rituals.

ARGENTINUM ASTRUM Society founded by Aleister Crowley after he was expelled from the Order of the Golden Dawn. The name Argentinum Astrum ('Silver Star') was generally not used. Instead, members of the society used this designation: A.·. A.·..

ARCHAEUS In Greek, the word means 'the ancient.' It is used by Cabalists to name the oldest manifested deity.

ARCHER-WIZARDS Makers of spellbound images. They often tried to insert into their waxen figures objects which had been parts of the intended victim—hair or the parings of nails. They flourished in the sixteenth century.

ARCHETYPE C. G. Jung and his followers believe in the existence of archetypes—symbolic ideas derived from the experience of the race and present in the individual's unconscious. The archetype controls the individual's ways of perceiving the world. The Devil is a universal archetype.

ARCHITECT (GREAT) See Great Architect.

ARCHONS The Gnostic sects, convinced that the world was thoroughly evil, thought that the supreme God was far away in a distant heaven. The world was assumed to be governed by lesser deities hostile to God or unaware of his existence. These deities were called Archons.

ARDAT-LILI In Semitic legend, a female demon who copulates with men.

ARMOR, YANN D' Pseudonym of Pierre Bourieux, French occultist.

ARNOLD OF VILLANOVA Thirteenth-century occultist. He is credited with invoking Satanic powers to help him in his medical practice.

ARNUPHIS Egyptian sorcerer. In the second century A.D., he is supposed to have saved Marcus Aurelius' army by inducing a downpour of rain.

AROE The Bororos of Brazil believe that the spirits of the dead merge into a collective being whom they call Aroe.

ARPHAXAT Ancient Persian sorcerer, killed by a thunderbolt.

ARRHETOPHORIA A Greek festival during which phalli and snakes fashioned from pastry were thrown into a pit.

ARS MORIENDI A book published in 1542 by Domenico Caparnica, Bishop of Fermo. 'The Art of Dying,' a collection of the teachings of the bishop's many predecessors, enjoyed great popularity. It showed the faithful how to resist diabolic temptations even until the moment of death.

ARTEMIS (DIANA) The Greek goddess of hunting and queen of wild beasts inspired a barbaric mystery cult in Sparta, where human beings were sacrificed to her.

ARTEPHIUS A twelfth-century occultist, he reputedly lived more than a thousand years, with the help of demons. He wrote *The Art of Prolonging Life,* according to tradition, at the age of 1025.

ARTISSON, ROBERT A demon who had intercourse with Alice Kyteler. He appeared sometimes as a man, sometimes, as a black dog or a cat.

ASCLEPIUS A work purporting to describe the magic rites used by the ancient Egyptians. It probably dates from the second or third century A.D.

ASEB The Egyptian fire god.

ASHAKKU In Mesopotamian religions, the demon of the head. He entered the body through sin and caused headaches.

ASHANTI The predominant tribe among the African tribes transported to Jamaica. Ashanti witchcraft (*obeah*) was antagonistic to Ashanti religion, but practitioners of the latter, proscribed by law in Jamaica, often turned to obeah in order to survive.

ASHIPU In ancient Mesopotamia, a priest specializing in the exorcism of disease-producing demons.

ASHMOG In the Avesta, a dragon or serpent with a camel's neck. Cabalists call it the flying camel.

ASHMOLE, ELIAS Seventeenth-century English alchemist.

ASHTAR VIDYA The most ancient Hindu work on magic, preserved only fragmentarily.

ASMODEUS In Jewish demonology, an evil spirit sometimes credited with causing matrimonial happiness. His cradle is the Avesta, the sacred book of the Zoroastrian religion. The Persians added the word *daeva* to the name Aeshma. *Aeshma daeva*, 'demon of lust,' later was identified as the king of the demons. The genie of concupiscence became a satellite of Satan in Christian theology.
Asmodeus was the name of the chief demon who possessed the body of Jeanne des Anges. He filled her mind with 'shameful things.'

ASMOUG In Mazdean religion, chief emissary of Ahriman, the Spirit of Evil. His function is to incite discord and kindle warlike feelings among the nations.

ASPIC A poisonous asp, one of the principal attributes of the Devil.

ASPILCUETTA, MARIE D' French witch. She was arrested during the reign of Henri IV. She confessed that she had attended the Sabbat.

ASS Through the ages the ass has been the symbol of evil (in Egyptian theology), stupidity and stubbornness, and sexuality. Though the ass appears in incantations used in black magic, the Devil never assumes his shape.

ASSASSINS A masonic and mystic order founded in Persia in the eleventh century by Hassan Sabah. The sufis who founded the order were addicted to hashish eating. They used hashish to induce celestial visions. The chief of the order was called the Old Man of the Mountains and wielded absolute power.

ASSYRIAN DEMONOLOGY The ancient Assyrians recognized a host of evil demons. The monuments of Chaldea prove the existence of an extremely complex demonology, including the *mas, lamma,* and *utuq;* the *alapi, alal,* and *nirgalli;* and the disease-engendering demon of the southwest wind. The mas, lamma, and utuq are divided into two classes, good and evil. The alal appear to be demons of destruction. The *labartu, labassu,* and *ahharu* are ghosts, phantoms, and vampires. The nirgalli are lion-headed and eagle-claw-footed demons. The *seirim* of the Israelites recall Assyrian carvings which depict evil spirits in the shape of goats.

ASTARA FOUNDATION A world-wide organization whose tenets are drawn in part from ancient mystery cults.

ASTAROTH Powerful grand duke in the western region of Hell. His wife is Astarte, a Phoenician moon goddess with elegant horns forming a crescent. He has the face of an ugly angel, rides a dragon, and holds a viper in his left hand. As treasurer of Hell, he wields great power. Wierus states that he knows both the past and the future. He is supposed to be one of the seven princes of Hell who visited Faust. Astaroth (Ashtaroth, Ashtoreth, Astarte, or Atargatis) was originally the Great Goddess of Canaan, equivalent to the Babylonian Ishtar. As the goddess of fertility, she was worshiped with lascivious rites. She became a male demon with bad breath.

ASTARTE Goddess of lust and sexuality. Known also as Astorath in Satanic circles. The blood of a sacrificed child, mixed with the wine from the chalice, is offered to her.

ASTHAR VIDYA The oldest Hindu work on magic. Only fragments survive.

ASTRAL BODY Modern occultism teaches that a 'body of light' leaves the corpse of a dead man and moves on to the astral plane of existence. His soul eventually moves on to higher planes, leaving the body of light on the astral plane as an astral corpse or body. The astral body retains a faint spark of life. It retains a desire to live again and can be drawn back to the ordinary world, where it can prolong its existence indefinitely by absorbing life-energy from living creatures.

ASTRAMPSYCHOS Ancient Chaldean sorcerer.

ASTROITE A precious stone said by Zoroaster to help one to appease the terrestrial demon, summon benevolent spirits, and obtain answers to questions put to them.

ASTROLATRY The cult of the stars as a means of divination. This type of cult was predominant in the Near East and in Mesopotamia. It was also in force among the Aztecs, in the pre-Columbian period.

ASTROLOGY In many pagan religions astrology played an important role in rituals and ceremonials and in the general beliefs of the people. This was particularly the case among the Egyptians, the Romans, and the Assyro-Babylonians. The movements of the heavenly bodies, the rising and setting of the sun, eclipses were studied in order to discover the arrangement of the cosmic system and its influence on the lives of men.

The Babylonians were the pioneers in this science. Their observations, from the third millennium on, were gradually systematized into formal prognostications, based on astrological and astronomical calculations, regarding the effectiveness of any human undertaking. The interpreters were the priests attached to a particular temple, and their decisions were accepted not only by the people at large but by the rulers themselves.

The Assyro-Babylonian deities, to whom were assigned in the divine scheme special areas of the heavens, were the arbiters of human fate as manifested by astrological science.

Among the Romans, astrology was carried to even greater lengths and greater exactitude. The entire cosmic system was put under minute observation. The orderliness of the heavenly bodies suggested to the professional astrologers the possibility of mathematical precision in forecasting human events. For the gods themselves had now become identified with the heavenly bodies. During the period of the Roman Empire, astrology exerted a powerful influence in major national policies and in the imperial decisions and decrees of the ruling emperor.

From Mesopotamia and the temples where astrological practices were in force, the science spread to Egypt. Greece was not greatly affected until after the death of

Alexander the Great in 323 B.C., when Oriental influences imposed themselves on Hellenistic life.

In Rome, every level of society felt the force of astrological predictions. In one particular direction, in medicine, astrology exercised a powerful influence that lasted for centuries. See Aquarius.

ASTRONOMOS An initiate into the mystery cult of ancient Thebes.

ASTRUM ARGENTINUM A secret society founded by Aleister Crowley. The scandalous behavior of those who entered his Abbey of Theleme in Sicily discredited the society.

ASURAS In Vedic mythology, these were demons, led by the serpent Vritra.

ASVINS Vedic deities possessed of many forms. Twin sons of the sun and the sky, they are among the most mysterious of all gods. In esoteric philosophy, they are the reincarnating principles.

ATARGATIS A Phrygian goddess corresponding to the Greek goddess Artemis. In Syria, she inspired a mystery cult. In Greece, she was worshiped as a manifestation of Aphrodite.

ATHAME A black-handled knife made or inherited by a witch.

ATHANASIUS Fourth-century Christian biographer. His account of the life of St. Anthony is the embodiment of theological speculation about the Devil during the fourth century. In his long struggle against the Devil, the saint was tempted in every way imaginable, for his decision to serve God 'was intolerable for the Devil who is the enemy of all good.' Fortunately, 'he who believed himself equal with God was outplayed by the adolescent.'

ATROPOS   See Moira.

ATTIS   In Asia Minor Attis was the god of fertility. His worship had also spread to Greece. His cult reflected occasions of lamentation at his death and rejoicing on his rebirth. In this respect his worship is akin to that of Adonis. Attis was loved by the goddess Cybele, who drove him into such a frenzy that he committed self-mutilation.

AUCH   In 551 the Council of Auch attacked witchcraft: 'those who, under the influence of the Devil, pronounce magical incantations.'

AUDUMLA   In Scandinavian mythology, the Cow of Creation, source of four streams of milk which fed the giant Ymir and his sons the Hrimthurses before the appearance of gods or men. She licked the salt of the primal ice-rocks to produce Bor, father of Odin, Wili, and We.

AUKERT   An Egyptian name for the underworld.

AULAK   Among the Arabs, a vampire demon.

AUMGN   Aleister Crowley's expansion of the Buddhist Om. It is 'a mantra of terrific power by virtue whereof [the magician] may apprehend the Universe.'

AURA   An emanation from a human being. It assumes various colors and indicates the character of the person.

AUTO-DA-FE   Torture by fire ordered by the Inquisition to force confessions of witchcraft.

AUXONNE NUNS From 1658 to 1663 nuns in the Ursuline convent of Auxonne were allegedly possessed by demons. The nuns made accusations of Lesbianism against their Mother Superior, who later was found innocent. Physicians testified that the nuns had never displayed any convincing signs of true demoniacal possession.

AVARUS A demon summoned by the French sorcerer Soubert.

AYM See Haborym.

AYPEROS Infernal prince who commands thirty-six legions. Represented as a vulture, he can foresee the future.

AYPHOS One of three demons obedient to the will of Nebiros, field marshal of Hell.

AZAEL According to the Book of Enoch, one of the leaders of the two hundred angels who rebelled against god.
In apocalyptic writings, the cosmic power of evil, identified with man's evil impulse and death.
The name is connected with the ritual of atonement and associated by Milton with Satan. In Genesis he is the leader of the sons of God who wedded the daughters of men. Rendered as 'scapegoat' in the King James Bible, Azael is understood to have borne the sins of the people away from them to the Devil.

AZILUT In the Cabala, the world of emanations. It is the great and highest prototype of the other worlds, the Great Sacred Seal by means of which all the worlds are copied.

AZKEEL One of the leaders of the two hundred fallen angels. According to the Book of Enoch, he rebelled against God and swore allegiance to Samiaza.

AZOTH In alchemy, mercury, treated as the creative principle in nature. It is symbolized by a cross bearing the letters TARO. Each combination of these letters has an occult meaning. Paracelsus owned a talismanic jewel in which a powerful spirit was supposed to dwell. His jewel was called the Azoth.

Book of the Devil
(Damerval; Paris, 1508)

B

BA In Egyptian religion, the soul, represented as a bird with the head of a human being. The Egyptians believed that the *ba* and the *ka* or genius, together with the *khu* or transfigured soul, could live on if the body of the deceased could be preserved. Hence arose the practice of mummification of the corpse, sheltering it in a tomb, and providing it with food.

BAAL According to the *Lemegeton*, the commander of the armies of Hell. The name Baal, 'lord,' was applied to many local deities in Syria and Palestine. The supreme Baal was the great fertility god of the Canaanites. Children were sacrificed to him.
In the Middle East, Baal was a generic name used by several religious cults. He is a Semitic god of fertility, whose worship was associated with gross sensuality. Among the Phoenicians, Chaldeans, and Canaanites he was the chief male divinity.
The term Baal was frequently used along with another designation: e.g. Baal-Peor, who was the Moabite god at Peor and whose worship was steeped in debauchery. In Biblical times he was at one time worshiped by the Israelites.

BAALBERITH A Canaanite god, 'lord of the covenant,' who became a demon in Jewish popular belief. He was one of many devils who took possession of Sister Madeleine de Demandolx of the Ursuline convent in southern France.

BAALZEBUB The god of Ekron. Beelzebul, the name used for Satan in the New Testament, mainly in reference to demoniac possession, comes from the name of the god of Ekron. In Hebrew the expression means 'Lord of the Flies.'

BABYLONIAN DEMONOLOGY Demons had a central place in Babylonian life. Animal-shaped demons inhabited the fields. Ghostly creatures, half man and half-animal, haunted graveyards. Generally called alu and gallu, they were designated more specifically as lilu (spooks), utukku or etimmu (restless ghosts of those who had met an untimely death), rabisu (vampires lying in ambush), etc. Ardat-lili and Lilitu were female demons who seduced men. Demons often banded together in groups of seven. Sickness was attributed to the influence of a demon. For example, ahhazu caused epidemics while lamastu caused fever and endangered the lives of pregnant women and children. Plants, minerals, hair, feathers, incantations, and exorcisms were frequently used in the unending struggle against demons.

BABYLONIAN INCANTATION A Babylonian magic text mentions both Ea and Marduk, gods of magic.
Bright oil, pure oil, shining oil, the purifying oil of the gods, oil which softens the sinews of man.
With the oil of the incantation of Ea, with the oil of the incantation of Marduk
I have made thee drip; with the oil of softening which Ea has given for soothing
I have anointed thee; the oil of life I have put on thee.

BABYLONIAN INVOCATION An invocation to the goddess Tasmitu to remove sickness and evil spells contains these words:
> I, son of . . ., whose god is . . ., whose goddess is . . .,
> In the evil of an eclipse of the Moon . . .,
> In the evil of the powers, of the portents, evil
>   and not good, which are in my palace and my land,
> Have turned toward thee! . . .
> May the consumption of my muscles be removed!
> May the poisons that are upon me be loosened!
> May the ban be torn away!

BACCHANALIA A Roman mystery cult, characterized by unbridled debauchery, celebrated in honor of Bacchus (Dionysus). It was represented by a decree of the Roman Senate in 186 B.C.

BACCHANTES Women dedicated to the worship of Bacchus (Dionysus). Dressed in skins of beasts, they roamed the country, filled with divinely inspired enthusiasm. They are vividly portrayed in Euripides' play, *Bacchae*. They also were known as Thyades.

BACON, ROGER Franciscan scholar (1214-1294) to whom legend ascribes the creation of an android. His scientific writings led to his imprisonment on the charge of witchcraft.

BACOTI Among the Tonkinese, a witch or sorcerer.

BAEL First king of Hell. His domain is the eastern section. He commands sixty-six legions. One of his three heads is shaped like a toad, another like a man, and the third like a cat. The head of the powers of evil has a harsh voice and is a good fighter. Those who invoke him become alert and cunning, and they learn how to become invisible when necessary.

BAETULUS (BAETYL) A meteorite or similar stone thought to be of divine origin and made the object of veneration. The Semites believed the baetyl (literally, 'house of God') to be the abode of a divinity. The Court of the Great Mosque at Mecca contains the Kaaba, a cubical stone building which since the time of Mohammed has sheltered the famous Black Stone — a meteorite fabled to have been given by Gabriel to Abraham.

BAGAHI LACA BACHABE An ancient formula for invoking a demon.

BAHIR A source book on the mystical Cabala. The word means 'luminous.' With the Zohar (Book of Splendor) it presents the basic teachings of Judaic mysticism.

BAHOMET Idol worshiped by the Knights Templar and, later, by those who took part in the Black Mass.

BAKER, STANLEY Two men identified by police officials as Satan cultists and carrying human bones in their pockets were held in Salinas, California, as suspects in the slaying of a social worker in July, 1970. Stanley Baker and his companion, Harry Stroup, were arrested in connection with the death of James Schlosser. Baker said he shot Schlosser then hacked the body into pieces and ate the heart. He told the officials he developed a fetish for human flesh after receiving a severe electrical shock. Both men were said to be Satanists.

BAKRU In Surinam, a corpse that walks about like a living person.

BALAAM One of the evil demons who possessed Sister Jeanne des Anges. Balaam's passion was 'all the more dangerous because it seemed less evil.' The *Lemegeton* identifies Balaam (Balan or Balam) as a three-headed devil who rides a bear, carries a hawk on his wrist, and predicts the future. He is said to have one head like a bull's, another like a man's, and a third like a ram's. He is often shown naked. In the Old Testament, Balaam is a greedy sorcerer; in the New Testament, a symbol of avarice, immorality, and idol-worship.

BALBERITH A demon who possessed Sister Madeleine, at Aix-en-Provence. He also listed the other demons possessing Madeleine, and he gave the special saints opposing these demons.

BALOMA The Trobriand Islanders believe that the baloma or soul leaves the body at death to lead a shadowy existence in another world. At the annual feast called *milamala* it returns to its familiar surroundings.

BALOR A giant whose eye blighted every Formorian on whom it was turned. The 'eye of Balor' is an expression used by the Irish to denote the Evil Eye.

BALZAC, HONORE DE A major figure of French literary Satanism. Honoré de Balzac (1799-1850) created Vautrin, the ruthless criminal whose overriding aim was to seek diabolic revenge against society. Balzac was addicted to occult theorizing. It has been said that his universe is the self-sufficient creation of a demiurge.

BAMBERG WITCH TRIALS Hundreds of persons accused of practicing witchcraft were burned in Bamberg, beginning with the administration of Bishop Johann Gottfried von Aschhausen (1609-1622) and continuing through that of Bishop Johann Georg II, who died in 1632.

BANSHEE (BANSHIE) In Irish and Scottish folklore, a female spirit supposed to warn families of the approaching death of a member, generally by wailing under the window of the house occupied by the person who is to die a day or two later. Old Nick in his role as harbinger of death and carrier of souls to the future world is related to the banshee.

BAPTAE In Greek mythology they were the priests of Cotyto, whose obscene rites were celebrated in Athens, at night. For the purpose of purification, the priests at certain times were dipped into water. Hence their name, which in Greek denotes 'those dipped in water.'

BAPTISM The religious ablution signifying purification or consecration appears in many non-Christian cultures. Baptism belonged to the earliest Chaldeo-Akkadian theurgy, was practiced in the Egyptian pyramids, had a place in the Eleusinian mysteries, and is preserved today among the descendants of the ancient Sabians, the Mandaeans.

Medieval theologians agreed that a would-be sorcerer must renounce baptism, which blots out man's original sin.

BARBATOS One of three demons in the service of Satanachia, commander of the first legion of Hell.

BARCLAY, MARGARET A Scottish housewife convicted of witchcraft, strangled, and burned at the stake in 1618. At her public trial, she recanted everything that she had confessed under the influence of a 'most safe and gentle torture.'

BARD The chanted spells of the Celtic poet or singer were supposed to give him superhuman powers. He combined the offices of singer, genealogist, and custodian of tribal lore.

BARDESANES An early Syrian writer (154-222 A.D.), called a Gnostic by some and a Christian by others. His teachings incorporate elements from Gnosticism, Christianity, astrology, Indian philosophy, and occultism.

BARDESANIAN SYSTEM A system worked out by Bardesanes and called by some a Cabala within a Cabala. A very old Gnostic system, the so-called 'Codex of the Nazarenes' contains doctrines formulated before Bardesanes as well as the ancient names of good and evil powers.

BARDO THODOL See Tibetan Book of the Dead.

BARI Among the Bororos of Brazil, the bari is a sorcerer associated with terrifying spirits that control wind and rain, sickness and death. He mediates between human beings and the evil spirits.

BARKERS Demoniacs who bark like dogs. Famous examples include the barkers of Jocelyn, in Brittany, France, and Spanish nuns of the seventeenth century.

BARON A demon who signed a pact with Gilles de Rais (1404-1440). To him Gilles de Rais sacrificed the hands and hearts of children in order to obtain the secret of the philosopher's stone.

BARON SAMEDI In Haitian Voodoo, god of the dead and guardian of their tombs.

BARRET French village where the Devil is supposed to have appeared in January 1953.

BARRETT, SIR WILLIAM FLETCHER British scientist and occultist (1845-1926). In *The Magus* (1891) he describes, with illustrations, demons, conjurations, spells, and necromancy. He differs from Michaélis in ascribing attributes to demons: Mammon is the prince of tempters; Asmodeus, the prince of evil vengefulness; Belzebuth, chief of the false gods. He also introduces new attributes for five demons: Pytho is the prince of the spirits of deceit; Belial, prince of iniquity; Merihim, prince of the spirits of pestilence; Abaddon, prince of war and evil; and Astaroth, prince of accusers and inquisitors. He believed in the existence of a spiritual world, survival after death, and the possibility of communicating with the dead. See Michaélis, Sébastien.

BASILEUS The Archon or high priest who presided over the Elusinian mysteries.

BASILIDEAN GNOSTICISM The doctrine taught by Basilides comprises a complicated cosmology. Basilides claimed to have received secret knowledge from the apostle Matthew. His writings, including a twenty-four volume gospel and commentary, were burned.

BASILIDES Second-century Gnostic teacher who lived in Alexandria. He dealt with the problem of good and evil in terms of Persian dualism.

BASILISK A legendary serpent, lizard, or dragon whose breath, and even evil look, was fatal. Born of an egg laid by a cock and incubated by a toad, the basilisk is one of the principal attributes of the Devil.

BASQUE WITCHES Wholesale burnings occurred in the Basque regions of France in 1609. Details are reported in Pierre de Lancre's *Tableau* (1612).

BAST In Egyptian religion, a lion-headed or cat-headed goddess whose cult originated in the protohistoric cult of the lion or lionness. Her worship was associated with the city of Bubastis. An aspect of Hathor, she was the symbol of sexual passion. Termed in inscriptions 'the lady of life,' she is commonly represented as holding a shield in one hand, a sistrum in the other, and a basket over one arm.

BAT A flying mammal generally associated with the witches' Sabbat.

BATAILLE, DOCTOR Fictitious name of Leo Taxil, author of sensational revelations published in *Le Diable au XIXe siècle,* beginning in 1892. Dr. Bataille claimed to have traveled widely, to have witnessed spirit manifestations, satanic initiation rites, and modern worshipers of Bahomet, and to have learned the secrets of Albert Pike's occult powers, Sophie Walder's conversion, etc. In 1897 Leo Taxil admitted publicly that he had fabricated all of Dr. Bataille's sensational revelations.

BATSAUM-PASHA A Turkish demon or spirit, invoked to produce good weather or rain.

BATHYM One of three demons in the service of Fleuretty, lieutenant general of the forces of Hell.

BATRAAL According to the Book of Enoch, one of the leaders of the two hundred angels who rebelled against God and swore allegiance to Samaiza.

BATTLE OF BEWITCHMENT See Boullan, Abbé.

BAUDELAIRE, CHARLES French poet. Satan figures prominently in the work of Charles Baudelaire (1821-1867), whose aphorism is frequently quoted: 'The neatest trick of the Devil is to convince us that he does not exist.'

Baudelaire's major poetic work, *The Flowers of Evil*, contains a remarkable hymn of praise to Satan, *Les Litanies de Satan*.

BAVENT, MADELEINE See Louviers, Nuns of.

BAXTER, RICHARD (1615-1691) A renowned Presbyterian author and teacher, he defended belief in witchcraft in *Certainty of the World of Spirits* (1691).

BAYEUX French town through which a witch in the shape of a dog prowls the streets by night, gnawing at bones. When struck with a key hard enough to draw blood, the dog again takes on human form.

BEAST In the Book of Revelation (13:1-3 and 11-14) two beasts appear: one rises from the sea, the other from the land. Both are cast into the lake of burning fire prepared for them throughout eternity. A third beast has the form of a great red dragon and a fourth has seven heads and ten horns (17:3 and 8-11). All four beasts represent Satan.

BEAST, THE GREAT See Number of the Beast.

BEASTS OF THE DEVIL Most prominent among animals associated with the Devil are the goat, serpent, lion, basilisk, toad, black cat, black horse, yellow dog, crab, devil-fish, and spider.

BECHARD One of the demons who may be invoked by a Satanist. One must summon him on Friday by writing 'Come Béchard' in a circle three or four times. He requires a nut as a pledge.

BECKFORD, WILLIAM Eighteenth-century English writer. He was interested in demonology and Oriental magic. He wrote *Vathek.*

BEELZEBUB An oracle deity of the Ekronites. He was worshiped by the Philistines and by idolatrous Hebrews who, in New Testament times, called him the prince of devils. The name, derived from Baalzebub, is used in the New Testament to identify Satan. In demonology, he is the prime minister of the infernal spirits. The name also appears as Beelzebul.

BEHEMOTH One of the seven demons who possessed Sister Jeanne des Anges. Behemoth often filled her mind with blasphemies and gave her 'a very strange aversion' to her vocation.

BEHERIT The Syriac name of Satan.

BEKKER, BALTHASAR In *De Betoverde Weereld* (The World Bewitched), published in 1691, Dr. Balthasar Bekker attacked the doctrines of witchcraft then prevalent and charged that they were invented by the papacy 'to warm the fires of purgatory and to fill the pockets of the clergy.'

BEL The Akkadian form of the Western Semitic word *Baal,* meaning 'lord,' ultimately associated with the rivals of the Hebraic God. In other settings, his name is recorded as Beli, Belus, Belenus, or Belinus.

BELFIEL, JEANNE DE See Loudun, Nuns of.

BELIAL The most vicious of all the demons, he drives a fiery chariot and is named, in the Book of Revelation, 'The Beast.' In apocalyptic writings Belial (or Beliar) is the cosmic power of evil, identified with death and the evil impulse in man. In The War of the Sons of Light and the Sons of Darkness, one of the Dead Sea scrolls, he appears as the leader of the forces of evil: 'His purpose is to bring about wickedness and guilt. All the spirits that are associated with him are but angels of destruction.'

BELL, BOOK, AND CANDLE The resources of the Church for excommunicating heretics were summed up in the phrase 'to curse by bell, book, and candle.'

BELLONA The Roman war goddess to whom priests offered their blood in sacrificial rites.

BELLONARII Priests who inflicted wounds on their bodies and offered the flowing blood to Bellona, the Roman war goddess.

BELLS They are supposed to ward off demons. Their sound forces demons to abandon the witches that they are taking to the Sabbat.

BELPHEGOR In obscene worship, a demon with a gaping mouth and a phallic-shaped tongue.

BELTANE In Celtic religion, this was a fertility festival, held in midsummer. A fire was kindled and a sacred tree, the oak, was burned, together with an image of the vegetation spirit. The mistletoe was cut, and human sacrifices were performed. The fire, the tree, and the victim all constituted fertility symbols.

BEMILUCIUS An obscure deity of the ancient Celts.

BENDIS In ancient Greek religion, a Thracian moon goddess. Proclus identified her with Persephone.

BENEDICT IX, Pope (1032-1044). Known before he ascended the throne of St. Peter as Teofilatto and later as 'The Boy Pope' (he was probably twelve when he became Pope), he is said to have worshiped demons and to have had their help in seducing women. He was the teacher of Sylvester II.

BENJEES In the East Indies, devil worshipers.

BENNU In Egyptian religion, the soul of Ra and guide of the gods in the underworld. Identified with the phoenix, the emblem signified immortality.

BERASIT A mystic word used by the Cabalists of Asia Minor. It is the first word of the Book of Genesis.

BERLIOZ, HECTOR French composer whose *Symphonie Fantastique* (1830) contains a musical interpretation of the witches' Sabbat.

BERNANOS, GEORGES One of the most important Catholic writers of the twentieth century. In his first novel, *Sous le Soleil de Satan*, Georges Bernanos (1888-1948) seems obsessed by incubi and diabolic machinations.

BES In Egyptian religion, an ancient phallic god, represented as standing on a lotus ready to devour his own progeny. Later, his image was widely used as an amulet, throughout the Greco-Roman world down to the Middle Ages.

BESTARBETO An obscure demonic or angelic power.

BETH ELOHIM A Cabalistic treatise on angels, demons, and souls. The Hebraic expression means 'house of god.'

BEWITCH To cast a spell over a person or gain power over him by charms or incantations. To injure by witchcraft. To seduce with erotic or evil intent.

BEYREVRA Indian demon, master of souls that roam through space. He has crooked nails. He used one of his nails to cut off one of Brahma's five heads.

BHUT Among the animistic Dravidians of India, a wicked spirit that haunts graveyards, animates the bodies of the dead, and devours human beings.

BILLIS African sorcerers who are credited with the power to prevent the growth of rice.

BILSON BOY One of a number of young imposters who made false accusations that caused others to be suspected of witchcraft. His real name was William Perry. In 1620 he accused an old woman of bewitching him. Later it was discovered that he had been trained by a priest to feign possession.

BINAH The third sephira, represented in the first triangle of the Tree of Life. In the Cabalistic system, it is the passive, female principle in God. It is called the Mother, the Throne, the Great Sea. It is the passive Understanding of God. Binah is symbolized by the cteis, cup, circle, diamond, and oval. Its deities include Hecate, goddess of witchcraft and sorcery.

BINSFELD, PETER German authority on witch-hunting (c. 1540-1603). He incited many trials for witchcraft and was widely quoted.

BISCAR, JEANNETTE A French sorceress, reputed to have been conveyed to a Sabbat in goat form by the Devil himself.

BISHOP, BRIDGET A black servant tried and convicted of practicing witchcraft in Massachusetts in 1692. She and several other servants implicated in the Salem affair may have been practicing a cult resembling voodoo.

BLACK BOOKS (GRIMOIRES) Manuals of magic, pseudepigraphically ascribed to Solomon, Albertus Magnus, certain Popes, and other karcists or wizards. Highly popular during the Middle Ages, they describe many occult practices, rituals, and ceremonies. Among the most notable: *Liber Spirituum;* the Hebrew manual called *Shemamphoras; Oupnekhat,* a Sanskrit manual translated into Persian and later into Latin (1802); *Grimoirium Verum,* by Alibeck the Egyptian (1517); *The Constitution of Honorius,* attributed to Pope Honorius III; *Little Albert; Red Dragon; Arbatel; Tonalamatl,* an ancient Mexican manual; *Y-Kim,* an obscure Chinese work assigned to the fourth millenniun B.C.; *Red Book of Appin; Hell's Coercion,* attributed to Johannes Faustus; *The Black Hen; The Great and Powerful Sea Ghost,* by Faustus; *Lemegeton, or the Lesser Key of Solomon,* which describes the demonic hierarchy; *The Key of Solomon,* ascribed to King Solomon; *The Testament of Solomon,* a tenth-century account of the building of the Temple by Solomon with the aid of demons; *Liber Pentaculorum; The Sage of the Pyramids; The Almadel;* and *The Book of Raziel,* reputedly derived from *The Book of Signs,* a handbook on magic attributed to Adam.

BLACK CAT Like the black pullet, the black cat plays an important role in magic. Long associated with the Devil and credited with having nine lives, the cat was worshiped by the ancient Egyptians. A maleficent companion of the Devil and witches who participate in Sabbat dances, the black cat is a harbinger of bad luck. Those who see him crossing the street before them must take defensive steps. The heretical Stadinghians were said to worship a black cat, kissing its genitalia as they did in the case of the Devil at the Sabbat.

BLACK DEATH Many people were charged with witchcraft and held responsible for the deaths of many victims of the plague which ravaged Europe in the fourteenth century.

BLACK DRAGON A popular grimoire. Attributed to Honorius, it contains instructions for summoning demons and making pacts. Each day of the week calls for a different procedure. On Monday, Lucifer is invoked; on Tuesday, Frimost; on Wednesday, Astaroth; on Thursday, Silcharde; on Friday, Bechard; on Saturday, Guland; and on Sunday, Surgat.

BLACK GLANCE Another name for the Evil Eye.

BLACK HEN Like the black dog, the black hen or pullet has long been associated with the Devil and witchcraft.

BLACK HORSE A symbol of death, the black horse is the Devil's steed.

BLACK MAN The Devil.

BLACK MASS The mysteries of witchcraft are inextricably interwoven with occult pagan cults which, despite unceasing attacks by Christianity, have flourished through the centuries. Pagan cults stress the distinction between Christian tenets and the beliefs of the 'Old Religion,' or witchcraft. The Black Mass, which attracted much attention during the Middle Ages, is an obscene travesty of Christianity. Its inverted rituals, lascivious formulas, and weird pronouncements raise and exalt the Archfiend. Long associated with the Witches' Sabbat, the Black Mass probably overlapped into its ceremonials, merging with it to produce one unit with the sole aim of forming an alliance with the dark forces of the universe and rejecting all tenets in conflict with the 'Old Religion.'

As it evolved during the Middle Ages, the Black Mass became a parody of the Christian Mass. Satan was the object of worship. The altar was dominated by an obscene figure of Christ or an infernal goat; candles were black; the chalice contained blood or human fat. Sometimes a nude woman was used as an altar, with the mass being celebrated on her buttocks or stomach. Presiding over the mass was a defrocked priest. The celebrants were nude except for a cassock adorned with Satanic symbols. The host was black.

Finally the Black Mass acquired a sinister importance of its own, becoming an independent ritual with its own locale and devotees, bound by their common interest in Satanism. People from all walks of life — lowly peasants and high-born ladies, priests and prelates, nobles and servants, were drawn by curiosity or avarice, by lust or hope, to worship the Archfiend, the Devil, Diabolus. At the height of the ceremonial, with the priestly officiant taking the leading role, an unbridled sexual orgy occurred. Brocken Mountain and the church of Blokula, in Sweden, were famous as meeting places for Black Mass participants.

Many paintings, etchings, and sculptures have tried to capture the wild, orgiastic nature of the rites, often involving sacrifices of crops and animals.

BLACK MASS CONSECRATION After the blood of a sacrificial child had been mixed with the contents of the chalice, these words were used to accompany the offering made to Satan:

> Astaroth, Asmodeus, I beg you to accept the sacrifice of this child which we now offer to you, so that we may receive the thanks we ask.

BLACK PRINCE A name designating the Devil.

BLACK PULLET A grimoire supposedly published in Egypt in 1740 but probably dating from the latter part of the eighteenth century. Also known as the *Black Hen*.

BLACK SHAMAN A shaman who is associated with malignant and magic forces.

BLACK STONE See Baetulus.

BLAKE, WILLIAM Haunted by apocalyptic visions, William Blake in his *The Marriage of Heaven and Hell* (1790) paved the way for many modern writers who, though they may deny both God and Satan, proclaim the victory of the latter.

BLANCHEFLEURE A Parisian Jewess who announced in 1600 that she had conceived by Satan and given birth to the Antichrist.

BLANCKENSTEIN TRIALS Chatrina Blanckenstein was acquitted of the charge of bewitching a small child. Her trial was held in Saxony in 1676. In 1689, her daughter confessed to a series of crimes, under torture, and was condemned to be burned alive.

BLOOD From time immemorial blood has been regarded as a vitalizing agent and has figured prominently in ritual sacrifices. In paleolithic times the bodies of the dead were put in pits containing ocher. The reddish ore may have been intended to provide the deceased with a substitute for the vitalizing agent.

The Greeks poured blood into graves to revive the spirits of the dead. In certain mystery cults, as in Mithraism, blood baptism was used to purify both body and soul. Demons are said to love blood. Whenever a necromantic act is performed, according to Gratian, author of the twelfth-century *Decretum*, 'blood is mixed with water so that they may be exorcised more readily by the color of the blood.'

BLUEBEARD Probably Gilles de Rais (Rays).

BOANTHROPY The technical term for metamorphosis into the shape of a cow.

BOAT OF THE SUN See Sektet.

BOCOR A voodoo adept. Unlike the *hungan,* who is endowed with supernatural powers, the bocor buys his gods. He relies on magic alone, not on prayers.

BODIN, JEAN French lawyer, philosopher, and demonologist (1529-1596). His *De la Démonomanie des sorciers* (Demonomania of Witches), published in 1580, derived from his personal experience as a judge at many trials.

BODY OF LIGHT A replica of the earthly body, except that it is made of subtler material. See Astral Body.

BOGEY (BOGY) A hobgoblin or specter. The Devil.

BOGEYMAN A goblin or bugbear. The Devil.

BOGOMILES A Bulgarian sect originating around the tenth century A.D. and teaching that the Creator had two sons, Satan and Christ or Logos.

BOGUET, HENRI French jurist. His *Discours des sorciers* (1602) examines the Sabbat, the powers and marks of witches, and punishments to be meted out. The appendix presents in seventy articles many different statutes and court decisions concerning witchcraft. The book is supposed to have resulted in the burning of more than six hundred witches in Burgundy.

BOKOR A Haitian necromancer. He exercises control over the spirits of the dead.

BOLINGBROKE, ROGER Fifteenth-century English wizard. He was hanged in London for trying to kill Henry VI by witchcraft.

BOLOS OF MENDES Author of the oldest known book on alchemy, *Physika kai Mystika,* The Physical and the Mystical, about 200 B.C.

BON The animistic religion of Tibetan tribesmen abounds in sorcery and barbarous practices. The ritual sacrifice of human beings is practiced.

BONAMPAK Wall paintings at Bonampak, the cultural center of the Mayan civilization, dramatize the sacrificial killing of prisoners of war.

BONA-OMA In Roman religion, a goddess of fertility who was also patroness of female occultists.

BONATTI, GUIDO Italian astrologer and adept in the black arts. Like Michael Scot, the thirteenth-century writer was consigned to Hell by Dante.

BONEWITS, ISAAC An occultist and serious student of magic, Isaac Bonewits was the first person to receive a college degree based on the study of the supernatural. In 1970 he received his bachelor of arts degree for 'studies in the field of magic' from the University of California in Berkeley. His expressed aim is to translate magic 'into modern terms that can be used in a parapsychological laboratory.'

BONIFARCE One of the demons who possessed Elisabeth Allier, a seventeenth-century French nun.

BOOK OF CHANGES See I Ching.

BOOK OF ENOCH Many demonological beliefs have their source in the apocryphal work attributed to Enoch and composed in the second century B.C. The Book of Genesis notes that the children of God chose the most beautiful daughters of men as their mates, and it makes Enoch a grandson of Adam.
The Book of Enoch relates that the two hundred children of God swore allegiance to their leader **Samiaza**. They came down to Aradis, near Mt. Armon. Each chose a wife and taught her the properties of trees and roots, magic spells, and witchcraft. The women gave birth to giants.
Anarchy, war, and massacres ensued. God charged Uriel with the task of warning Noah of the coming flood. To Raphael he entrusted the mission of capturing Azaziel, one of the angels responsible for the revolt against God. God ordered Raphael to bind him hand and foot, pile sharp, heavy stones on him, and envelop him in darkness. Samiaza and the other rebellious angels were to be chained under the earth for seventy generations, until the final Judgment. Their sons were to be slaughtered. At the Final Judgment, rebellious angels and their chiefs were to be condemned to be hurled into the depths of a fiery pit, where they would suffer endless torment.

The leaders of the two hundred angels were, in addition to Samiaza: Urakabarameel, Akikel, Tamiel, Ramuel, Danel, Azael, Amers, Batraal, Amane, Zavehe, Samsavael, Ertrael, Turel, Yomael, and Zazel.

The fallen angels are credited by Enoch with engendering a race of evil spirits whose mission is to torture mankind.

BOOK OF FORMATION Hebraic treatise of great antiquity. It uses mystical numerical calculations based on the values of letters to expound the creation of the world. Also called Sepher Yetzirah, Sefer Yezirah.

BOOK OF MOSES The standard magicians' code of the Middle Ages. It contained a complicated ritual for the induction of neophytes.

BOOK OF THE DEAD An Egyptian handbook for guiding the souls of the dead through the underworld.

BOOKS ON WITCHCRAFT The first book on witchcraft was Johannes Nider's *Formicarius*, written in 1435 and published in 1475. The first printed work was Alphonsus de Spina's *Fortalicium Fidei* (1845). Jean Vineti, in a work written in 1450, *Tractatus contrademonum invocatores*, described witchcraft as heresy. The idea of the Sabbat was developed in *Errores Gazariorum*, also written in 1450. The first work written in French was *La Vauderie Lyonois*, compiled by the inquisitor of Lyon. J. Spenger and H. Kramer compiled the *Malleus Maleficarum*, which became the handbook of the inquisitors.

BORDELON, LAURENT Author of some thirty works on witchcraft, Laurent Bordelon (1635-1730) has been called the Don Quixote of demonography. The French writer ridiculed both witchcraft and the harsh measures used to repress it.

BOS, FRANCOISE French witch accused of having sexual relations with an incubus disguised as the 'Captain of the Holy Ghost.' She was burned on July 30, 1606.

BOTIS One of three infernal demons in the service of Agaliarept, commander of the second legion of Hell.

BOTOCUDO A primitive tribe of South America, more properly called the Kaingang. They have evolved elaborate techniques of imitative magic, closely related to animism, in their attempts to control the weather. The fundamental religious outlook of the Kaingang is animistic. Their religion is not the expression of an inner need but a naïve projection of a peculiar psycho-physical orientation which focuses attention on the fundamental distinction between one's own body and all other bodies.

Death sets in motion awesome forces of destruction, causing the Kaingang to mobilize all their emotional resources. When death is momentarily actualized in the form of the *kupleng* or ghost-soul of the deceased, the most elaborate ritual forms are used to protect the living. The spouse or *thupaya* stands in greatest danger and must remove all traces of old contacts with the deceased. The thupaya must free himself from the kupleng quickly, and he performs rites designed to rid him of his personal fear as well as to protect the community. He leaves camp alone, abstains from eating cooked food, and sleeps alone at night. When he kills an animal, he opens its belly and rubs the blood on himself to 'wash off' the hunting formerly done for his wife.

BOUGET, HENRI French lawyer and demonographer (c. 1550-1619). He was the author of *Discours des sorciers*, which went through twelve editions in twenty years and became a standard legal guide.

BOULLAN, ABBE Leader of the Work of Mercy, a mysterious sect founded by Pierre Vintras, and central figure of the great 'battle of bewitchment' that raged in the 1880's and 1890's. Prior to his affiliation with the Work of Mercy, the Abbé Boullan and a nun called Adèle Chevalier had founded the Society for the Reparation of Souls. A defrocked priest, Boullan had a pentagram tattooed at the corner of his left eye and celebrated Mass in vestments displaying an inverted crucifix. He specialized in exorcism and recommended consecrated hosts mixed with feces for nuns possessed by demons. On December 8, 1860, he ceremoniously sacrificed his and Adèle Chevalier's child, as the high point of a Mass. He announced in 1875 that he was a reincarnation of John the Baptist and the new head of the Work of Mercy. He taught nuns to enjoy sexual intercourse with his own astral body and to hypnotize themselves into thinking that they were having intercourse with Christ and the saints. Stanislas de Guaita claimed that the practical result of Boullan's belief in union with God through the sex act was unlimited promiscuity. Guaita and Oswald Wirth broke with Boullan and initiated the battle of bewitchment by announcing that they had judged him and condemned him. Huysmans, one of the partisans of Jean-Antoine Boullan, called him 'a very learned and intelligent priest' in his novel *La Bas*. The Abbé was also known as Dr. Johannes. The Satanic orgies that he proposed to his parishioners were called 'Life Union.' One of his co-workers as the Supreme Head of the Church of Carmel was the Head Priestess, Mme. Thibault.

BOULLE, FATHER THOMAS See Louviers, Nuns of.

BOURIEUX, PIERRE Breton magician who wrote many articles on occultism under the name of Yann d'Armor. His mysterious death in 1949, exploited by the press, drew thousands of visitors to Ker Guy, the manor in which he had lived. The next year Ker Guy was destroyed by a fire that was unanimously attributed to the Devil.

BOURIGNON, ANTOINETTE A French mystic (1616-1680) who started a convent for orphan girls in Lille, France. The novices of Lille exploited the credulity of Madame Bourignon, claiming that they had intercourse with the Devil.

BOUVET, LESIEUR Seventeenth-century provost general of the French armies in Italy. On the basis of his personal experience, he wrote *Manieres admirables,* a technical manual for witch-hunters.

BOVET, RICHARD English writer, author of *Pandaemonium* (1684), a collection containing commentaries on witchcraft and fifteen amusing ghost stories.

BRAGADINI, MARK ANTONY Sixteenth-century Italian sorcerer. He was beheaded for boasting that he had used demonic forces to transmute metals.

BRAGGA In 563 the Second Council of Bragga branded as heretical the belief that the Devil 'by his own power created thunder, lightning, storm and drought.'

BREAKING OF THE TOAD Travesty on the breaking of the Host. At the Black Mass, the officiant uttered a curse, using the name of Philip IV, as the toad was sliced open. It was Philip IV who persecuted the Templars.

BRETHREN OF THE CROSS A Thuringian sect charged in 1453 with practicing flagellation and celebrating orgies in secret by night. They were said to believe that Satan would regain his lost power and expel Christ from heaven.

BRIAREUS In Greek mythology, a monster with a hundred hands.

BRIGUE, JEHENNE DE See Paris Witch Trial.

BRINVILLIERS, MARIE-MARGUERITE DE Famous French demoniac. She was possessed by the Devil at the age of seven.

BROCKEN Highest mountain peak in Harz Mountains in central Germany. Long associated in popular legend with Walpurgis Night or witches' Sabbat. One scene in Goethe's *Faust* has its setting here.

BROOM Goya captioned one of his satirical drawings of two witches borne through the air on a broomstick: 'The broom . . ., besides being useful for sweeping, can . . . be changed into a mule that runs so fast that even the Devil cannot keep pace with it.'

BRUCOLACAS In contemporary Greek, an expression designating vampires.

BRUXA A Portuguese witch. In isolated country districts she still commands attention. In 1968, for example, a bruxa was tried in Lisbon for practicing medicine without a license.

BRYNHIL In Norse mythology, the goddess who chose the warriors who were to die on the battlefield and be conducted to Valhalla. She was the daughter of Odin and the chief of the Valkyries.

BUER One of three demons in the service of Agaliarept, commander of the second legion of Hell.

BUGGERMAN A dialectical term for the Devil.

BUIRMAN, FRANZ One of the bloodiest magistrates of the seventeenth century. He went so far as to burn as a witch his own executor in the town of Sieburg.

BULL In antiquity and in the ancient mystery cults, the bull symbolized the potency of the male principle.

BULLS, PAPAL The basis for witchhunts in Europe was laid by papal bulls issued by John XXII, Eugene IV, Innocent VIII, Alexander VI, and Leo X. In *Super illius specula* (1326) John XXII censured those 'who worship demons and make offer sacrifices to them.' Eugene IV (1437) criticized those who 'make ill use of the Eucharist and the elements of baptism.' In *Summis desiderantes affectibus* (1484) Innocent VIII charged that 'many people of both sexes . . . turn away from the Catholic faith and indulge in orgies with incubi and succubi.' In *Cum acceperimus* Alexander VI charged the Lombards with practicing 'diabolical incantations and superstitions.'

BULWER-LYTTON, EDWARD English novelist and occultist (1803-1873). His many writings include a collection of fantastic tales, *The Pilgrims of the Rhine* (1834); *Zanoni* (1842), dealing with occultism; and *The Haunted and the Haunters* (1861), a series of ghost stories.

BUNOT, LEON A hunchback regarded as a witch by the people of Saint-Andre-de-Briouze and killed by Victor Delorme on November 26, 1948. Delorme accused him of threatening to loose 'the red dog.'

BURROUGHS, GEORGE New England clergyman. He was one of the most eminent victims of witchcraft. Cotton Mather concluded that the thirty testimonies against him 'were enough to fix the character of a witch upon him.' He was put to death in 1692. He maintained his innocence to the end, reciting the Lord's Prayer on the scaffold. Mather pacified the other on-lookers, who believed that no witch could recite the Lord's Prayer without stumbling, by suggesting that the Devil was most dangerous when he assumed the role of an angel of light.

BURTON BOY Thomas Darling, a disturbed English youth living in Burton, began making unsubstantiated charges against others in 1596. John Darrell staged a performance in which he exorcised the demon that was torturing the youth.

BURYING ALIVE The practice of burying alive human beings or animals in the hope of attaining permanence for buildings is associated with the privilege of collecting rent and the idea of offering sacrifice in payment of debt due.

BWAGA'U Among the Trobriand Islanders, these are male sorcerers.

BYRON, LORD In *Manfred* (1817) and *Cain* (1821) Lord Byron was a prime mover in the exaltation of Satan in literature. In the latter work Cain becomes a sinister man of genius, a victim of his compassion for mankind.

C

CAACRINOLAAS In medieval demonology, a powerful demon generally identified as the grand president of Hell.

CABALA A body of occult doctrine. Originally Jewish, the Cabala has been adopted by many modern occultists. It is *hokmah nistarah,* 'hidden wisdom,' transmitted secretly from generation to generation since the time of Abraham, who received it from God. Modern occultists maintain that the most profound secrets of the Cabala are not recorded in accessible form but are passed on by word of mouth to those who are worthy of them or embodied in ancient documents which have never left the hands of initiates.

Many of the elements of the Cabala appear also in Gnosticism, which makes knowledge of the divine the supreme aim of man. Knowledge which comes through divine inspiration or sacred traditions based on divine inspiration, transforms the knowing subject, making him a sharer in the divine being.

The written part of the Cabala consists of numerous commentaries by various authors, most of them unknown. The most important of the older works are the *Sepher Yetzirah* (Book of Formation), written in Hebrew between the third and sixth centuries A.D., and the *Zohar* or *Sepher ha-Zohar* (Book of Splendor), written in Aramaic, probably by Moses de Leon, in Spain, around 1300.

The Cabalistic system of occult theosophy had a profound effect on medieval literature and is the source of much medieval and modern magic and demonology. It teaches that creation is the process of emanation, that man is a microcosm, and that every element of Scripture has a hidden sense. According to the Cabala, all men are endowed with magical powers which they themselves may develop. God is the original principle of all being. All things are created through emanation. The triumph of morality and goodness among men can overcome the powers of evil. Once man's mind has achieved full control, the Messiah will restore the world to a perfect state.

First used by Jewish rabbis and handed down orally through chosen disciples, the Cabalistic system became popular only after parts of it had been committed to writing. One branch of the system deals specifically with mystic operations, involving anagrams, names of spirits, etc. Underlying much of the thinking of the Cabalists is the notion that writing is the means through which man can penetrate into the divine mysteries. Also Cabbala, Kabala, Kabalah, etc.

CABALISTIC CIRCLE *The Great Grimoire* gives directions for making a magic circle:
You will begin by making a circle with the goatskin . . . , nailing it down with four nails. Then you will take your blood stone and trace a triangle inside the circle, beginning with the direction of the east. . . .
After which, the karcist will gather his assistants into the circle . . . , placing the two candlesticks with the two verbena wreaths on the right and the left of the inner triangle. . . .
After all that has been previously mentioned has been performed, you will pronounce the following words:
'I offer you, O mighty Adonai, this purest incense. . . . I offer it, O great and potent Adonai, Eloim, Ariel, and Jehovah, with all my soul and all my heart.'

CABALISTIC SYMBOLS Hebraic mysticism has four secret symbols associated with the four letters comprising the name of God: the wand is associated with I, the cup of libation with H, the sword with V, and the shekel of gold with H.

CABALISTS Some occultists perverted the teachings of the Hebraic Cabala and made it a collection of recipes for gaining power over demons and controlling the elements. Cabalists are supposed to renounce women in favor of sylphs and nymphs, who become immortal. Zedechias in the eighth century is supposed to have caused regiments of sylphs to appear publicly and invite men to join them in their kingdom. Cabalists were supposed to be able to locate lost objects by invoking certain demons and saying aloud the word *Agla.*

CABIRI A group of gods worshiped in Hellenistic times. Their cult was known for its obscene practices. The Cabiric mysteries of Samothrace were second in repute to the Eleusinian mysteries.

CADIERE, CATHERINE French nun, born at Toulon in 1709. She created a scandal by charging a highly respected Jesuit, Father Girard, with bewitching her, and seducing her. The Parlement at Aix dismissed her charges.

CADUCEUS Hermes' magic wand. The entwined serpents, one black and the other white, represent good and evil, disease and health.

CAGLIOSTRO The real name of the occultist, alchemist, and magician known throughout Europe as Count Alessandro Cagliostro was Giuseppe Balsamo (1745-1795). He acquired a fortune by selling love potions and magic elixirs. His achievements included the manufacture of a diamond by alchemical means, conjuring up a dead woman, and founding The Egyptian Lodge.

CAINITES A heretical sect who glorified as heroes Cain, Esau, and the Sodomites. They paid homage to Korah, a Hebrew who was destroyed after he led a rebellion against Moses, and to Judas, whom they credited with freeing mankind from Jesus. See Ophites.

CALALU A herb used by the *obeah* man in the West Indies. Jamaican slaves were induced to join a secret society in the belief that after their initiation they would be beyond the control of the white man. After receiving an infusion of the herb, the slave danced until he collapsed and fell into a profound sleep. The obeah man then rubbed him with another substance that removed the effects of the calalu and the memory of all that had happened to him after he stopped dancing.

CALI Queen of demons and sultaness, according to Collin de Plancy. Human victims were sacrificed to her.

CALMECAC In ancient Mexico, an institution where the occult arts were studied.

CALMET, AUGUSTIN French Benedictine monk (1672-1756). He wrote books on witchcraft, lycanthropy, and demonology.

CALUNDRONIUS A stone endowed with magic properties. It can be used for apotropaic purposes against demons, enchantments, and spells.

CALVARY According to an ancient belief, Satan was present on Calvary when Christ was crucified. Like a bird of prey, he perched on one arm of the Cross.

CAMBIONS The offspring of succubi and incubi.

CAMPANELLA, TOMASO Italian occultist (1560-c. 1639). A Dominican friar, he turned to the black arts after being imprisoned on charges of heresy.

CAMUS, ALBERT French novelist, dramatist, and essayist. Albert Camus (1913-1960) created Meursault, the protagonist of *L'Etranger* (1942), called by Papini 'the loathsome personification of existentialist Satanism.'

CANCER In the mystery cult of Orpheus, the entrance of the soul into incarnation. Cabalistically, it signifies the vital organs of the grand old man of the skies and therefore the life forces.

CANIDIA A sorceress often mentioned by Horace. She cast spells, using wax figures, and succeeded in making the moon descend from the heavens.

CANON EPISCOPI Until the thirteenth century the Church held that witchcraft was an illusion or fantasy originating in dreams and that belief in witchcraft was therefore heretical. The earlier view is presented in the Canon or Capitulum Episcopi. Of uncertain origin, the Canon Episcopi was incorporated in the *Corpus Juri Canonici* in the twelfth century and became a part of the Canon Law.

CANTRIP A spell cast by a witch.

CAPEAU, LOUISE See Aix-en-Provence.

CAPNOMANCY Divination by observation of fumes rising from poppies thrown on live coals.

CARCASSONNE French city long associated with witchcraft. Angela de Labarthe was burned at Carcassonne in 1274, charged with giving birth to a monstrous child, offspring of the Devil. The Inquisition found 74 persons in the vicinity guilty of practicing black magic between 1330 and 1335. In the latter part of the fourteenth century, six hundred persons living in Carcassonne and Toulouse were burned as witches.

CARDAN, JEROME French occultist (1501-1576). He claimed to have his own familiar demon, called Scaliger.

CARDINAL POINTS In Egyptian religions, the gods of the four cardinal points watched over the intestines of the dead. They were Amseti, Hapi, Tuamutef, and Qebhsennuf.

CARDUCCI, GIOSUE Italian poet (1835-1907) and Nobel laureate. He praised the great spirit of Evil in his poem 'Inno a Satana' (1863).

CARMEL CHURCH A Satanic church organized in the late nineteenth century in Lyon, France, by Jean-Antoine Boullan. The Eglise de Carmel was the center for liturgical ceremonies to ransom souls. Sacrilegious orgies were performed in the name of 'Union de Vie' (Life Union).

CAROLINA CODE The criminal code of the Holy Roman Empire. Introduced in 1532, during the reign of Charles V, it was derived from the famous Bamberg code regarding capital offenses (1508) and was followed in witchcraft trials.

CARPOCRATES Second-century founder of a Gnostic sect (the Carpocratians) stressing prior existence and metempsychosis. The sect was popular in Alexandria but disappeared in the sixth century.

CARPZOV, BENEDICT Professor and member of the supreme court of Leipzig (1595-1666). He recommended seventeen kinds of torture for witches, and the 'thirty-six decisions' which he handed down became illustrious precedents, making him the guiding spirit of Protestant tribunals. He is credited with signing the death warrants of thousands of persons accused of witchcraft.

CARTAPHILUS, JOSEPH The name ascribed to the Wandering Jew in the sixteenth century.

CASSIEL Chief of the spirits, according to the *Book of Spirits.*

CASTEL DEL MONTE A castle built in Italy by Frederick II in the thirteenth century. It was a replica of Solomon's Temple and was supposed to shelter the Master of the World, elected by the eight orders of knighthood.

CASTELMEZZANO A mountainous region of southern Italy, reputed to be the present capital of sorcery. Earlier capitals were Toledo, Loudun, and Prague.

CAT (BLACK) The black cat is widely regarded as the Devil's accomplice and as an ill omen when crossing the road in front of a traveler.

CATALIN Legendary Irish wizard.

CATERINO, AMBROISE Dominican theologian whose real name was Lancelot Politi (1483-1553). His *De gloria bonorum angelorum et lapsu malorum,* published in Lyon in 1552, attributes Satan's rebellion to jealousy and indignation provoked by God's failure to make him the incarnation of the Word. His grief and disappointment changed first to indignation, then hatred, and finally rebelliousness.

CATHARS (CATHARISTS, CATHARITES) A widespread movement, closely linked with witchcraft, prominent over most of Europe from the tenth to the fourteenth century. It originated in eastern Europe and included a belief in the Manichaean principle of a God of good and a God of evil. Satan, the God of evil, ruled over the world, which was the same as Hell. Pope Innocent III organized a crusade against the Cathars in southern France. They were charged with worshiping the Devil in the form of a goat or a cat at meetings labeled 'synagogues of Satan' by Catholics. Under torture some of them confessed to flying through the air on broomsticks or greased poles, slaughtering and eating stolen children, etc.

CATHERINE DE MEDICI Queen of France and noted astrologer (1519-1589). Her enemies accused her of enlisting the aid of demons.

CATHOLIC RITE OF EXORCISM The rite of exorcism prescribed in the Catholic Ritual is administered when the following signs appear: ability to communicate in foreign tongues, knowledge of secret facts, and manifestation of obviously superhuman strength.

CATO Roman statesman and writer (234-149 B.C.). He used the following incantation for a dislocated bone:
Huat hanat huat
Ista pista sista
Domiabo damnaustra.

CATS The 'first pet of civilization' has long been associated with sacred rites, superstitions, and magic. The cat was held sacred in ancient India. As an Egyptian deity, it was supposed to have oracular powers. The entire city of Bubastis was dedicated to feline worship, and a festival honoring the sacred animal was attended each May by more than half a million pilgrims.

The most prominent of the feline goddesses was Ubasti, represented in bronze as a cat-headed woman. Prayer and sacrifice were elements of the cult. Dead cats were embalmed and sent to Bubastis for burial.

The cat also had great prestige in Britain, where sacred rites were held in its honor. In Scandinavian countries, Freya was the cat-goddess, and her chariot was said to be drawn by two cats.

CAUCHEMAR The French word meaning 'nightmare' contains the root of the verb *caucher* ('trample') and the Old Teutonic noun *mara* ('demon'). See Mare.

CAULDRON OF REGENERATION A witch ceremony, also called 'Drawing down the Moon,' practiced in England on or about December 12. Spirit is poured over leaves thrown into a cauldron set in the middle of a magic circle. The spirit is lighted and Bacchus, the god of wine and fertility, is invoked by a chant led by a witch-priestess.

CAYM Grand master of Hell. He generally appears as an elegant man with the head and wings of a blackbird. When he appears as a human being, he carries a tapered saber. The cleverest Sophist in Hell had an encounter with him. Caym understands birds, oxen, dogs, and the sound of waves. He knows the future. At times he appears as a man adorned by a tuft and a peacock's tail. He commands thirty legions.

CAZOTTE, JACQUES Eighteenth-century French occultist and seer. He foretold the deaths of many leading figures of the Revolution, including his own.

CELLINI, BENVENUTO Italian goldsmith, sculptor, and autobiographer (1500-1571). In his famous autobiography he describes a conjuration which he witnessed in Rome.

CEMETERY Appropriate setting for the practice of black magic. Corpses, werewolves, vampires, specters, and coffin-nails all have a part in necromancy.

CERBERUS Three-headed offspring of Typhon and Echidna. The giant dog watch guarded the Greek underworld, allowing no one to escape. Orpheus alone succeeded in putting him to sleep. Hercules overpowered him and brought him to the surface of the world.

CERNUNNOS Stag-god of Gaul. According to Murray's theory, the Devil appeared in animal form at the witches' Sabbat because he was the pagan horned god of Europe. Cernunnos, a god of fertility and the underworld, has been proposed as the pagan god.

CHALCHIUATL In Aztec religion, human blood drawn from sacrificial victims and used to nourish the sun god.

CHALDEAN INCANTATION The following incantation is from the Akkadian-Chaldean inscriptions in the royal library at Nineveh, dating from the second millennium B.C. It involves sympathetic magic and the casting of spells.
He who forges the image, he who enchants —
The spiteful face, the evil eye,
The mischievous mouth, the mischievous tongue,
The mischievous lips, the mischievous words,
Spirit of the Sky, remember!
Spirit of the Earth, remember!

CHALDEANS (CHALDAEI) An ancient Semitic tribe occupying the estuaries of the Tigris and Euphrates. They became the learned Cabalists of Babylonia. In Roman times they were the interpreters of astrological phenomena until their great power caused them to be banished from Rome.

CHAMBRE ARDENTE Star chamber established by Louis XIV to investigate poisoning among the French nobles, between 1679 and 1682. Witchcraft was a pervasive theme. The name is also applied to other tribunals that conducted witchcraft trials.

CHAMOS One of the demons listed by John Wier. Chemosh was worshiped as a god by the Moabites.

CHAM-ZOROASTER Reputed to be the first sorcerer to appear after the Flood. His four sons were Cush, Mizraim, Phut, and Canaan, lords of magic, respectively, over Africa, Egypt, the desert tribes, and Phoenicia.

CHANDRAKANTA In Hindu mythology, a fabulous gem credited with occult and magical properties. It is supposed to be formed of the moon's congealed rays.

CHAOS In Greek religion, the oldest of the gods, the father of Night and Hell.

CHARLEMAGNE Also called Charles I and Charles the Great, Charlemagne (742-814) ordered bishops to make their rounds each year and 'to prohibit pagan practices.' These included divination, sorcery, and incantations.

CHARMS and AMULETS In many pagan religions verbal charms in the form of spells and incantations, were employed in rituals and ceremonies associated with religious cults. Amulets or talismans, material charms, were similarly in use, for protection against disease, disaster, or evil forces. Such amulets consisted of animal teeth or claws, roots of plants, human bones or hair, arrow heads, phallic objects, tusks, feathers, written magic formulas, and inscribed objects.

CHARON In classical mythology, the deity who ferried the dead over the Styx, collecting as his fee an obol which had been placed in the mouth of the passenger.

CHARUN The Etruscan demon of death.

CHATEAUBRIAND At the beginning of the nineteenth century François René de Chateaubriand published *The Genius of Christianity*, introducing Satan into Romantic literature. In *The Martyrs* (1809) Satan became the protagonist. Chateaubriand followed the example of Milton in glorifying the Fallen Angel and setting the stage for his rehabilitation.

CHELMSFORD WITCHES One of the first trials for witchcraft in England, following enactment of Queen Elizabeth's Statute of 1563, was held at Chelmsford in the summer of 1566. The proceedings were published in a sensational chapbook: *The Examination and Confessions of Certain Witches*. . . . Highly imaginative stories of children were accepted as evidence against three defendants, Elizabeth Francis, Agnes Waterhouse, and Joan Waterhouse.

CHEMOSH The supreme god of the Moabites. Human sacrifices were offered to appease him.

CHEU KYONGS In Tibetan mysticism, a group of beings of diabolical origin controlled by a magician.

CHEVALIER, ADELE French nun, co-founder of the Society for the Reparation of Souls. Adèle Chevalier claimed to have heard supernatural voices and to have been miraculously healed of a disease by the Virgin Mary. She bore a child to Abbé Boullan, who sacrificed it ceremoniously, as the high point of a Mass, on December 8, 1860.

CHILDBIRTH An ancient superstition among the Greeks was that a witch could hasten or delay childbirth by standing in front of the door of the expectant mother with crossed legs and intertwined fingers. In later times the Devil was credited with siring monsters, serpents, and werewolves.

CHILDREN OF THE DEVIL During the whole period of the Middle Ages deformed and misshapen children were often regarded as the offspring of the Devil; hence they were mercilessly destroyed. Angelle de Labarthe, in 1265, confessed that she had borne the Devil a son with the head of a wolf and the tail of a serpent, and that she was obliged to feed it on the flesh of infants.

CHILD SACRIFICES The Hebrew scriptures attribute the custom of child sacrifice to Tyre, the Phoenician capital. Carthaginian stelae show that children were sacrificed to Baal Hammon and to Tanit. Many people still believe that the Carthaginians systematically sacrificed their firstborn male children to one or more gods, and that the sacrifices performed at Carthage were a legacy from Tyre. Sacrifices were made to the gods to obtain favors and were conducted according to prescribed rituals. The sacrificial rite, called *molek*, was a secret one. It may have involved throat-cutting and the placing of the dead body in a sacred pit or *tophet*, where the flesh was burned.

CHORONZON A mighty demon conjured up by Aleister Crowley in the Algerian desert. Some occultists claim that he was possessed by the demon for the rest of his life. Choronzon appeared, shouting the words that will open the gates of hell: *Zazas, Zazas, Nasatanada, Zazas.*

CHRISM Consecrated oil. Pope Fabian declared it an effective antidote against the Devil.

CHTHONIAN DEITIES Gods or spirits of the underworld. Propitiatory and magical rites are characteristic of chthonian worship among the Greeks. In classical mythology, they include Pluto, Demeter, Persephone, Hermes, Zeus Chthonios. Much earlier, the Mesopotamians made seals and reliefs showing deities growing from mountains and plants growing from the hands of the deities. The best known of these chthonian deities is Tammuz.

CHURCH OF SATAN A church founded in 1966 by Anton LaVey, self-styled High Priest and Doctor of Satanic Theology. The creed of the San Francisco church is set forth in the *Satanic Bible,* written by LaVey in 1969. He claims that his church has seven thousand members. Lifetime membership costs $20.00. He calls his religion one of indulgence and 'controlled selfishness.'

CHWEZI Mythical hero-gods forming the basis of divination cults among the Nyoro people of Uganda.

CHYNDONAX A magician-priest of the Druids.

CIDEVILLE PARSONAGE Site of disturbances recorded in 1850 in Normandy. Thirty-four witnesses confirmed that two boys, pupils of Father Tinel, were subject to poltergeist annoyances after they had been touched by the village simpleton. Father Tinel forced Thorel to beg one of the boys for forgiveness when Thorel entered the parsonage, presumably to determine the effectiveness of his sorcery. The boy identified Thorel as the specter that had been haunting him for two weeks.

CIHUATETEO In Aztec religion, malefic female demons. They were the spirits of women who had died in childbirth.

CIMERIES One of the devils listed in the *Lemegeton*. He rides a black horse and has dominion over all the spirits of Africa. His name probably derives from the Cimmerians, mentioned by Homer.

CIRCE A sorceress whose attempts to keep Odysseus and his men under her spell are recounted by Homer. The mandrake, a frequent ingredient in love-philtres, is also called the plant of Circe since her witch-brew is traditionally thought to contain infusions of mandrake.

CIRCLE Sorcerers protected themselves from the fury of evil spirits by retreating inside a magic circle. Generally, there were two circles, a smaller one inscribed in a large one. In the East the outer circle was seven feet square, elsewhere about nine feet square. Between the parallel lines marking off the larger circle and between the two circles were inscribed the holy names of God and other occult characters. See Magic Circle.

CLEMENTIUS OF BUCY A French peasant who taught that the altar of a Catholic church was the mouth of Hell.

He also taught that to marry and beget children was sinful. His followers avoided this sin by practicing homosexuality. His doctrines were popular at the beginning of the twelfth century.

CLOTHO   See Moira.

CLOVEN HOOVES   Henry More found irrefutable proof that Sabbats were attended by witches and devils with cloven hooves.

COCK   An occult bird much appreciated in ancient augury and symbolism. According to the Zohar, the cock crows three times before the death of a person. The bird was sacred to Aesculapius. The cock's crow made the demons flee and brought the Sabbat to an end. To delay or stifle the sound witches rubbed the cock's head with olive oil and put a garland of vine-branches around its neck.

COFFEE   Once considered Satan's drink as well as the nectar of the gods, coffee was discovered by a goat-herding Coptic monk some seventeen centuries ago. Pope Clement VIII is said to have made this statement about coffee: 'This Satan's drink is so delicious it would be a pity to let infidels have exclusive use of it. We shall baptize it and make it a Christian beverage.'

COFFIN-NAILS   When used to pierce a picture or image of an enemy, coffin-nails are supposed to bring about his death.

COFFIN-RITE   The final rite of initiation in the ancient mysteries of Egypt, Greece, and elsewhere. The last and supreme secrets of occultism could be revealed to the adept only after he had passed through an allegorical ceremony of death and resurrection into new light.

COHOBA A narcotic snuff prepared from the seeds of a subtropical plant, the *huilca,* and used by the Incas to induce a hypnotic state accompanied by visions.

COLLIN DE PLANCY, ALBIN-SIMON DE Nephew of Danton and author of the *Dictionnaire infernale.* Collin (1793-1887) rewrote his famous dictionary five times. Victor Hugo used it in writing *The Hunchback of Notre Dame.*

COMMUNISM In his *Dictionary* Collin de Plancy defines communism as a 'doctrine that denies original sin and consequently demons. . . . It is a summation of a host of heresies and the surest way to reduce man to the state of savagery.'

CONFESSION In witchcraft trials confession might be obtained directly or by accusation. Torture was used to force confessions. In his *Cautio Criminalis* (1632) Friedrich von Spee states that 'the result is the same whether the witch confesses or not. If she confesses, her guilt is clear. . . . If she does not confess, her torture is repeated twice, three times, four times. . . . Once she has been arrested and put in chains, she must be guilty.'

CONJUNCTION A demonic spell which prevents the consummation of marriage. The means of effecting conjunction, also called the witches' knot, vary according to the authority consulted. The *Petit Albert,* a medieval handbook of magic, prescribes the killing of a wolf and removal of its organ. When the person to be bewitched is near, he should be called by name. When the victim answers, the 'organ is to be tied with a lace of white thread and the bewitched will be as impotent in the marriage act as if he had been castrated.' See Ligature.

CONJURATION The *Great Key of Solomon* gives the following directions for invoking a spirit for the purpose of making a pact with him. Here the pact is to be made with Lucifuge.

Emperor Lucifer, Master of all the rebellious spirits, I beg you to be favorable in the invocation that I make to your great Minister Lucifuge Rofocale, as I wish to make a pact with him. . . .

O great Lucifuge! I beg you to leave your abode . . . and to speak to me. Otherwise I shall constrain you by the power of the great living God, his dear Son, and the Holy Spirit.

Obey promptly, or you will be tortured eternally by the force of the potent words of the Great Key of Solomon that he himself used to bind the rebellious spirits to accept his pact.

So come forth instanter! or I shall torture you endlessly by the force of these powerful words from the Key: Agion, Telagram, vaycheon stimulamaton y ezpares retragrammaton oryoram irion esytion existion eryona onera brasim moym messias soster Emanuel Saboot Adonai, te adoro et invoco.

CONJURATION OF LUCIFUGE *The Great Grimoire* gives the formula for summoning Lucifuge Rofocale:

I conjure you, O spirit, to appear within a minute by the power of Great Adonai, by Eloim, by Ariel, Johavam, Agla, Tagla, Mathon, Oarios, Almouzin, Arios, Membrot, Varvis, Pithona, Magots, Silphae, Rabost, Salamandrae, Tabost, Gnomus, Terreae, Coelis, Godens, Aqua, Gingua, Anua, Etituamus, Zariatnctmik.

CONJURATIONS One desiring to summon the Devil must adhere to certain rules. Lucifer may be invoked on Monday at dawn, provided the conjurer wears a new stole and surplice and offers a live mouse as a pledge. Frimost can be summoned only between nine and ten p.m. on Tuesday; he requires as a pledge only a pebble found during the day. Astaroth will appear between ten and eleven on Wednesday if he is invoked in the name of the Father, Son, Holy Ghost, and the Virgin Mary. See also Silcharde, Béchard, Guland, and Surgat.

CONSTANTINOPLE, COUNCIL OF In 547 the Council of Constantinople declared Satan to be eternal.

CORAL It is supposed to have the power to ward off the evil eye, stop bleeding, and reveal the presence of poisons in foods. In Italy it is worn as a talisman or as a charm to protect one's virility.

CORELLI, MARIE English novelist (1855-1924). Her works on occult themes include the following: *The Secret Power, The Sorrow of Satan,* and *The Soul of Lilith.*

CORINTHUS The earliest Gnostic of whom there is any mention. He lived in the second century A.D.

CORPOREAL DEMONS Adam Tanner states in *Tractatus Theologicus* (1629) that demons often form bodies from impure air or vapors and exhalations or clouds mixed with air. To the air water is added, earth, mud, sulphur, resin, wood. Sometimes too there are added bones from the corpses of animals or condemned men: at times too from the semen of beasts or men and such like matter.

CORPUS HERMETICUM Pseudo-Egyptian philosophical writings dating from the second century A.D. The collection is a blend of Platonic, Stoic, Judaic, and Persian doctrines dealing with the ascent of the soul, regenerative processes through which the soul frees itself from the material world, etc.

CORY, GILES The most courageous of those tortured at the Salem witchcraft trials. He died under torture in 1692.

CORYBANTES Priests of Cybele. Their wild ritualistic dances degenerated into orgies of self-mutilation. In Rome the priests were known as Galli; in Greece they were called Curetes.

CROSSROADS Some ancient European tribes offered human sacrifices at crossroads. In the Middle Ages criminals and suicides often were buried at crossroads.

COSTA BEN LUCA Ninth-century astrologer and occultist. His influence was marked during the Middle Ages.

COURILS Little demons that force their victims to dance until overcome by exhaustion. They are found in Finistère, in northwestern France.

COVEN A term that first appeared in 1662, when one of the Auldearn Witches, Isobel Gowdie, confessed that 'there are thirteen persons in each coven.' Various theories have been proposed: that the coven is a survival of the Stone Age religion of the Horned God, thirteen being the maximum number of men and women who can dance inside a nine-foot circle; that it appeals to women who cherish the survival of the matriarchal society that once was dominant; and that heretical Catharists, under the influence of mystery religions of the East, used the coven to parody Christianity.

The notion of a coven of twelve witches headed by a devil or leader disguised as a devil has been upheld by Margaret Murray. Alex Keiller has found in a number of instances that the prevalence of thirteen is unfounded.

CROUCH, NATHANIEL English occultist. (c. 1632-1728). Author of forty-five different works, published in England. Under the pseudonym of R. B. he wrote *The Kingdom of*

Darkness (1688), one of the most extreme statements ever made in defense of the prevalence of Satanic practices.

CROWLEY, ALEISTER Scottish Satanist (1875-1947), founder of a cult violently opposed to Christianity, and editor and author of many works on the occult. His numerous magical writings include many articles published in *The Equinox* (a journal which he founded), contributions to a number of obscure magazines, *The Kabbalah Unveiled, Magick in Theory and Practice,* and *Moonchild,* an occult suspense tale.

Crowley claimed to be a reincarnation of Edward Dee. After he died at Hastings in 1947, his orgiastic 'Hymn to Pan' was recited during the funeral services held for him in the chapel of the Brighton crematorium and a Black Mass was administered at his grave by his passionate disciples. See Great Beast.

CRUX ANSATA A variant Latin designation for the Egyptian ankh.

CURETES The Greek name for the priests of Cybele, called Corybantes in Asia and Galli in Rome. Pythagoras is said to have been an initiate.

CYBELE This Phrygian goddess, who was called the Great Mother of the Gods, was the source of a widespread cult in antiquity. She was depicted as traveling in a chariot drawn by lions. When the forests of Ida and Berecyntus were shaken by storms, the tumult thus occasioned represented her lamentations for her lover Attis' death. Through the woods her dedicated votaries followed her, their clamorous shouts intermingling with the beating of tambourines, the shrill notes of flutes, the resounding echoes of castanets and cymbals. The adherents, roused to ecstatic frenzy by the din and the throbbing instruments, were filled with a sense of rapture, with total communion with the divinity.

The rites of this cult were characterized by wild orgies and febrile dancing. Many devotees, in a paroxysm of passion, castrated themselves, in the belief that thus they would become one with Cybele.

Cybele was an earth goddess, the mother of all nature. Her consort was the equally divine Attis or Papas. The processional features associated with her ceremonials included bands of exultantly chanting votaries, solemn priests marching in resplendent robes, all barefooted, all carrying emblems and insignia of the deity. Then, in recurrent waves of sorrow, arose the litanies over the death of the young Attis. But the mourning soon ceased. For at his resurrection there followed jubilations and hymns glorifying his rebirth.

CYNOCEPHALIA A herb used to protect the possessor against evil enchantments. If plucked out of the ground, however, it may cause instant death. Such was the view of Pliny the Elder.

CYTHRAWL In Celtic cosmogony, the power of evil.

CZARNOBOG In Slavic mythology, this is an evil deity, akin to the Zoroastrian Ahriman, the Spirit of Evil.

D

DABO French town in the Moselle region. Pierre de Lutzbelbourg is supposed to have entombed his wife Ida, a witch, in one of the towers of a château in Dabo.

DADOUCHOS A Greek expression meaning 'a torch-bearer'. He was an official who performed certain sacred rites in the mystery cult of Demeter.

DADUCHUS In the Eleusinian mysteries, the torch-bearer, one of four celebrants. The office probably symbolized Demeter's search for her daughter.

DAEMON (DAIMON) In Greek, a general term for a supernatural power or being. Homer used the word *daemon* almost interchangeably with *theos*, 'god.' Theos stresses the personality of the supernatural power, daemon his activity, regularly applied to a sudden supernatural intervention not ascribed to a particular deity. The word daemon came to mean the power determining the fate of an individual. Like Socrates, a man could have his own personal daemon. The dead of the golden age were regarded first as daemons, then as a little lower than the gods but higher than mankind.

DAGON A demon, according to lists compiled by medieval demonologists. Dagon was the great god of the Philistines. They placed the Ark in his temple after capturing it from the Israelites.

DALKEITH Site of a Scottish trial in which Christine Wilson was condemned because she had bled when compelled to touch a corpse.

DAMNUM MINATUM A threat of evil made by a sorcerer or witch. See Maleficia.

DANAIDES In Greek mythology, the fifty daughters of Danaus, who commanded them to kill the fifty sons of his twin brother Aegyptus. In Hades, the daughters were compelled to pour water forever into a vessel full of holes as punishment for their crimes.

DANEAU, LAMBERT Famous Calvinist theologian, author of *Les Sorciers* (1564), translated into English in 1575 as *A Dialogue of Witches*.

DANEL One of the leaders of the fallen angels. According to the Book of Enoch, he rebelled against God and swore allegiance to Samiaza.

DARLING, THOMAS See Burton Boy.

DARRELL, JOHN English exorcist whose excesses led in 1603 to publication of Canon 72, outlawing exorcism.

DASHWOOD, SIR FRANCIS A wealthy English profligate who dabbled in Satanism and mysticism. He transformed the ancient ruins of the Cistercian abbey of Medmenham into a lavish brothel, equipped with a library of rare pornographic books and adorned with friezes and engravings depicting lascivious scenes. Setting himself up as Superior of the Friars of Medmenham, he officiated during the ritualistic celebration of the Black Mass. He died in 1781.

DASNI See Devil Worshipers.

DAVID, FATHER PIERRE See Louviers, Nuns of.

DEATH Medieval theologians held that Satan made a final assault on his victims as they lay on their deathbeds, preventing repentance or nullifying it. Satan's fiends could catch the soul in its flight and make it their eternal companion.

DEATH PACTS Two Italian philosophers, Marsilio Ficino and his friend Michel Mercanti, promised each other that the first of them to die would return to tell the other what life beyond the grave was like. At the hour of his death Ficino is supposed to have appeared before his friend, mounted on a white horse. The Marquis of Rambouillet had made a similar pact with his friend the Marquis of Précy in the time of Louis XIV. He appeared at Paris on the day following his death in Flanders. Harry Houdini (Ehrich Weiss) made a death pact which has yet to be consummated.

DECUMA See Parca.

DEE, JOHN English scholar, mathematician, and occultist (1527-1608). He was imprisoned for practicing enchantment against Mary, Queen of England. He wrote *Liber Mysteriorum* (Book of Mysteries).

DEFEAT OF SATAN The battle against Satan and his fall is described in the Book of Revelation (12:7-9): 'Michael and his angels battled with the dragon, and the dragon and his angels fought... And that great dragon was cast down, the ancient serpent, he who is called the devil and Satan, who leads astray the whole world; and he was cast down to the earth, and with him his angels were cast down.'

DEFENSES AGAINST DEMONS The sign of the cross is the most powerful weapon against the Devil. Next comes holy water, then bells, the relics of saints, and certain natural objects — gems such as chrysolite and agate, plants such as garlic and rue, salt, the cock, and a herb called by the French *permanable,* which can enchant demons.

DEIKNYMENA An expression used in the Eleusinian mystery cult to refer to esoteric truths taught by demonstration.

DELORT, CATHERINE See Georgel, Anne Marie de.

DEL RIO, MARTIN ANTOINE Famous Jesuit scholar (1551-1608), author of *Disquisitionum Magicarum,* one of the most complete handbooks on witchcraft.

DE MAGIS An occult treatise (1591) in which Johann Georg Godelman defines sorcerers as those who by evil spells, dire curses, and the sending of foul spirits, by potions prepared by the Devil or through illicit arts from corpses of hanged men, harm and destroy the health and lives of men and beasts.

DEMANDOLX, MADELEINE DE See Aix-en-Provence.

DEMETER (CERES) In Greek legend, Demeter was a corn goddess who presided over harvests. When her daughter Persephone was carried off by Hades (Pluto) to the Underworld, Demeter went in search of her as far as Eleusis. Persephone was returned by Zeus (Jupiter) to the upper earth, but had to spend part of each year underground. Symbolically, this myth applies to the rotation of the season and the harvest and the death and rebirth of the produce of the earth.

A mystery cult developed from this legend, with special festivals honoring the goddess and rituals that offered immortal life to the initiated, in harmony with the annual decay and revival of the earth's produce.

The mysteries, known as the Eleusinian Mysteries, were so called on account of Demeter's arrival in Eleusis.

DEMIURGE In Greek, the word means 'artisan.' It was used by Plato to designate the creator of the universe. The Gnostics, Marcionites, Paulicians, and other heretical sects used it to designate the evil power responsible for matter. Also called Demiurgus or Demiurgos.

DEMOGORGON An obscure Roman deity associated with the Underworld. In the late Roman Empire, he was invoked in magic rites.

DEMON A word used to denote a lower order of supernatural beings, generally thought to be hostile to mankind. Belief in such beings is widespread. The ancient Mesopotamians lived in fear of demons, commonly represented in their art with human bodies and animal heads. Both the Babylonians and Assyrians thought the demons were evil spirits who came from beneath the earth or ghosts of the unburied dead. In Greece, the word *daimon* had a good as well as a bad connotation. Socrates had a familiar demon who warned him when he was on the point of making a wrong decision. The rise of Christianity, with its condemnation of the spirits of the pagan world, assumed to be in league with the Devil, transformed demons into malevolent spirits.

DEMON In Haitian voodoo cults a vampire, the male counterpart of the *loup-garou*. Children protect themselves against the demon by carrying countercharms such as cassava bread, black thread, or ashes.

DEMONIAC A person possessed by an evil spirit. Christ healed persons thus possessed (Matthew 10: 1; Mark 3:10; Luke 9: 1, 10, 17).

DEMONIACAL POSSESSION The Church has always recognized the possibility of demoniacal possession and uses the order of exorcists to combat it. Only priests who have obtained permission from a bishop may exorcise demons. Possession, often intermittent, is of different degrees. The limbs and organs of the victim are assumed to be under the control of an alien agent.

DEMON LOCUSTS In the fifth chapter of the Book of Revelation the Angel of the Bottomless Pit is identified as the chief of the demon locusts. They are described as having the bodies of war-horses, the faces of human beings, clashing wings, and the tails of scorpions.

DEMONOLATRY Worship of spirits, ghosts, or demonic powers. Demonolatry frequently involves the use of magic rites of propitiation or aversion.

DEMONOLOGY Scientific study of demons, forming a part of theology. Also, the description of popular beliefs in demons.

DEMON PREACHER English sorcerer whose real name was John Fian. He was said to have preached repeatedly to a number of notorious witches at a church in North Berwick. He was burned at the stake in 1591.

DEMONS, LISTS OF See Michaélis, Sébastien, and Barrett, Francis.

DEO In the Eleusinian mysteries, Deo was the mystic name of Demeter.

DESCENT INTO HELL In many pagan religions myth and legends describe visits of both deities and mortals to the Underworld, the realm of the dead. Such descriptions appear in the mythology of the Greeks and the Romans, the Babylonians, and the Egyptians.

The purpose of the infernal visit may vary. It may be a matter of curiosity, or to secure a favor from the gods of the Lower Regions, or rescue a soul. In the Hellenistic mysteries the descent was associated with certain secret initiatory rites.

The Apostles' Creed contains the statement that Christ 'descended into Hell.' The Catholic Church teaches that the soul of Christ went to Limbo. There the souls of the just remained until Christ ascended and opened to them the Kingdom of Heaven.

DESERT The Bible contains many references to the desert as the dwelling place of wicked angels or evil spirits. Monasticism began in the desert, where the Christian heroes struggled against the forces of Satan. See Azazel, Scapegoat, St. Anthony.

DESTROYER (THE) One of the epithets applied to Satan. The literal meaning of the Hebrew word Abaddon, the name used to identify the leader of the demon locusts described in the ninth chapter of the Book of Revelation, is 'the destroyer.' The first or highest of the Hindu Trimurti (trinity) is also called 'the destroyer.' The worship of the Hindu god Shiva is grounded on the idea that pure being is attained only after material fetters have been destroyed.

DEV The Persian name of Satan.

DEVA In the Zoroastrian religion, a maleficent spirit, the enemy of men and of Ormazd. In Hinduism, it is the general designation for God. In ancient Aryan religion, the Devas were the 'bright heavenly ones,' sons of Dyaus, father of the sky. *Deva* is the Sanskrit derived from the Indo-European root seen in Latin *deux,* Greek *Theos,* and English *devil.*

DEVAKI In Hindu mythology, the mother of Krishna.

DEV AZUR In the Zoroastrian religion, he was the demon of evil desires.

DEVI Mother goddess worshiped by the Shaktas as the personification of the female creative principle of the universe.

DEVIL The word devil is derived from Greek *diabolos,* 'slanderer,' 'accuser.' Generically, it designates a spirit of evil. In Jewish and Christian theology, it designates the arch adversary of God and man, the supreme spirit of evil. The Devil is recognized as the chief of the fallen angels. In dualist systems of theology, he is recognized as the source of evil.

In the Old Testament the Devil is rarely mentioned. Here he appears as the tempter and tormenter, the master of deceit.

Christian doctrine makes the beatific vision accessible to men and angels alike, but only after they have been tested. Some of the angels failed the divine test (the exact nature of their failure is controversial). One devil — Satan, Beelzebul, or Lucifer — is assumed to have seduced others. Some scholars make Lucifer and Satan one and the same, Lucifer being the name by which Satan was called before he failed the divine test and was cast out of heaven.

The New Testament gives the Devil power over the world and mankind. Even though Christ redeemed man and destroyed the Devil's power, God still permits the Devil to tempt man through his nature or body.

The Catholic Church teaches that the Devil will not be bound in Hell until the last day. He was created by God, as were his wicked companions. All were good and by their own fault fell into sin. The devils still tempt and persecute mankind. They are pure spirits with an intelligence of a high order. Each has a will obstinately bent on evil. They are intelligent individuals responsible for their own deeds. See Demon, Lucifer, Satan.

DEVIL AND PSYCHOANALYSIS In Rosette Dubal's work *La Psychanalyse du Diable* (1953) the Devil is the incarnation of the mean father and also of the great god Pan.

DEVIL OF THE TAROT In the Tarot, the Devil is the fifteenth mystery, combining the four primal elements of fire, air, water, and earth.

DEVILS Alphonsus de Spina identified ten varieties of devils:
1. Fates.
2. Poltergeists, who create mischief by night.
3. Incubi and succubi, who pollute nuns by night.
4. Marching hosts, who sound like hordes of men.
5. Familiar demons, who eat and drink with men.
6. Nightmare demons, who disturb men's dreams.
7. Demons formed from semen and the odor accompanying copulation. These demons cause men to have erotic dreams so that they can 'receive their emission and make the reform a new spirit.'
8. Deceptive demons, who appear now as men, now as women.
9. Clean demons, who assault only holy men.
10. Demons who cause old women to believe that they fly to Sabbats.

DEVIL'S GARTER Name given to an imperfect rainbow.

DEVIL'S MARK A mark of identification made by the Devil to seal a compact. According to Ludovico Maria Sinistrari's *De Demonialitate* (1700), the Devil imprints on a witch some mark, especially on those whose constancy he suspects. That mark, however, is not always of the same shape or figure; sometimes it is the likeness of a hare, sometimes like a toad's foot, sometimes a spider, a puppy, a doormouse. It is imprinted on the most secret parts of the body; with men, under the eyelids or perhaps under the armpits. . . .

DEVIL'S NUMBER Four is the Devil's own number, according to Talmudic computation.

DEVIL'S RAINBOW A rainbow with a flawed arc.

DEVIL'S SEAL See Devil's Mark.

DEVIL WORSHIPERS A sect numbering some 50,000 adherents, residing mainly in the vicinity of Mosul. They call themselves Dasni but are known by their neighbors as Devil Worshipers or Yezidis. Probably an offshoot of Mazdaism, their cult contains elements of Christianity and Islam. The Devil is regarded as the chief of the angelic hosts. He suffers punishment now but will eventually be restored to his former high station. They regard the Devil as the creative agent of the Supreme God and try to propitiate him as the source of evil. They avoid calling his name, and they represent him as a peacock. The name of the sect literally means 'God-worshippers.' The cult is probably a syncretism of Mazdan, Christian, and Mohammedan elements. Adherents worship both a good supreme god and subordinate gods. The chief of their subordinate gods, Melek Taus, represented as a peacock, is apparently the author of evil and therefore descended from Adam alone.

DIABOLIC HOSTS John Wier concluded that the diabolic monarchy consisted of 72 princes and 7,405,926 devils. He determined that the devils were grouped in 1,111 legions of 6,666 each. He distinguished six kinds of demons, refined by later theologians as follows: (1) Igneous demons, who never descend to the earth; (2) Aerial demons, who roam through the air and appear on occasion as men; (3) Terrestrial ones, who dwell obscurely among men or set snares for hunters and travelers; (4) Aquatics, who cause storms at sea; (5) Subterraneans, who dwell in caves and are very spiteful; and (6) Lucifuges, who shun the light of day and assume corporeal features by night.

DIABOLIC PACT Though a pact between the Devil or one of his henchmen and a man or woman may vary in detail, it always includes:
1. Preparation for the pact (abstinence from meat, etc.).
2. An invocation in the form of a ritual accompanied by the sacrifice of a black fowl, fire, etc.
3. A complex set of formulas.
4. The appearance of the devil.
5. Signing the pact with blood drawn from the left arm. On signing the pact, the individual 'loses his double' — that is, he casts no shadow and his image cannot be seen in a mirror.

DIABOLIC TRINITY Giovanni Papini, in *The Devil's Notes for a Future Diabology*, identifies three distinguishable persons in the Devil, similar to those of the Trinity: the Rebel (Father) who seeks to replace the Creator; the tempter (Son) who invites man to imitate God; and the Collaborator (Comforter) who torments men on earth.

DIABOLISM IN THE CHURCH Dualistic beliefs persisted throughout the Middle Ages. Sects influenced by Manichaeism include the Paulicians, the Bogomils, and the Cathari, or Albigensians. Within these sects there were apparently secret groups of Luciferians who worshiped the Devil. The Luciferians named the object of their cult Satanaël (the Satan-God). Members of a chapter of Luciferians were burned at the stake at Orléans in 1022. Devil-worship among the Cathari of Milan was recorded by Matthew Peris in 1236. A bull issued in 1233 by Gregory IX describes the initiatory rites of the Luciferians.

DIAKKA In occultism and theosophy, Phantoms or 'spooks.' They are the communicating and materializing spirits of mediums and spiritualists.

DIANAE In 1318, Pope John XXII said that a group of magicians at his court in Avignon had copulated with demonesses called Dianae.

DIGONNET A beggar in whom the Abbé Drevet claimed to recognize the prophet Elijah. The movement founded by the Abbé Drevet was identified with Satanism and caused a schism in 1847.

DILETTANTI CLUB A riotous group, famous in eighteenth-century England for its orgiastic practices.

DIODORUS OF CATANIA Ancient sorcerer, burned alive in an oven.

DIONYSIAN MYSTERIES An ancient cult that originated in Phrygia and spread to other regions. The rites, honoring the god Dionysus, god of the vine and fertility, were marked by frenzied orgies. These practices were inspired by the deity himself who made his presence felt within the votaries. They were proof of the immanence of Dionysus.

DIONYSIUS THE AREOPAGITE A convert of St. Paul at Athens, he was later identified with St. Denis. About the year 500, a Christian Neoplatonist forged some writings in his name. *Of the Heavenly Hierarchy* transformed the whole angelic world, making the Devil and his hosts pure spirit-beings. Hugh of St. Victor and St. Thomas fortified the theory of the pseudo-Dionysius and made it an incontrovertible truth.

DIONYSUS (BACCHUS, LIBER) In classical mythology, the god of wine and fertility. His cult was widespread in Thrace, where the Thracian women were particularly dedicated to his orgiastic rites. The women, Maenads, in their ecstatic frenzy, abandoned their homes, roamed the fields and hillsides, dancing, swinging their flaming torches. In their passion they caught and tore apart animals, sometimes even children, and devoured the flesh, thus acquiring communion with the divinity. Dionysus himself at times appeared to them in the form of some animal, usually a bull. Celebrations, of a milder type, were also held on Mount Parnassus.

In the mystic cult, Dionysus was associated with the Lower Regions. This cult became highly popular in Hellenistic and later on in Roman times. The cult of Dionysus as practiced by his devotees is presented dramatically in Euripides' tragedy *The Bacchae*.

Modern scholars surmise that memories of the cult of Dionysus survived and influenced the Sabbat. In animal form, the Greek deity sometimes appeared as a goat. At Eleutherai he was called Melanaigis, 'he with the black goatskin.' Like other fertility deities, he was associated with the underworld. He was attended by satyrs, lustful goat-spirits, for whom he served as the object of orgiastic rites.

DIS In Roman religion, an underworld deity, identical with the Greek God Pluto. His worship was introduced into

Rome with that of Proserpina in 249 B.C. He is also called *Dis pater.*

The Celts claimed descent from Dis. In Norse mythology Dis is a generic title referring to any of several supernatural beings, including the Valkyries, Norns, and tutelary spirits. The Slavs, like the Celts and the Teutons, revered an evil demon much like the three-faced one portrayed by Dante as Dis: a red face in the middle, a whitish-yellow face on the right side, and a black face on the left side. Dis recalls the three-headed hoar-giant of the Edda, Hrim-Grimnir, as well as Triglaf, the Slavic deity.

DISMISSING A SPIRIT *True Grimoire,* a medieval book, gives the formula for discharging a spirit once its task is accomplished.

I am pleased and contented with thee, Prince Lucifer, for the moment. Leave thou in peace now, and go in quiet and without trouble. Do not forget our pact, or I shall blast thee with my Wand. Amen.

DITHEISM In Greek the term means 'twice god.' It was a Zoroastrian tenet, postulating the existence of two supreme gods, one good and the other evil. The beneficent deity was Ahura Mazda, his opponent was Ahriman, the Spirit of Evil.

DITTAMY An aromatic plant growing on Mount Dicte and Mount Ida in Crete. It possesses occult and mystical properties. The evergreen shrub was sacred to the moon goddesses and had a place in many magical performances. Occultists claim that it cures somnambulism. Pharmacy attributes to the plant strongly sedative and quieting properties.

DIVAN CLUB A Satanical group that flourished in eighteenth-century England.

DIVINATION In antiquity, various forms of divination were in vogue. They centered on dreams and their interpretation, augury, oracles, astrological calculations. Responses and and other deductions were held to be inspired by divine guidance.

In the early Christian centuries pagan divination was viewed as being under the domination of malefic demons.

DOCRE, CANON In *Là-Bas* (1891) Huysmans describes a Black Mass said by an aging and villainous priest, Canon Docre. Naked except for his dark red chasuble and a scarlet, two-horned cap, Docre kneels before an altar, hails Satan as a reasonable, just God, king of the disinherited, etc., and calls upon the Devil to grant his followers riches, glory, and power. The worshipers writhe and scream hysterically as Docre consecrates and defiles the host in orgasm, hurling it to the floor.

DOG The Devil's accomplice. Dogs are also faithful companions of necromancers. The Devil assumes the shape of a dog to help the necromancer without arousing suspicion, but his presence is betrayed by his black hair. Early magicians believed that demons appeared as dogs. Plutarch relates that a black dog came to Cimon to announce his impending death. Early Christians drove dogs away from their churches. The Furies were called the dogs of hell, and black dogs in ancient times were sacrificed to infernal deities.

DRAGON OF REVELATION A group of Waldensians near Turin were accused in 1388 of worshiping the Great Dragon of Revelation. More powerful than God, he was said to have created the earth.

DRAVIDIAN SPIRITS The Dravidians, a non-Ayran race inhabiting southern India, believe that the universe is peopled by many evil spirits. Their religion is marked by demophobia, and they perform animal sacrifices to propitiate local gods and ward off evil spirits that might cause disease and disaster.

DREAMS Demonologists assume that dreams of the supernatural come from Hell.

DREVET, ABBE A religious movement founded by the Abbé Drevet at Saint-Jean-de-Bonnefond, in France, and attributed to Satanism. The nineteenth-century priest claimed that he recognized the prophet Elijah in a filthy beggar named Digonnet. The movement led to a schism in 1847.

DRUJ In Zoroastrian religion, a word designating Lie, Falsehood, Untruth, originating in the wrong moral choice made by the individual between the Twin Spirits (Twin Mainyu). The Druj was personified in later Avestan writings as a foul hag or demon.

DRUJO DEMANA In Zoroastrian sacred literature, the House of the Lie where the wicked dead reside.

DRUMMER OF TEDWORTH A poltergeist who haunted the house of John Mompesson, an English justice of the peace, beginning in 1661. William Drury, a vagrant drummer whose instrument was confiscated by order of Mompesson, was said to be the cause of disturbances — apparitions, flying objects, levitations, drumbeats heard by night — that occurred whenever he was in the vicinity. Joseph Glanvil gave a firsthand account of the affair in *Sadducismus Triumphatus* (1668). A play dealing with the subject, *The Drummer* (1716), was written by J. Addison. Other writings on the subject include W. Scott's *Woodstock* (1826) and a short poem by Edith Sitwell (1935).

DRURY, WILLIAM See Drummer of Tedworth.

DUALISM The doctrine that good and evil, two opposing principles, dominate the universe. In all dualist sects there is a tendency to exalt the Devil as God's eternal rival. Some sects influenced by Manichaeism — the Paulicians, Bogomils, and Cathari or Albigensians — apparently contained secret groups who worshiped the Devil. These groups, called Luciferians, worshiped him under the name of Satanaël or Sammaël. The eleventh-century Bulgarian Bogomils held that Satanaël had seduced Eve and that he, not Adam, was the father of Cain.

DUCASSE, ISIDORE See Lautréamont.

DUGPAS A Tibetan sect (literally, 'Red Caps') whose members, since the fourteenth century, have given themselves over to sorcery, drunkenness, and immorality.

DUMISANI, NKAYIPI An African witch doctor. See Zulus.

DUNCAN, GILLY See North Berwick Witches.

DUNCAN, HELEN A British medium sentenced under the Witchcraft Act of 1735 to nine months imprisonment. Mrs. Helen Duncan was convicted on Friday, April 3, 1944, following a trial that lasted seven days.

DURGA One of the many names of the Hindu goddess of destruction, Kali. Appearing in early epics as Uma, she may have been worshiped by the aborigines. The Durga-puja festival honors her as a war goddess.

DUSES Demons accused by the Gauls of copulating frequently with women.

DUSII Demons abiding in caves and woods. They are mentioned in the writings of St. Augustine. See Duses.

DWELLER In occultism, the malefic astral counterpart of a dead person.

DYBBUK In Jewish folklore, a wandering spirit or soul. It enters a human body and possesses it. Exorcism requires the talents of devout men. A. Anski's play on the subject received wide popularity.

E

EARTH-PLANET In mysticism, the seven stages of the earth-planet are the Polarian period, the Hyperborean period, the Lemurian period, the Atlantean Period, the Seven Seals, and the Seven Trumpets.

ECKANKAR According to advertisements that appear in popular magazines, an ancient science of Soul Travel.

ECKHART, MEISTER German mystic (1260-1327). Dominican writer, is called the Father of German Mysticism.

ECTOPLASM The material form of the astral body. It is a vapory substance believed to surround mediums and emit a smell of ozone.

EDISON, THOMAS ALVA American inventor (1847-1931). His diary reveals that he worked on a device to facilitate communication between the living and the dead.

EDMONDS, JOHN WORTH A distinguished jurist and influential American spiritualist (1816-1874). He investigated the mysterious rapping sounds heard near Rochester, New York, by the Fox sisters, developed the gift for mediumship, and received communications from Bacon, Swedenborg, and others.

EDN In the Rosicrucian mystic system, these letters represent the Latin words 'Ex Deo Nascimur,' meaning 'out of God we are born.'

EGBO An occult cult of West Africa.

EGERIA In Roman religion, a fountain nymph. She was supposed to have given advice to Numa Pompilius, the second king of Rome.

EGGREGORE In occultism, a collective phenonenon embracing the evocation of images such as flying saucers and the suns of Fatima.

EGYPT During the early centuries of Christianity Egypt, the land of desolation and malediction, was widely known as the Devil's domain. The whole country was peopled by pious monks, the Desert Fathers, who gladly called themselves the athletes of God. It was in Egypt that St. Anthony founded the first monastic order.

EGYPTIAN BOOK OF THE DEAD A collection of the inscriptions found on papyrus, the walls of buildings, monuments, and tombs. These ancient Egyptian writings embody the rituals and magic associated with the burial of the dead and their passage into the afterlife.

EGYPTIAN INCANTATION Among the incantations used by the ancient Egyptians is the following, inscribed on a magic tablet. It is an incantation against noxious animals. Mako is a mystic crocodile, Set a deity, and Re (Ra) the Egyptian prototype of man.
 Come to me, O Lord of Gods!
 Drive far from me the lions coming from the earth,
  the crocodiles issuing from the river, the mouth of all biting reptiles coming out of their holes!

Stop, crocodile Mako, son of Set!
Do not wave thy tail:
Do not work thy arms:
Do not open thy mouth.
May water become as a burning fire before thee!
The spear of the seventy-seven gods is on thine eyes:
The arm of the seventy-seven gods is on thine eye:
Thou who wast fastened with metal claws to the bark of Ra,
Stop, crocodile Mako, son of Set!

EGYPTIAN INVOCATION The series of names in the following invocation refers to magically transfigured names of the Egyptian gods Osiris and Seth.
O Oualbpaga!
O Kammara!
O Kamalo!
O Karhenmon!
O Amagaaa!

EGYPTIAN LODGE An occult society founded by Count Alessandro Cagliostro (1745-1795).

EHEIEH One of the Mystic Names used to summon demons.

EKIMMU In ancient Mesopotamia, a spirit who tortured the living when they failed to remember him with offerings. In Assyrian demonology, a vampire demon.

EL One of the Nine Mystic Names used to summon demons.

EL ADONAI TZABAOTH One of the Nine Mystic Names used to summon demons.

ELEAZOR An exorcist who, according to Josephus, drove

out a demon in the presence of Emperor Vespasian.

ELEMENTALS In occultism, four classes of beings: undines who inhabit water, gnomes who dwell in the earth, salamanders who live in fire, and sylphs who inhabit the air.

ELEUSINIA A Greek festival held in honor of Demeter (Ceres). The festival was celebrated at Eleusis, in Attica, then it was transferred to Rome, where it was observed until the reign of the Emperor Theodosius in the fourth century A.D.
The festival was part of a mystery cult, wrapped in secrecy and scrupulously guarded against profane eyes. The mystery cult revolved around the vegetation myth of Demeter and her daughter Persephone.
Both sexes were initiated into the rites. The cult promised happiness after death. Various mystic and dramatic performances took place at appointed times. The hierophants were required to observe chastity and celibacy during the period of the festival and also to perform certain prescribed rituals. They tended the altar, offered sacrifices. In Greece the festival continued for nine days.

ELEUSINIAN INITIATES In the Eleusinian mysteries men, women and children were eligible for initiation into this mystery cult.

ELEUSINIAN MYSTERIES In ancient Greek religion, the cult of Demeter was associated with the city of Eleusis. The members of the cult comprised a triad: Demeter, Kore the Maid, that is, Persephone, the daughter of Demeter, and Triptolemus, an agricultural deity.

ELEUTHERAI The Greek village from which the cult of Dionysus spread to Athens.

ELFAME See Queen of Elfame.

ELFIN See Queen of Elfame.

ELICH, PHILIP LUDWIG Sixteenth-century German demonographer. He wrote *Daemonomagia* (1607).

ELOAH VA-DAATH One of the Nine Mystic Names used to summon demons.

ELOHIM GIBOR One of the Nine Mystic Names used to summon demons.

ELOHIM TZABAOTH One of the Nine Mystic Names used to summon demons.

EMEN-HETAN Words shouted by a witch as she exits through the chimney on her way to the Sabbat. French witches ride on broomsticks greased with the fat of an unbaptized infant. Italian witches ride on goats.

EMERALD TABLE A tablet of emerald on which are engraved Phoenician characters. It is said to have been discovered by Abraham's wife Sarah (or by Alexander the Great) in a cave, where it was held by the lifeless fingers of Hermes Trismegistus. Hermes Thrice Greatest was reputed to be the grandson of Adam and the builder of the Egyptian pyramids. The Emerald Table is supposed to be extremely mysterious. No two translations of the Latin version which has been known since the eleventh century, or of the earlier Arabic versions, seem to agree. The opening sentence of the Latin version states the occult doctrine of 'as below, so above,' which is the foundation of astrology and a key element of Cabalistic lore: quod superius est sicut quod inferius et quod inferius est sicut quod superius ad perpetranda miracula rei unius ('that which is above is like that which is below and that which is below is like that which is above, to achieve the wonders of the one thing').

EMMA In Japanese folklore, the chief judge of the Hell. He presides over Meifu, the dark tribunal.

EMPUSA A foul female demon associated with Hecate. She had the vampire's lust for human flesh.

ENCAUSSE, GERARD Author of several treatises on the occult sciences: *The Tarot of the Gipsies, The Kabbala, the Knowledge of the Magi.* He founded a theosophical group known as Isis. Also known as Papus.

END OF DAYS In Judaic tradition, the Day of Judgment, involving the battle between Gog and Magog.

ENDOR, WITCH OF According to the Bible (Samuel 28) King Saul, fearing an attack from the Philistines, consulted the Witch of Endor. She conjured up his predecessor Samuel to advise him.

ENERGUMEN A demoniac. The name was used in the early history of the Church to designate the unfortunate members of a distinct class among Christians.

ENKI AND NINHURSAG A Sumerian myth containing elements which reappear in the biblical account of the Garden of Eden. The Sumerian Paradise is called Dilmun. Trouble occurs after Enki, the water god, brings fruits to Uttu, his greatgranddaughter, then commits the sinful act of eating eight plants plucked for him by his messenger, the two-faced god Isumud. Ninhursag utters a curse against Enki, saying that until he dies she will not look upon him with the 'eye of life.'

ENLIL AND NINLIL A Sumerian myth concerning the underworld. Enlil, the air god, and Ninlil, the air goddess, unite to produce Nanna, the moon god. After Enlil is banished to the underworld, Ninlil follows him and is impregnated by him under three different guises. She gives birth to three underworld deities: Nergal, Ninazu, and a third deity whose name is unknown.

ENOCH Seventh of the ten antediluvian patriarchs mentioned in the Book of Genesis. In occultism, he is identical with the Egyptian Thoth, the Phoenician Cadmus, and the Greek Palamedes. See Enoch, Book of.

ENOCH, BOOK OF A collection of parts of many works by Pharisaic writers in Palestine and Hellenistic Jews in Egypt. The Book of Enoch is the source quoted by the first Fathers who sought the origin of demons. Written in the first and second centuries B.C., the First Book survives through Ethiopic, Greek, and Latin versions. The Second Book, written about the beginning of the Christian era, survives only in a Slavonic version. The Book of Enoch led the Fathers to the conclusion that evil angels, seduced by their own passions, copulated with the sons of men and produced giant demons. See Book of Enoch.

ENOCHIAN A language used in the Church of Satan. Anton LaVey, founder of the church, claims that the language, used in his *Satanic Bible,* antedates Sanskrit.

ENUMA ELISH The Mesopotamian myth of creation, set forth in a long Akkadian poem known from its two opening words ('When above'). It dates from the first dynasty of Babylon and seeks to glorify Marduk, supreme god and creator of the universe. In the beginning, according to the poem, there was only the primeval sweet-water ocean, personified by Apsu, and the primeval salt-water ocean, personified by Tiamat.

These two divine principles, representing living, uncreated matter, became the father (Apsu) and mother (Tiamat) of a vast number of troublesome gods. Apsu was slain, but Tiamat continued the struggle, giving birth to a host of hideous monsters. The gods elected Marduk as their champion. He killed the mother goddess, split her body in two with his sword, and divided the waters, forming heaven and earth. He fashioned the stars, perhaps plant and animal life (portions of the text are missing), and finally mixed earth with the blood of the slain god Kingu to produce man, the servant of the gods.

ENVY According to many of the early Church Fathers, the cause of Lucifer's fall was not pride but envy — envy of man. This view was held by St. Justin, St. Irenaeus, Tertullian, and St. Cyprian. The idea dominant today — that pride caused the Devil's fall — was first sustained by Origen.

EPHESIAN MYSTERIES Ceremonies, rites, and occult instruction associated with the temple of the goddess Diana in Ephesus.

EPHIALTES The demon believed to cause nightmare.

EPOPTEIA The culmination of the sacred rites in the Eleusinian mystery cult. At this point the initiates were introduced to mystical 'things said, things done, things shown.'

EPWORTH POLTERGEIST Disturbances which occurred between December, 1716, and January, 1717, in the parsonage at Epsworth, England, where Samuel Wesley was minister. The poltergeist manifestations seemed to involve the minister's daughter Hetty, sister of John Wesley, founder of Methodism.

EREBUS Name given by the Greeks to the dark region above Hades, the region through which souls passed in traveling to their destination.

ERESHKIGAL In the Sumero-Akkadian pantheon, Ereshkigal is 'lady of the great place' (queen of the underworld). In Sumerian texts, she is said to reign in her palace, ever on guard over the fount of life. The evil demon, Death, is her offspring and servant.

ERICHTHO In Lucan's *Pharsalia*, a witch 'who had kept on good terms with the infernal powers by squatting in tombs' and who succeeded in making a ghost enter the body of a corpse and provide answers to questions posed by Pompey.

ERTRAEL According to the Book of Enoch, one of the leaders of the rebellious angels who swore allegiance to Samiaza.

ESBAT A term designating the Sabbat.

ESOTERIC DOCTRINE Occultists claim to possess a body of mystical teachings known to the highly evolved adepts in all ages. They believe that the esoteric doctrine, which incorporates elements of truth found in the aggregate of all the world's religions but only partially in any one religion, has been held since time immemorial by exalted seers who promulgate parts of it to the world when the need arises.

ESOTERIC FICTION Imaginative works incorporating esoteric themes include: L. Adams Beck, *The House of Fulfillment;* Algernon Blackwood, *The Garden of Survival;* E. G. Bulwer-Lytton, *The Coming Race, Zanoni;* Rider Haggard, *She, Ayesha;* Lafcadio Hearn, *Karm;* Arthur Machen, *Tales Strange and Supernatural;* Talbot Mundy, *Winds of the World.*

ESPIRITISMO A cult rooted in African and Voodoo practices. It is widespread among black and Spanish-speaking people in the United States. This form of spiritism deals heavily in curses and charms. Master Gambling Oil is used to anoint the armpits of gamblers, essence of Bendover to control minds, and Chango candles to achieve evil purposes.

ESSENES Members of an ancient Jewish mystic sect possessing a vast collection of esoteric literature. Their library at Qumran was discovered in 1947.

ETRUSCAN CULT OF THE DEAD The chief Etruscan underworld deity was a colossal goddess. The Satanic figure of Charun (Charon) appears in many representations. The Etruscans communicated with the underworld deities by deep wells lined with stone.

EUCHARIST The consecrated elements of bread and wine used in Holy Communion. The role played by the host, the body of Christ, in popular superstition and magic throughout the Middle Ages was recognized as early as the fourth century. The Jews, the Devil's brood, were accused of using the wafer of the Eucharist in their own diabolic undertakings. The wafer became a favorite ingredient in magical potions. Pope Alexander VI is said to have worn a consecrated host to ward off harm and death. The Jews were said to offer the host to the Devil in their magic practices. It assumed a significant role in witchcraft. Christians convicted of desecrating the Eucharist were forced to wear yellow felt patches in the shape of a host.

EUCHITES An early Christian sect who believed that each man had a congenital devil that could be expelled only by constant prayer. Its members repudiated the sacraments and moral law. They worshiped Lucifer as the oldest son of the Creator and paid homage to matter. They accepted incest and sodomy, and openly derided virginity. Their sect spread from Mesopotamia into Thracia in the twelfth century and into Bohemia and Germany. In conformity with the decrees of the Council of Treves, the Euchites were persecuted by the Dominicans after 1231.

EURYNOMUS In Greek mythology, a dark, cannibalistic demon. Pausanias identifies the demon as one who 'eats off all the flesh of corpses' and describes Polygnotus' painting of him in these terms: 'He is of a color between blue and black, like that of meatflies; he is showing his teeth and is seated; under him is spread a vulture's skin.'

EUSEBIUS Early Christian writer (d. 309). He ascribed the origin of witchcraft to the evil angels who introduced the black arts to men.

EVANGELIUM NICODEMI An apocryphal document dating from the third century. It describes Christ's descent into hell and a session of Satan's court (sanhedrin).

EVIL EYE Superstitions prevalent almost universally attribute to certain peculiarly endowed individuals a baleful influence which brings bad luck to those on whom they cast their eyes. The common people often try to counteract the Evil Eye by wearing special charms or amulets.

EXECUTION OF WITCHES The number of persons executed as witches is unknown. G. Lincoln Burr estimated in 1914 that at least one hundred thousand victims had been executed in Germany. A sixteenth-century authority told Spina that he had used ten executioners to put an end to a thousand witches in one year. The last witches were executed in Holland in 1610; in England in 1684; in America in 1692; in Scotland in 1727; in France in 1745 (although the death penalty for witchcraft had been outlawed in 1731, isolated executions occurred in 1826 and 1856); in Germany in 1775; in Switzerland in 1782; in Italy in 1791; and in Poland in 1793.

EXORCISM The act or process of expelling evil spirits by means of magical or religious ceremonies, regularly practiced by the ancient Egyptians, Assyrians, and Babylonians. Methods used to drive out evil spirits include words or incantations, flagellation, and sacrificial acts. According to Catholic doctrine, exorcism must be performed by a priest and with the permission of a bishop. The rite is prescribed in the *Rituale Romanum*. Foreign missionaries are still asked in some instances to use the rite.

EXORCISM, THE RITE OF As prescribed in the *Rituale Romanum,* the rite of exorcism begins with the litany of the Saints, the Pater Noster, two prayers for the demoniac, and a warning to the unclean spirit. Then the exorcist reads one or more passages from the Gospels, puts his right hand on the head of the possessed, invokes the name of God in a short prayer, and pronounces three long exorcisms of the demon, accompanying them by signs of the cross.

EXORCIST In the Catholic Church, the second of the minor orders. The duties of the exorcist are 'to cast out devils, to warn the people that non-communicants should make room for the communicants, and to pour the water needed in divine service.' Today the order is only a step to the priesthood. In the early Church, anyone who had the gift of exorcism could use it.

EYE OF BALOR Term used by the Irish to denote the Evil Eye.

EYE OF HORUS Amulet worn by Egyptians to protect themselves against evil forces. Also called *utchat*.

EYMERIC, NICOLAS Late fourteenth-century Dominican inquisitor, author of the *Directorium Inquisitorum*. He collated civil and ecclesiastical documents dealing with witchcraft. The handbook states:
> Any magical operation involves abandonment of the faith, apostasy, *by virtue of a pact with the Devil . . .,* so that those who practice magic must be treated as heretics.

EZRA A famous Cabalist whose full name was Rabbi Azariel ben Manahem. Also known as Azareel and Azriel, he is the author of a work on the Ten Sephiroth. He lived in Spain in the twelfth century.

EZZELINO DA ROMANO Ruthless tyrant of Verona. Ezzelino da Romano (1194-1259) was said by his mother, Adelinda, to be the son of Lucifer.

The Devil Receives the Soul of a Sinner
Detail of altarpiece; 15th Century, artist unknown
(Barcelona: Museum of Catalonian Art)

F

FABRE D'OLIVET, ANTOINE Eighteenth-century French occultist who attempted to revive the Pythagorean mystical system.

FAKIR A Hindu dervish or worker of miracles.

FALK, CAIN CHENUL First-century Cabalist, reputed to have communicated with spirits.

FALK, HAYYIM SAMUEL JACOB Mystic Cabalist (c. 1708-1782), denounced as a follower of the false Messiah, Sabbatai Zevi.

FALLEN ANGELS During the patristic period, apocryphal scriptures, particularly the Book of Enoch, had considerable influence on the concept of demons. Justin Martyr, Tertullian, Cyprian, and others held that the demons were the sons of the fallen angels and human mothers. See Azazel, Lucibel, Semiazas.

FALL OF SATAN The Book of Revelation (chap. 12) describes a dragon whose tail sweeps a third of the stars and who is vanquished by Michael and his angels. Jerome saw in this text a description of Satan's fall. Petrus Lombardus used the passage to prove that Satan had perverted a portion of the angels. St. Thomas followed his example, and later theologians based their doctrine of the fall of the wicked angels on the passage.

Medieval theologians speculated at length about the fall of Satan. The Dominican school, which included Albertus Magnus as well as St. Thomas, held that the Devil sinned through pride because he tried to obtain, independently of God, a natural beatitude. Duns Scotus (d. 1309) and the Franciscan school held that the Devil sinned through pride because of his desire for equality with God. In the sixteenth century, Francisco de Suarez tried to reconcile both views. He set forth the opinion that the Devil sinned because he desired to unite hypostatically with the Word.

FALL OF THE DEMONS The Book of Enoch places the fall of the demons in the time of Noah. Origen labeled this account a fable and made Satan's sin antedate the appearance of the human race.

FAMA FRATERNITATIS A document published in 1614, telling of the long journeys of the reputed founder of the Rosicrucian order, Christian Rosenkreuz.

FAMILIARS Attendant demons attached to a witch. They sometimes assumed the shape of a human being but appeared more frequently as animals: goats, lizards, ferrets, moles, birds, dogs, apes. They are identified by names in demonological writings: Phrin, Rapho, Robin, Zewuiel. Agrippa von Nettesheim had a black dog called Monsieur. Jehanneret Reynal-le-Boiteux, a French warlock of the fifteenth century, had a familiar named Josaphat. Oliver Cromwell is supposed to have had a familiar called Grimoald.

FARRUSARRABBA Afrasiab, identified by the Scythians with Ahriman, probably was known by the Turanians as Farrusarrabba.

FASCINATION The power to bewitch or enchant has been attributed to those who possess the Evil Eye (*glamour* in Scotland, *mauvais oeil* in France, *böser Blick* in Germany, *mal occhio* or *la iettatura* in Italy). Derived from the Latin *fascinum*, fascination implies the act of casting a spell. The term is also used for a charm to counter the Evil Eye, generally a phallus.

FATES In Greek and Roman religion, the goddesses of fate or destiny. In Greek they are called Moirai and designated individually as Clotho, Lachesis, and Atropos. In Latin the three fates (*Fatae* or *Parcae*) are known as Nona, Decuma, and Morta.

FATHER OF LIES A name given to the Devil (John 8:44).

FATHERS OF THE DESERT All Christian monasticism derives from the monks and hermits of the Egyptian deserts in the fourth century. St. Anthony, the father of all monks, and Paul, the first hermit, are among the most famous. They were celebrated for their perseverance in resisting the temptations of the Devil and his legions.

FAUN Originally an Italian deity of the fields (Faunus), the idea of the faun later became amalgamated with that of the satyr and Faunus was identified with Pan. A faun is depicted as having the shape of a human, pointed ears, small horns, and sometimes the tail of a goat. Sometimes a faun is conceived as half human and half ghost.

FAUST Whether legendary or real, Faust is the prototype of the man who has sold his soul to the Devil in exchange for youth and honors. He practiced magic in Prague, invoked spirits in Wittemberg, and claimed to have ridden through Hell astride Belzebuth. He performed miraculous cures, flew through the air, was cursed by Luther, and was imprisoned. At the end of the pact, the Devil caused him to suffer a horrible death. Afterwards he appeared several times to his faithful servant Christopher Wagner.

FEAR OF THE DEAD Prehistoric men evidently sought to protect the living against the dead by tying the corpse up in a foetus-like position soon after death. It would seem that many primitive rites are directed, not toward helping the dead, but toward protecting the living. Cemeteries are widely regarded with fear and awe.

FEAST OF FOOLS A medieval celebration providing participants unlimited orgiastic opportunities. Though condemned in 1445 by the Faculty of Theology in the University of Paris and attributed to 'original sin and the snares of devils,' the Feast continued far into the seventeenth century.

FEBRIS In Roman religion, an evil spirit, worshiped in order to prevent her from doing harm.

FENRINS In Norse mythology, a treacherous wolf, the offspring of Loki and Angerbotha.

FERN In European folklore, the fern seed is used to acquire treasures from the powers of darkness.

FETISHISM Any form of belief in fetishes, which are material substances or objects assumed to be the abode of supernatural spirits or powers. The essential idea of fetishism, that spiritual powers reside in material objects, finds expression in the reverence of primitive and advanced peoples for sacred places, trees, relics, etc. The mistletoe of the Druids, the Cross, and great numbers of amulets and charms attest to the tendency to adopt fetishistic beliefs.
The word fetishism is derived from Portuguese *feitico*,

which first meant a charm and was applied to relics, rosaries, and images thought to possess magic qualities. Portuguese explorers applied the word to objects worshipped by the natives of West Africa. Fetishism was used by Auguste Comte to explain his theory of early religion. He believed that primitive men could reach the stage of star worship without a priesthood. Fetishism, according to him, allowed free exercise to man's innate tendency to attribute to all external bodies 'a life analogous to his own with a difference of mere intensity.'

FEVER-DEMON A terrifying demon feared by the early Semitic tribes inhabiting Mesopotamia. He had the head of a lion, the limbs of a panther, and the teeth of an ass. A black dog nibbled at his breasts, and terrible serpents writhed in his hands. He generally entered the body of a victim through sin. A person who failed to observe a religious ceremonial or who committed theft or murder became the fever-demon's prime target. Fever in the body of a victim was proof of the demon's presence.

FEYERABEND, SIGMUND Editor of one of the most curious works of Protestant demonology, the *Theatrum Diabolorum*. One of the contributors, Borrhaus, calculated the number of devils to be not less than 2,665,866,746,664.

FIAN, DR. JOHN See North Berwick Witches.

FIRST FESTIVAL OF OCCULT ARTS In April, 1970, a rock-music center, New York City's Fillmore East, hosted the 'First Festival of Occult Arts.' Witches and mediums, according to news reports, were among those present.

FLAGELLANTS The practice of self-castigation as a religious rite. In 1444 some hundred European flagellants were condemned to the stake.

FLAMING ANGEL An opera by Prokofiev. A medieval German setting is used by the composer to complement eerie sounds befitting sexual obsession and devil worship.

FLEURETTY Lieutenant General of the Infernal spirits. He controls Bathim, Pursan, and Abigar. He has the power to perform any task by night.

FLOWER SISTERS Margaret and Philippa Flower were executed at Lincoln, England, in 1618, after they had been convicted of using magic to cause the death of Lord Henry Rosse.

FLUDD, ROBERT The chief of the fire-philosophers was generally known by his Latin name, Robertus de Fluctibus (1574-1637). A celebrated English Philosopher and Hermetist (1574-1634), he was a voluminous writer on mystic and occult subjects.
He wrote *Mosaical Philosophy* and *Summum Bonum*, treatises in defense of necromancy.

FLYING OINTMENT Medieval witches frequently confessed to flying to the Sabbat. They rubbed themselves with flying ointment and uttered appropriate spells in order to prepare for the flight. Some of the ingredients of their flying ointment were capable of inducing delusions. Recipes frequently included aconite, belladonna, hellebore root, hemlock, soot or baby's fat, and bat's blood. Flying ointment may be traced back to classical times. Apuleius' *Golden Ass* contains the account of a witch who smeared her body with ointment and recited a spell in order to turn herself into a bird. Prierias, Luther's adversary, thought that flying ointment was made from boiled, unbaptized children.

FOCALOR The name by which the Devil is called in the *Lemegeton*, where he appears as a man with wings.

FOETOR JUDAICUS Medieval Christians ascribed an unpleasant odor, the so-called *foetor judaicus*, to the 'demonic' Jew. Baptism was supposed to carry away the stench, leaving the Jew with a fragrance 'sweeter than that of ambrosia.'

FORAU One of three demons obedient to the will of Sargatanas, brigadier general of the legions of Hell.

FORCAS In medieval demonology, the grand president of Hell. He commands twenty-nine legions, appears in the shape of a robust, white-haired man, and teaches logic, rhetoric, and other subjects.

FORKED OBJECTS In occultism, forked objects are viewed as Satanic symbols since they are associated with the horns on the Goat-Fiend as manifested during the Witches' Sabbat.

FORMICARIUS A fifteenth-century Dominican preacher and writer, Joseph Nider, wrote one of the best treatises on the practice of witchcraft in his day. The title means 'The Book of Ants.'

FORTUNE-TELLING Using palmistry, crystal-gazing, dream interpretation, etc. to predict the future is a grave sin, according to the teachings of Catholicism, if the aid of spirits is invoked.

FOX SISTERS In 1847, at Hydesville, New York, Margaret and Katie Fox claimed that they were hearing sounds produced by a spirit. These raps were followed by the movement of furniture. By using the raps as signals, the Fox family was able to establish communication with the ghost of Charles Haynes, a man who had been killed a few years earlier by his neighbor. Margaret and Katie, with the help of their sister Lea, initiated a groundswell of interest in spiritualism and became eminently successful as mediums.

FRAGARACH   A sword to which the Irish attributed magic properties.

FRANCISCUS OF PIACENZA   A converted Jew who in 1602 published a catalogue of secret Jewish afflictions. According to medieval superstitions, the Jews brought about the death of Christ and must forever bear the signs of their iniquity. It was fitting that the Devil's brood should suffer hemorrhages, hemorrhoids, scrofula, and various other diseases for which the sole effective therapeutic agent was Christian blood.

FREYA   In Scandinavian demonology, goddess of love and queen of the Underworld. Witches held their meetings on Friday, her sacred day.

FRIARS OF MEDMENHAM   An eighteenth-century coterie led by Sir Francis Dashwood. Their private cells, refectory, and secluded gardens were established on the ruins of the Cistercian abbey of Medmenham, in Bucks, England.

FRIMOST   One of the demons who can be invoked by mortals. He can be summoned only between nine and ten o'clock on Tuesday night. He requires as a pledge the first pebble that the conjurer has found during the day.

FROGS   Associated with witchcraft and black magic, but less important in these practices than toads.

FUCHSIN   A demon succubus known to Johannes Junius.

FUMAROTH   A demon swallowed by a woman in childbirth. She had neglected to make the sign of the Cross before drinking a cup of water. The incident is reported in the Life of Saint Bononio (d. 1026).

FURFUR Count of Hell. He reveals himself as an angel or a winged stag with human arms and a flaming tail. He commands twenty-six legions and controls storms. He lies unless confined in a magic triangle.

Detail of center panel of *The Last Judgment*
Altarpiece by S. Lochner
(Cologne Museum)

G

GADREL According to the Book of Enoch, the name of the archangel who seduced Eve.

GAEA In Greek religion, an earth goddess who was the object of many local cults. She was the daughter of Chaos and mother of Uranus and the Titans.

GALIGAI, LEONORA Accused of bewitching people and sacrificing cocks to demons, Leonora Galigai was beheaded and burned in Paris on July 8, 1617.

GALLI Priests of the Phrygian goddess Cybele. They castrated themselves in dedication to her and smeared the blood on her statue. They also sprinkled the blood on their fellow priests and drank it to show their total immersion in the identity of the goddess.

GALLU A demon feared by the inhabitants of ancient Mesopotamia. He looked like a furious bull and roamed by night through deserted streets.

GANDILLON See Saint-Claude.

GARDNER, GERALD British authority on witchcraft, author of *The Meaning of Witchcraft* and *Witchcraft Today*. He tried to bring together available information on the surviving members of what he considered to be a fragmented cult that had existed since the Stone Age. He maintained that some modern covens stress theology, others ritual, and others occultism. He dressed ostentatiously, cultivated a devilish appearance, and was frequently seen on the television screen. He died in 1964.

GARLIC Worn as a necklace, garlic is supposed to protect one against vampires.

GARM In Teutonic mythology, a demon hellhound, similar to the classical Cerberus. He has four eyes and blood-dripping jaws.

GARNIER, GILLES Werewolf who frequently attacked youngsters in Dole, France. Arrested in 1573, he confessed that he had killed two boys and one girl. He was burned alive in 1574.

GAUFRIDI, LOUIS French wizard, executed in 1611. He was known as the Prince of Sorcerers.

GEBER A ninth-century Arabic occultist.

GEBURAH A Cabalistic term denoting the fifth Sephira, a passive, female potency. It is the sphere of Mars and stands opposite Hesed in the second triangle of the Tree of Life. Its symbols are the sword, spear, scourge, and chain, as well as the pentagon and the Tudor rose, both symbols of 5.

GEHENNA In Jewish history, a valley near Jerusalem, called the Valley of Hinnon, where children were sacrificed to Moloch. Later used as a place for burning refuse, it is referred to in the New Testament as Hell.

GEILER VON KAYSERSBERG, JOHANN Theologian and author of a sermon on werewolves. He believed that so-called werewolves were actually wolves under the control of demons. His writings on witchcraft, published in the same book of sermons, titled *Die Emeis* (1517), were the first to be published in German.

GEMATRIA A division of the practical Cabala, showing the numerical values of letters and analogies between words and phrases.

GEORGEL, ANNE MARIE DE Catherine Delort and Anne Marie de Georgel, two elderly witches of Toulouse, gave the earliest accounts of the Sabbat. In 1335 they confessed that they had served Satan for the past twenty years. They described the he-goat worshiped by those who attended the Sabbat and many of the excesses associated with his worship. They believed that the Devil was God's equal; he ruled the earth while God ruled the sky.

GERBERT (SYLVESTER II) Consecrated Pope Sylvester II in 999, Gerbert reigned until 1003. A great statesman and scholar, he collected manuscripts of the classical scholars. His fame led Cardinal Benno to designate him as the first of a long line of magician popes. William of Malmesbury added a compact with the devil and the story of a bronze head that gave oracular responses.

GERYON In Greek mythology, a monster with three bodies and powerful wings. He was killed by Hercules.

GHIRLANDA DELLE STREGHE The Italian word for ligature.

GHOST DANCE A ceremony in which American Indian dancers regard themselves as being in touch with the dead.

GHOSTS In ancient Greek religion, the Greeks acknowledged ghostly and evil spirits that harassed human beings. Among such monstrous creatures were Kurko, Sybaris, Empousa, Gello, and Mormo.

GHOULS Evil beings who rob graves and feed on corpses. They are among the most dangerous of demons. The name was originally given by Arabs to demons that lurk in dark places, ready to seize their prey.

GIB-CATS Old English terms for tom-cats. They were associated with witchcraft.

GIDE, ANDRE French writer, author of the Satanic text *Les Caves du Vatican*. André Gide (1869-1951) presented his theory of the "gratuitous crime" in *The Caves of the Vatican* (1913). His diabolic theory is illustrated by the crime committed by the hero, Lafcadio. Gide admitted in his last work that 'If I believed in the Devil. . . I would say that I have a pact with him.' He popularized the notion that no work of art is possible without the Devil's collaboration.

GILO Famous sixth-century witch. She was said to devour small children.

GJOLL In Teutonic mythology, the river of Hell, guarded by Garm.

GLANVILL, JOSEPH One of the earliest researchers in the field of psychic phenomena, Joseph Glanvill (1636-1680) wrote *Sadducismus* (London, 1681) to prove the existence of witchcraft. The work, which presents 26 case histories, wielded great influence.

GLASYALABOLAS One of the seventy-two devils listed in the *Lemegeton*. He teaches all of the arts and sciences, but he also incites murder.

GLOBE OF FIRE Albertus Magnus assumed that the demons pulled along behind them, wherever they went, a globe of fire which enveloped and tortured them but remained invisible to human eyes.

GLOSOPETRA A stone to which magic properties were attributed. It is said to have fallen from heaven during a waning moon. It was shaped like a human tongue.

GLASYALABOLAS One of the three demons who serve Nebiros, field marshal and inspector general of Hell.

GNOMES Elemental spirits or deformed dwarfs. They guard mines and hidden treasures. They live like men and are friendly creatures. The Rosicrucians identify them with the spirits of the elements.

GNOMIDE A female gnome.

GNOSIS A periodical specializing in Satanism, published by Aleister Crowley.

GNOSTICISM A religious system centered in Alexandria and embracing some seventy esoteric sects. The Gnostics took their name from the Greek term for knowledge. Absolute, complete knowledge was at the core of their doctrine. They also posited a series of emanations from the One Supreme Being. Matter was evil. Later, Gnostics adopted magic practices. Notable adherents included Marcion, Bardesanes, Valentinus, and Carpocrates.

GNOSTIC SECTS After Christianity became the official religion of the Roman Empire, Gnostic theories kept alive by heretical sects in the East were transmitted to the West. The Messalians of Armenia moved westward after the fourth century; by the eleventh century they had reached the Balkans. The Paulicians moved into the Balkans in 872. The Messalians and the Paulicians influenced the beliefs of the Bogomils, who had settled in Bulgaria by the year 950, and in Bosnia, Italy, and France by the twelfth century. The Bogomils gained control over the Cathars, who held that the world belonged to Satan, that

Satan governed the human body and all material and temporal things, and that marriage was an abomination since it was designed to procreate children. Because they seemed to encourage debauchery — even though the high adepts lived in strict austerity — the Cathars were accused of devil worship.

GO A Greek mystery cult that was observed at Phyle. It celebrated the deity Go.

GOAT According to popular legend, the Devil's creation, symbolic of lechery. The goat in medieval folklore appears as the symbol of Judaism and the Jewish God. The goat's beard or goatee, a supposedly characteristic feature of the Jewish physiognomy, was also considered to be a physical token of the Jew's Satanism. The Devil, frequently represented as having goat's horns, often took the form of a goat. In this shape he was worshiped by his devotees, who often sacrificed a goat to him.
Satan appears at the Sabbat in diverse forms, but as the Devil himself and as Leonard, patron of witches and wizards, he appears in the form of a three-horned goat. The middle horn serves as a torch to illuminate the area. The sight of the black-crowned beast inspires terror. His long tail covers a face-like rump on which the faithful bestow their kisses.

GOAT OF MENDES Symbol of the Black Mass.

GOBLINS Grotesque, ugly spirits. They may be evil and malicious or merely mischievous.

GODELMAN, JOHANN GEORG German student of the occult, author of a treatise defining sorcerers. See *De Magis*.

GOD OF THIS WORLD A name applied to Satan by St. Paul.

GOETY Derived from a Greek word meaning 'witchcraft,' the archaic term designates the black art or magic.

GOG AND MAGOG In apocalyptic writings, these names symbolize the world hostile to Israel.

GOGARD In the Avesta, the Tree of Life.

GOLDEN BOUGH In Graeco-Roman tradition, the Golden Bough was plucked by Aeneas before he descended to the underworld. It was supposed to be a certain bough in a grove near Aricia, on the shores of Lake Nemi, where the most famous shrine of Diana stood. The officiating priest at the shrine was the 'King of the Wood.' Before succeeding to the office he had to slay the reigning king in a duel, a feat which he could accomplish only after plucking the golden bough. Sir James George Frazer started from the mysterious ritual of the wood divinities at Nemi and elaborated a series of studies in primitive religion, his monumental *The Golden Bough*. The book contains detailed accounts of an amazing variety of cults devised by man to control celestial bodies and terrestrial elements, leading to the development of what has been termed the vitalistic view of religion.

GOLEM In Jewish legend, a red-clay statue brought to life by the famed Rabbi of Prague, Judah Loew ben Bezaleel (1520-1609); hence, an artificial man. Loew brought the statue to life by uttering certain formulas and writing on its forehead the word 'Emet,' the magic term for Truth or Life-God. The statue returned to dust when the inscription was erased or replaced by 'Death.'

GOOD FRIDAY Though the Sabbat might take place on any night ordained by Satan, it usually was associated with Good Friday.

GORGONS Three fabled sisters — Stheno, Euryale, and Medusa — with snaky hair. Their frightful aspect could turn the beholder to stone.

GOSPEL OF TRUTH A mystical treatise that belongs in the corpus of Gnostic writings.

GOURD An *obeah* man uses a gourd or calabash containing grave dirt, bones, teeth, etc. to cast a spell. He places the container near the intended victim. If the victim fails to succumb to fear, the obeah man may resort to poison.

GOWDIE, ISOBEL A Scottish witch whose four confessions in 1662 provide a basis for the notion of a thirteen-member coven. She confessed to having met the Devil in the church at Auldearne in 1647, made a pact with him, received his mark on her shoulder, and been rebaptized in her own blood which the Devil had sucked from her.

GOYA, FRANCISCO JOSE DE Noted Spanish artist (1746-1828). Many of his paintings deal with Satanic themes.

GOZU In Japanese folklore, a steer-headed demon who assists Kongo, the sheriff of hell.

GRAHAS Hindu demons who cause the death of infants.

GRAIL According to one legend, the Grail is a chalice carved from an emerald that fell from Lucifer's brow.

GRAM In Norse legend, a sword to which magic powers were attributed.

GRAND GRIMOIRE Famous French handbook on magic. It probably dates from the eighteenth century.

GRANDIER, URBAIN See Loudun Nuns.

GREAT ARCHITECT Name used by some masonic groups to designate the Devil, according to Margiotta, *Le Palladisme.*

GREAT BEAST (THE) Title of John Symonds' biography of Aleister Crowley. *The Great Beast* describes Crowley's attempt to take over the leadership of the Order of the Golden Dawn. Samuel Mathers, the Visible Head, sent a vampire to attack Crowley, who 'smote her with her own current of evil.' Crowley's bloodhounds were all killed, but he retaliated by summoning up Beelzebub and forty-nine demons to attack Mathers.

GREAT BELOW The Sumerian term for the realm of the dead.

GREAT DRAGON The leader of the losing faction in the war that arose in heaven (Rev. 12: 7-9). 'Michael and his angels fought against the dragon; and the dragon and his angels fought, but they were defeated . . . and the great dragon was thrown down, that ancient serpent who is called the Devil and Satan, the deceiver of the whole world.'

GREAT DRAGON OF REVELATION In 1388 a man confessed under torture that a group of Waldensians near Turin worshiped the Great Dragon of Revelation, the creator of the world.

GREAT GODDESS The Minoans are considered to have worshiped a Great Goddess who ruled over the universe, including the Nether Regions. Most other nature cults included the mother goddess, or Great Goddess, as a central figure. In the Mediterranean area, the traditional mother goddesses were Astarte in Phoenicia, Isis in Egypt, Cybele in Phrygia, Dana in the Celtic lands, and Demeter in Greece. Though Cybele was the only one to be given the official sanction of the state, every mystery religion except Mithraism (which was for men only) had a Mother Goddess.

GREAT WITCH OF BALWERY The name popularly given to Margaret Aiken, a sixteenth-century Scotswoman who, in order to save her own life, went about the country detecting other so-called emissaries of the Devil.

GREGORY THE GREAT Pope Gregory I (r. 590-604), known as St. Gregory and as Gregory the Great, is often cited as an authority by St. Thomas. He advocated an unusual theory of redemption, based on God's deception of the Devil. See Redemption.

GREGORY OF NYASSA Fourth-century Greek Church Father. He attributed the revolt of Satan and his angels to man's material origin. He assumed that the intelligible world was governed by the angels before the creation of man. They revolted when the Creator used earth to fashion a creature in the divine image.

GRENIER, JEAN A French youth who, at the age of fourteen, confessed to three girls that he was a werewolf. In 1603 was sentenced to life imprisonment.

GRESEL One of the demons who possessed Sister Jeanne des Anges. She managed to drive him out as soon as she understood what he was doing with her.

GRESIL One of the demons who possessed Louise Capeau. See Aix-en-Provence.

GRESILLONS See Thumbscrews.

GRIFFIN A monster, half lion and half eagle, used as a symbol of Set, the Egyptian demon of death and evil.

GRILLANDUS, PAULUS Author of *Tractatus de Hereticis et Sortilegiis* (Treatise on Heretics and Witches), one of the most influential works on witchcraft published in the sixteenth century.

GRIMOIRE A magician's handbook. Medieval grimoires were falsely attributed to Solomon, Alexander the Great, and Hippocrates. See Black Books.

GRIMOIRE OF HONORIUS One of the most diabolical handbooks on magic ever written. It overflows with impassioned appeals to God and pious statements, yet prescribes the most ruthless steps for summoning the Devil: slaughtering a lamb, tearing out the eyes of a black cock, etc. The grimoire probably dates from the sixteenth century. It was first published in Rome in 1670.

GRIMOIRIUM VERUM An eighteenth-century French grimoire based on the *Key of Solomon*. It purports to have been published by Alibeck the Egyptian in 1517.

GRIS-GRIS Protective amulets worn by African tribesmen.

GROTIUS, HUGO Dutch jurist. Huig de Groot (1583-1645), known today as Hugo Grotius, may have inspired Milton's *Paradise Lost*. His tragedy *Adamus Exul* explores the question of Adam's temptation and suggests that Satan seduced Eve only after he had failed to convince Adam of his eternal loyalty.

GUAITA, STANISLAS DE Morphine addict and founder of the Kabbalistic Order of the Rose-Cross in Paris. Stanislas de Guaita (1861-1897) engaged in the celebrated 'battle of bewitchment' with Abbé Boullan. Huysmans became convinced that he, too, was an intended victim of Guaita's witchcraft. After Boullan died, on January 4, 1893, both Huysmans and Jules Bois, another of Boullan's supporters, believed his death had been caused by Guaita. Bois published violent attacks on Guaita and fought a duel with him. Bois' supporters believed that his gun had fired and that they had magically kept Guaita's bullet from leaving the pistol. Guaita died of an overdose of drugs.

GUAZZO, FRANCESCO MARIA Early seventeenth-century friar, author of the encyclopedic *Compendium Maleficarum* (1608). His handbook was intended to expose and classify the practices of witchcraft.

GUI, BERNARD A Dominican inquisitor responsible for classifying types of heresy and witchcraft. Between 1307 and 1323 he burned 632 heretics in Toulouse, France. His guide, *Practica contra infectos labe hereticae pravitatis*, recommends the use of torture in the event all other means of saving a lost soul fail.

GUIBOURG, ABBE Seventeenth-century French priest who officiated at Black Masses. He is supposed to have helped Catherine La Voisin to persuade Madame de Montespan, mistress of Louis XIV, to take part in obscene ceremonies.

GUILLAUME DE PARIS Medieval sorcerer credited with producing, by Satanic aid, statues endowed with human speech.

GUILLAUME DE POSTEL French occultist (1510-1581). He became professor of Oriental languages and mathematics in Paris. He was imprisoned by the Inquisition. He wrote *The Key of Things Kept Secret from the Foundation of the World*.

GULAND A demon who may be summoned on Saturday. The conjurer may invoke him between eleven and midnight by writing inside a circle 'Do not enter, Guland; Do not enter, Guland.' When he appears, he must be offered burnt bread. Then he will answer any question immediately.

GULLVEIG In Norse mythology, a goddess whose burning by the Aesir brought about war with the Vanir. It is said in the Edda that during the Golden Age, before man developed his lust for gold, the whole earth was happy. But when the bewitching enchantress came, she arose more beautiful each time from the fire into which she was cast three times, and she filled the souls of gods and men with unappeasable longing.

GUNA-GUNA Black magic as practiced by the Indonesians, especially at Java.

GUSEYN One of three infernal demons in the service of Agaliarept, commander of the second legion of Hell.

GUYA VIDYA The secret knowledge of mystic Mantras.

GYAN-BEN-GIAN King of the Peris or Sylphs in the mythology of the Iranians.

St. Wolfgang and the Devil
Michael Pacher
(Munich: Alte Pinakothek)

H

HABORYM Duke of Hell. He has three heads: that of a cat, man, and snake. He sits astride a viper, holding a torch. He commands twenty-six legions and is the demon of holocausts.

HACKS, CHARLES Nineteenth-century German physician. He is believed to have written, under the pseudonym of Dr. Bataille, *Le Diable au XIX siècle,* a work incorporating his views on Satanism and his personal occult experiences.

HADAD See Adad.

HADES In Greek mythology, the grim god of the underworld. He was the son of Cronus and Rhea and brother of Zeus and Poseidon. As the realm of the dead, Hades was conceived as a dark, gloomy abode. The earliest description of the land of the dead is found in Homer. The shades of the dead, both good and evil, passed by an entrance guarded by a three-headed watchdog, Cerberus. Beyond was the Styx, over which the souls of those who had been properly buried were ferried by Charon. Hades (Pluto) and Persephone presided over the souls brought to them by the psychopompos Hermes. Achilles declared that he would rather be a servant on earth than a ruler in Hades. Tantalus, the Danaides, Eisyphus, and Ixion, among others, bore witness to the tortures inflicted upon the wicked.

HAECKE, FATHER LOUIS VAN The model for Huysmans' Canon Docre. Haecke, according to Huysmans, was a Satanist who lured the young into his clutches, corrupted them, and initiated them into diabolical practices. Haecke was chaplain of the Holy Blood at Bruges.

HAIR In occult philosophy, hair is considered to be the natural receptacle of the vital essence which often escapes with other emanations from the body. With various sects, cutting of the hair and beard has been regarded as a sign of defilement.
In many religions, hair is given deep significance. Shaving the head signifies humiliation, punishment, or penance. The tonsure dates from the beginning of Christianity and signifies renunciation of the world. In Greece, youths offered hair to the gods at the initiation rites.
Recently, a play titled *Hair* popularized the notion of the advent of the Age of Aquarius.

HAIZMANN, CHRISTOPH Bavarian painter who confessed in 1677 that he had twice sold himself to Satan. Through exorcism he managed finally to regain possession of both pacts. In his autobiography he illustrated the seven appearances of the Devil: Satan had appeared to him first as a man with a black dog and last as a dragon. Freud used Haizmann's confession to illustrate his theory of schizophrenia.

HAJASCHAR In the Cabala, the powers of light, which are creative but inferior forces.

HALF-PEOPLE See Tornait.

HALLOWEEN See All Hallow's Eve.

HAMAN A stone shaped like a ram's horn, used in unveiling cosmic mysteries.

HAMARTIGENIA A short poem by Prudentius. It sets forth the notion that the Devil attempted to persuade the other angels that he was the creator of himself and therefore did not owe his existence to God. It also states that the Devil boasted of having created matter. The Devil's assertion of self-creation was revived by Rupert von Deutz in the eleventh Century, in his treatise *De victoria verbi Dei*.

HAMSA The founder of the mystic sect of the Druses of Mount Lebanon.

HAND OF GLORY A human hand especially prepared for use in necromantic practices. The sorcerer took the hand of a hanged man, wrapped it in a shroud, and pickled it in a jar. Two weeks later it was exposed to the sun or dried in an oven.

HANPA Assyrian demon, king of the evil spirits of the air.

HANSA In Hindu mythology, the white goose (or swan), the vehicle of the Asvins and, later, of Brahma. The mystical bird is analogous in occultism to the pelican of the Rosicrucians.

HANUMAN The monkey god of the *Ramayana*, the son of Vayu, the wind god, and a she-demon. He helped Rama, the Avatar of Vishnu, to conquer Ravana, who had abducted Rama's wife Situ, bringing about the celebrated war described in the Hindu epic poem.

HAOMA In Mazdaism, a drink prepared from the juice of the haoma plant with milk and sugar. It was used in the rites of the cult, and symbolized the drink of immortality.

HAPI In Egyptian religion, one of seven deities associated with funerary rites.

HARSHANA A Hindu god who presides over offerings to the dead.

HAWKWEED A plant that is supposed to ward off demons. It must be gathered by old women walking backwards on St. John's Eve.

HEART OF MAN A work which appeared anonymously, first in French and then in German (1732). It contains a series of illustrations representing the human heart as a battlefield of the powers of good and evil.

HEATING CHAIR An instrument of torture used by the Inquisition.

HEBON An ancient Italian deity, identified with Bacchus.

HECATE In classical mythology, a triple goddess, patroness of witchcraft. She is mentioned by Hesiod, the Greek poet. She is depicted as being accompanied by the souls of the dead. Dogs howl at her approach. Her statues were in three forms: as Selene, the moon, in heaven; as Artemis, the huntress, on earth; and as Persephone, Queen of the Underworld. Her name is associated with sinister rites and sacrifices. Her emissaries were a ghastly ghoul called Mormo and Empusa.

HECATESIA A Greek festival in honor of the goddess Hecate. In Athens it was celebrated with a public banquet during the New Moon.

HEISTERBACH, CAESARIUS VON Author of *Dialogus Miraculorum,* a book written mainly for the information of young monks. Its fame is attributable to the information it contains concerning common beliefs of the age in which Heisterbach lived (he died c. 1245). In it he makes the Devil responsible for thunder-storms, floods, diseases, strange noises, etc.

HEKAKONTALITHOS A stone used in demonic offerings in occult rites.

HEKAU In Egyptian religion, a magic formula used to achieve the wishes of the spirit of the deceased.

HELA In Norse mythology, the daughter of Loki. She was the goddess of death and presided over the underworld in Neiflheim.

HELENA Companion of Simon Magus. According to his enemies, Helena was a prostitute whom he had met at Tyre. She was the first conception (the Ennoea) of God, but through her conjunction with matter, she had become enslaved to its evil influence and had been in a constant state of transmigration. She had occupied many bodies, including that of Helen of Troy.

HELL The abode of the wicked after death, corresponding to Gehenna, Tartarus, Nifelheim, etc. Of Teutonic origin, the word originally signified a hollow space of underground cave. The word is used in the Old Testament to translate the Hebrew Sheol and in the New Testament to translate both the Hebrew Gehenna and the Greek Hades. In Teutonic mythology, it is the realm of Hel, Loki's daughter. Most of the ancient religions taught that punishment awaited sinners in a future life.
Catholicism holds that punishment is not equal for all, and that only those marked by grave, deliberate and unrepented sin are punished. After the Last Judgment the bodies of the lost will remain in Hell with their souls. Their punishment will never end.

HELHEIM In Norse mythology, the realm of Hel (Hela), goddess of the underworld. The dark, misty region is encircled by the river Gjöll.

HELL FIRE CLUB A group of men who joined with Sir Francis Dashwood (d. 1781) to establish a Satanic circle known as the Friars of Medmenham. Their so-called abbey was actually a lavish, lust-ridden brothel.

HENNU In Egyptian religion, the sacred boat containing the shrine of Seker, god of the dead.

HENRI III The sixteenth-century French king was accused of participating in black masses at the Louvre. He was also accused of 'sleeping with Terragon,' his familiar spirit.

HERACLITUS Greek philosopher who flourished about 500 B.C. Diogenes Laertius credits him with the statement, 'All the parts of the world are filled with spirits or with demons.'

HERMAS A Christian believed to have been the brother of John Cassian. He was the author of *The Shepherd*, a book published about 150 A.D. The book sets forth the theory that 'every man has close by him two angels, the one an angel of holiness, the other an angel of perversion.'

HERMES In classical mythology, the messenger of the gods, son of Zeus and Maia. He was also god of science and invention; guardian of roads, boundaries, and commerce; and (as psychopompos) conductor of the dead to Hades. The Romans identified him with Mercury.

HERMES TRISMEGISTUS Late name of Hermes (literally, 'Hermes thrice greatest'), as identified with the Egyptian god Thoth. He was the reputed author of all sacred books —forty-two volumes subdivided into six groups, only parts of which have survived and been translated into English: *Poimandres* ('Perfect Sermon'), the basis of all later Hermetic literature; excerpts by Stobaeus; and fragments from Zosimus, Fulgentius, and the Church Fathers.

His name is also assigned to many works on magic and alchemy. He is supposed to have written these magic terms in hieroglyphics: arbakoriph, obaob, abniob, baiax, chenor, ora, oresion, ousiri, pneuamousiri.

HERMETICA A body of literature attributed to the Egyptian god Thoth. See Hermes Trismegistus.

HERMETIC WRITINGS A body of writings, known as the Corpus Hermeticum, attributed to Hermes Trismegistus, who is identified with the Egyptian god Thoth. The writings are dialogues between Hermes and his son Tat or between Hermes and Asclepius. The first treatise in this corpus is called Poimandres. Together, these writings represent Hellenistic mysticism.

HERMETISM Doctrines or practices derived from the teachings of Hermes Trismegistus.

HERMETISTS They were mystics, devoted to the writings of Hermes Trismegistus. They constituted an esoteric sodality, whose purpose was to achieve mystical experience.

HERODIAS One of the names of the divine patron of witchcraft. Herodias was the enemy of John the Baptist. Burchard, Bishop of Worms, says that the pagan goddess of the night-riders of the Middle Ages was also called Herodias and Holda. John of Salisbury says that the ignorant believed that the Queen of Night or Herodias summoned them to meetings by night.

HESED One of the sephiroth in the second triangle of the Tree of Life. In cabalistic teachings, Hesed stands for the force behind all constructive energy, justice, peace, love. It is a masculine force, represented by the number 4. Its symbols are the sceptre, wand, and crook.

HEX See Maleficia.

HEXAGRAM A six-pointed figure used to control demons. Also known as the Shield of David.

HEXEN In Germanic folklore, witches with the power to cast spells and to appear in various guises. Their male counterparts were called werewolves.

HEYDON, JOHN English astrologer and occultist. He lived in the seventeenth century and called himself a Rosicrucian.

HIDDEN WISDOM See Hokmah Nistarah.

HIERARCHY OF DEMONS According to *The Key of Solomon*, the three principal infernal spirits are Lucifer, Beelzebub, and Astorath. They are, respectively, Emperor, Prime Minister, and Grand Duke. After them come the superior spirits that are subject to them: Lucifuge, Prime Minister; Satanachia, Grand General; Agaliarept, Grand General; Fleuretty, Lieutenant General; Sargatanas, Brigadier; and Nebiros, Field Marshal. They have at their command millions of lower spirits in addition to the eighteen spirits immediately subordinate to themselves: Baël, Agares, Marbas, Pruslas, Aamon, Barbatos, Buer, Gusoyn, Botis, Bathim, Pursan, Abigar, Loray, Valefar, Foraü, Ayperos, Nuberus, and Glasyabolas.

HIERARCHY OF HELL John Wier's complete hierarchy of hell includes the supreme chieftain, Beelzebuth; Satan, who occupies second place; Euronymous, Prince of Death; Moloch, Prince of the Land of Tears; Pluto, Prince of Fire; Baalberith, Proserpine, Astaroth, Adramelek, Nergal, Chamos, Melchom, Behemoth, and Dagon; Baal, Commander of the Armies of Hell; Lucifer, who dispenses justice; Asmodeus, who is in charge of the gambling-houses; the Antichrist, reduced to a mime and juggler;

and demonic ambassadors to England (Mammon), Turkey (Belial), Russia (Rimon), and Spain (Thamuz).

HIEROPHANT The chief priest of the Eleusinian mysteries. He represented the Demiurge.

HIPNOS (SOMNUS) Classical personification of Sleep, regarded as the brother of Death. Both lived in the underworld.

HIQUET In Egyptian religion, the frog goddess, one of the symbols of immortality.

HISI The principle of evil in Finland's epic poem, the *Kalevala*.

HISTORIA MONACHORUM IN AEGYPTO A collection of personal accounts of the misdeeds of demons inhabiting the land of Egypt. The testimonials of various monks, collected before 410, depict Satan and his accomplices as deformed and ugly. The earliest Christian artists had given them the harmonious bodies of satyrs and fauns.

HITLER, ADOLPH The German dictator whose policies and deeds have been labeled diabolical by many of his opponents is rumored to have been affiliated with a Satanical sect.

HOBOMOCO An evil spirit feared by certain Algonquian tribes.

HOD The eighth sephira, the sphere of mental faculties, imagination, inspiration, and intuition, in Cabalistic teachings. It is a female force, opposing Netsah in the third triangle of the Tree of Life.

HOGARTH, WILLIAM Famous English painter and engraver (1697-1764). In 1762 he published an album designed to combat the extravagances of witchcraft.

HOKMAH The positive, active, thrusting, male force represented by sephira 2 on the cabalistic diagram of the Tree of Life and in Greek mythology by Uranus, the wise god who impregnated Earth, engendering Nature and man. The Hokmah corresponds to the spirit brooding on the waters in Genesis and to the Logos in the Gospel Of St. John. Its symbols are the phallus, the tower, and the straight line, which connects two points. It stands below Kether and opposite Binah in the first triangle of the Tree.

HOKMAH NISTARAH These Hebrew words mean 'the hidden wisdom' and designate a body of occult knowledge that has supposedly been handed down from generation to generation since the time of Abraham. Published materials do not contain its most profound secrets, which are closely guarded by initiates.

HOLDA One of the names of the Queen of the Night, the divine patron of witchcraft. She was originally a Teutonic goddess.

HOLLER In Norse mythology, the god of death. He causes sickness and disaster. He drags men into his cave, where he tortures them.

HOLY WATER Together with the sign of the cross, holy water is used to exorcise demons.

HOMUNCULUS A little man, manikin, or dwarf. The offspring of the sun and the moon, he was conceived without any sexual union. The idea of man fashioned artificially, using sperm and blood, was popularized by Paracelsus.

HONO KURUMA In Japanese folklore, the fiery cart that transports the wicked to hell.

HONORIUS See Grimoire of Honorius.

HOPKINS, MATTHEW (d. 1646) Notorious witchfinder. Claiming that he had the Devil's list of all the witches in England, he brought hundreds of suspects to the point of confession by torturing them unmercifully. According to one report, from 1645 to 1646, over a period of fourteen months, he 'sent to the gallows more witches than all other witch-hunters of England.'

HORNED HAND A sign of recognition used by occultists. It is made by raising the index finger and the little finger while turning down the middle fingers and thumb. It is supposed to make the Devil powerless when held to the light.

HORNS Horns, associated mainly with the great goat of the witches' Sabbat, and all forked or two-pointed objects recall the Devil. They deny the One (God) and proclaim the Two (God and the Devil).

HORON In Canaanite religion, the deity who presides over death. Identified with Mot.

HRIM-GRIMNIR The three-headed hoar-giant of the Edda. He lives at the door of death.

HUANG LAO A religious movement which involved divination and alchemy, and which provided Taoism with some of its essential features.

HUEBENER, LOUISE The 'official witch' of Los Angeles. Recently she led a witchcraft festival that drew thousands to the Hollywood bowl. The purpose of the 'world's largest spellcast,' she said, was 'to increase sexual vitality.'

HUGO, VICTOR The versatile French man of letters who called himself the 'voice of his century' developed his theory of the redemption of Satan in *Satan Pardoned*. The leader of the Romantic school, he was also an ardent student of the occult.

HUITZILOPOCHTLI In Aztec religion, the sun god. The Aztec version of his death at the end of each day and his rebirth the following dawn is comparable to myths involving the cults of Demeter, Isis-Osiris, and Cybele-Attis.

HUMAN SACRIFICES The offering of human victims in propitiatory rites is one of the principal features of devil-worship. The Bible is filled with references to the evil practice of sacrificing 'sons and daughters to devils' or exposing them to 'the fire of Moloch.' The Aztecs stained the temples of Huitzilopochtli with the blood of thousands of victims. Greek legends indicate that the practice was widespread in the ancient world. Polyxena, for example, was sacrificed on the tomb of Achilles to ensure the safe return of the Greeks.

The Canaanites offered human victims as man's supreme gift to the gods on the occasion of great public disasters. The ceremonial killing of human beings is generally associated with peoples who have advanced beyond the state of savagery. The practice of sacrificing one individual to atone for the wrongs of the group is widespread. Human sacrifice is frequently associated with Satanism.

HUNGAN A voodoo priest, endowed with supernatural powers. A typical ceremony within the confines of the family mingles African and Christian elements. Tables set up on a sacred place are laden with food for the gods.

The hungan makes occult signs on the ground, using cornmeal as a marker. Then a bush priest conducts a lengthy ritual, based on the Catholic litany and designed to show that voodoo does not conflict with Christianity. The hungan invokes the loa, to determine the fee to be paid by those present. Sacrificial animals are offered to persuade the loa to take possession of the worshippers. Those possessed by the loa run, jump, roll on the ground, stamp out live embers with their feet, etc. Animals then are slaughtered, cooked, and placed in the house of worship. A calabash filled with their blood is set on the altar. The door is closed to allow the gods to enjoy their meal undisturbed. A few hours later, the hungan tells the worshipers that the loa have finished, and that they may have the food that remains. The whole ceremony lasts at least two full days and nights. A voodoo dance that follows the closed ceremony is open to the public. Observers have surmised that possession substitutes a second personality for the normal personality of the possessed, and that seizures result from innate neurotic tendencies as well as from a cultural tradition that stimulates seizures.

HUNS In the sixth century Jornandes popularized the notion that the Huns were the offspring of demons and the evil witches of barbarism.

HUTGIN A demon who takes pleasure in conversing with men and doing them favors.

HUYSMANS, JORIS KARL (1848-1907) French novelist, author of *Là-Bas,* a novel on Satanism. 'The Principle of Evil and the Principle of Good,' he wrote, 'the God of light and the God of Darkness, two streams contend for the soul. . . . It is quite evident that the God of light is in the eclipse, that Evil reigns over the world, as master.'

HYDEVILLE The town in New York made famous by the Fox sisters. In 1848 Margaret, Catharine, and Leah Fox caused their neighbors to believe that spirits were communicating with them by means of tappings — one tap for no, three for yes. These tappings marked the beginning of an upsurge of interest in spiritualism throughout America.

I

IACCHAGOGI Bearers of the statue of Iacchus (Bacchus) at the Eleusinian mysteries.

IALDABAOTH In alchemy, the demiurge who lies captive in the darkness of matter. He is that part of the deity that has been swallowed up in his own creation, the dark god who reverts to his original state of luminosity in the mystery of the alchemical transmutation. In Hebrew legend, he is the supreme archon. The Hebrew word means 'child of chaos' and suggests a parallel between Ialdabaoth and Baal, Kronos, and Saturn. In the writings of the Gnostics, he is the evil spirit who created the Lower World.

IAMBLICHUS A Syrian Neoplatonic philosopher who was born c. 250 and died c. 325 A.D. In Rome, he studied under Porphyry, also a Syrian, who was a pupil of the Neoplatonist Plotinus. Iamblichus founded a school of his own in his native Syria. Among his other works is a noted defense of magic, entitled *De Mysteriis Aegyptiis* (The Egyptian Mystery Cults).

He initiated the attempt to construct on the basis of Neo-Platonism a complete theology encompassing every myth, rite, and divinity associated with paganism.

IAO (IHAHO) A mystic name embodying the symbols of the male and female generative principles. According to Clement of Alexandria, it was worn by the initiates of the mysteries of Serapis.

IBLIS The Devil of Islam. According to the sacred book of the Yezidi, the Book of Revelation and the Black Book, Iblis is a fallen archangel. He damned himself because of his exclusive love of the idea of divinity. God pardoned him and entrusted to him the government of the world and the oversight of souls. The minister of God, called Malak Tawus or 'Peacock Angel,' is deemed worthy of adoration by the so-called 'Devil-Worshipers.'

IBN GABIROL An eleventh-century Jewish poet, philosopher, and Cabalist, Solomon Ben Judah Ibn Gabirol, also known as Avicebron, was born in Malaga and died in Valencia. His chief philosophical work *Fons Vitae* (Fountain of Life) introduced Neo-Platonism into Europe. In his system, universal matter emanates from the essence of God and universal form from His will. All beings are composed of matter and form. *Fons Vitae* is supposed to reveal some of the secrets of the speculative Cabala.

I CHING The most ancient of the Chinese classics, based on the interpretation of various arrangements of divided and undivided lines. *I Ching* ('The Book of Changes'), still used in divination, is believed to contain the key to Chinese philosophy. Legend attributes the eight diagrams from which the work derives to Fu Hsi (2953-2838 B.C.). From the markings on the back of a turtle, Fu Hsi is said to have constructed the circular arrangement of the eight trigrams from which the whole system of *I Ching* was developed.

ICHTHUS In Greek, this term means 'fish.' It was the name given to the son of Atargatis, who is identified with Cybele. The cult of Cybele worshiped fish, and the consumption of fish was hence forbidden to her priests.

ICU The Yoruba god of death. In Cuba, the *santero* conducts a mystic rite to protect a patient near death from Icú.

IDISI In Teutonic mythology, demonic female spirits.

IDOLATRY The worship of idols includes the cult of demons (demonolatry), animals (zoolatry), and spirits of various kinds (animism). Fetishism is related to idolatry.

IGNEOUS DEMONS One of six classes of demons identified by medieval theologians. They never descend to the earth from the air to have commerce with sorcerers.

IGNIS FATUUS A luminous apparition frequently seen in swamps.

ILLAPA The Incan god of the underworld. Also called Katoylla.

ILLUMINATI An expression (literally, 'the enlightened ones') applied in the fifteenth century to certain occultists.

ILLUYANKA A dragon killed by the Hittite Weather God of Heaven.

IMAGE MAKING Bernardus Guilonis (1261-1331) described the fashioning of two images:
He made and fashioned two images of wax with lead from fishing nets: moulded the lead: collected flies, spiders, frogs, snake skin, and a great many other items and placed them under the images along with conjurations and invocations of the demons. Then he drew blood from some part of his own body and mixed it with the blood of the frog and offered or gave it to the invoked demons.

IMHETEP Ancient sorcerer-priest of Egypt.

IMPERATOR A famous control said by Stainton Moses to have announced his presence on September 19, 1872. He claimed later to be Malchias, leader of a group of spirits working to elevate mankind.

INCANTATRIX The medieval designation of a witch.

INCARNATION OF SATAN The Devil is supposed to have taken on the disguise of flesh many times. Judas said that Satan was incarnated in him when he betrayed Christ. Nero was believed to be the incarnation of Satan, and after him, Attila, Theodoric, Ezzelino da Romano, Frederick II, Ivan the Terrible, Napoleon, Hitler, and Stalin.

INCENSE OF ABRAMELIN A mixture of cinnamon, myrrh, olive oil, and galingal. The fragrant mixture is used in summoning a spirit.

INCOMMUNICABLE AXIOM A key to the occult. When deciphered, it makes the occultist omnipotent. It is embodied in the four letters of the Tetragram, in the Cabalistic transcription of Azoth and Inri, and in the monogram on Constantine's standard (XP).

INCUBUS An evil spirit supposed to lie upon sleeping women and have intercourse with them. According to a papal bull issued by Pope Innocent in 1484:
Many persons of both sexes, forgetful of their own salvation, have abused incubi and succubi.
Some Church Fathers maintain that an incubus is an angel whose lust for women brought about his fall. He corresponds to the succubus who appears to men. When associated with a particular witch, both are known as familiars. The incubus is called by other names: *follet* (French), *alp* (German), *folletto* (Italian), *duende* (Spanish).

INFERNALIA Title of a famous work by Charles Nodier. It is a collection of materials dealing with Hell.

INFERNO Hell or a place likened to it. In the first part of Dante's *Divine Comedy*, Hell is depicted as a vast pit in which the souls of the damned suffer.

INFESTATIONS Acts of violence attributed to maleficent spirits.

INNOCENT VIII Author of one of the key documents in the campaign of the Church against witchcraft. The papal bull which he issued on December 5, 1484, stressed the duty of men to combat the Devil and served as justification for the merciless persecution of those accused of sorcery.

INSTITOR, HENRICUS See Kramer, Heinrich.

INSUFFLATION According to St. Augustine, one of the most ancient traditions of the Church was insufflation, or breathing into the face of a person who had been baptized to signify the expelling of the evil spirit and the introduction of the good Spirit of God.

INVOCATION OF A DEMON Among the ancient formulas for invoking demons are these: Palas aron azinomas; Bagahi laca Bachabé; and utterance of the nine divine and mystic names — Eheieh, Iod, Tetragrammaton Elohim, El, Elohim Gibor, Eloah Va-Daath, El Adonai Tzabaoth, Elohim Tzabaoth, Shaddai.

INQUISITION The redoubtable institution for the suppression of heresy was developed under Innocent III (1227-1241). In 1233 Gregory IX entrusted its operation to the Dominicans. In 1451 Nicholas V allowed the Inquisition to move against those accused of witchcraft. Innocent VIII and his successors issued papal bulls reinforcing the decision of Nicholas V. Tortures, both physical and mental, were approved by most of the pontiffs. The excesses of the Inquisition, including the deaths of thousands of apostates, heretics, Jews, and presumed witches, came to an end long before the institution was formally abolished, in 1772 in France and in 1834 in Spain.

INUATS Among Eskimos, spirits capable of assuming human form.

IOD One of the Nine Mystic Names used to summon demons.

IO-TE-PUKENGA A Maori supernatural being conceived as the source of all things and ruler of the world.

IPSISSIMUS The highest of the ten grades or ranks in Aleister Crowley's cabalistic system.
The first and highest sephira, the sphere of God, 'is beyond all comprehension of those of lower degrees.' The Ipsissimus is 'free from all limitations' He wields the magical power which belongs to man as the potential God.

IRENAEUS Bishop of Lyon. Irenaeus (130-202) established the right of Satan to rule over men. Sin gave men over to the Devil.

IRKALLA Variant of Ereshkigal, Sumerian queen of the underworld.

IRON Because meteoric iron was used by man long before it was smelted, iron can be used effectively against demons. Since it first came from the heavens, demons fear it.

IROQUOIAN WITCHCRAFT The Iroquoian tribes attributed disease to the mind of the patient, to physical injuries, and to witchcraft. The body was thought to be inhabited by a single soul occupying all its parts. Witchcraft was used to introduce foreign articles into the body and thereby produce sickness.

IRUNGU One of several spirits involved in the Nyoro cult. When he is 'in the head' of a medium, Irungu divines for clients willing to pay a fee for his services.

ISAAC THE BLIND Medieval French Jew (fl. 1190-1200) credited with reviving interest in the mystical teachings of the ancient rabbis.

ISACAARON One of the demons who possessed Sister Jeanne des Anges. Isacaaron filled her imagination with strange, shameful notions. She describes his passion as violent and says that he 'went to extremes and blinded reason.'

ISANGOMA An African witch doctor. See Zulus.
She accompanied witches to the Sabbat in Alsace,

ISEIA A festival that was observed in honor of Isis. The votaries, in commemoration of Isis as a corn-goddess, carried offerings of wheat and barley. The celebration itself was marked by orgiastic rites, and continued for nine days. The obscenities were so flagrant that the festival was abolished by the Romans. But the Emperor Commodus re-established it.

ISHTAR A Sumerian-Akkadian goddess, identified with Astarte. She was called by Hammurabi, King of Babylon, 'the lady of battles.' In Babylonia and Assyria she was depicted as a lion, holding a weapon in her hand. Ishtar was the goddess of carnal love and in Uruk, in Mesopotamia, she had her temple of Eanna. In one myth, she is the sister of Ereshkigal, Queen of the underworld in Sumerian legend.
Ishtar was the most widely celebrated deity in the entire Middle East, and temples dedicated to her were to be found in every principal city.

ISIASI Priest of the goddess Isis. In their hands they carried a branch of sea-wormwood, and chanted the praises of the goddess at dawn and in the evening. They dressed in linen robes. Their heads were shaven. They practiced continence and abstained from the use of sheep, pig, and salt.

ISIS In Egyptian religion, Isis is the supreme, the most widely worshipped goddess. Sister and consort of Osiris, mother of Harus, all three form the triad that was most dominant in Egyptian religious life.

The cult in time spread to Asia Minor and the entire Mediterranean world as well.

Isis is the daughter of Seb and Nut. She gave burial to the mutilated body of her consort Osiris. Her cult involved his death and his rebirth, accompanied with lamentation and jubilation respectively.

Identified with Demeter, who too represents a vegetation cult, Isis has many aspects, attributes, and functions.

She watches over sailors. She presides over magic arts, and she is the moon-goddess.

Isis was eagerly adopted into the Greek cities, and in Rome her temples were constantly filled with votaries. During the last four centuries B.C. and far into the fourth century A.D. her worship prevailed in the ancient world. She had temples in Egypt, Greece, Rome, and Asia Minor.

Isis had her official priests and her special festivals. Among the practices of her cult were the interpretation of dreams, lavish banquets, resplendent processions, and dances to the accompaniment of tambourines, cymbals, the sistrum, and other musical instruments.

Isis is identified with Aphrodite too, with Hathor, and with numerous other divinities, so that, to avoid offense, she was often addressed as 'O Thou, of countless names.' She was Ceres and Juno, Diana the huntress and Bellona the ear-goddess, Hecate, of the Lower Regions, Cybele the Phrygian Mighty Mother of the Gods. In this polyform aspect she was known as Myrionyma, the deity of one thousand names. One inscription in Latin reads: To you, goddess Isis, who are one and all things. Isis is the eternal divinity, without beginning, without end.

The Roman philosopher and novelist Apuleius, who flourished in the second century A.D., describes the rites of the cult of Isis in his amazing novel the *Metamorphoses*. Isis is sometimes represented as a woman with cow's horns, and holding a sistrum. She is also depicted veiled, her head topped with flowers, with the earth at her feet. Again, she is winged, with a quiver over her shoulder, or holding a flaming torch or a cornucopia.

ITTA African witch doctor, particularly influential among the Zulus.

IUDICIUM AQUAE See Swimming.

IXCOZAUHQUI Another name for the Aztec fire god, Xiuhtecuhtli.

IXION In Greek mythology, a king who was punished in Tartarus, the region below Hades, for aspiring to the love of Hera. There he was bound to an endlessly revolving wheel.

IXTAB In Maya religion, the goddess of suicides. She is an evil spirit, seducing and killing men at crossroads.

Devils
(N. Y. Public Library Collection)

J

JAINA CROSS The same as the swastika. Similar to Thor's hammer.

JALARUPA One of the most occult signs of the Zodiac. The Sanskrit word means 'water-body, form.' It figures on the banner of Kama, god of love.

JAMES VI King of Scotland and author of *Demonology*. His statute of 1604 intensified the campaign against witchcraft.

JAMES, WILLIAM American psychologist and philosopher (1842-1910). He founded the American Society for Psychical Research and maintained a lifelong interest in the supernatural. James Hervey Hyslop discusses James' return after death, in a book titled *Contact with the Other World*.

JAPANESE EXORCISM A procedure practiced by the Japanese involves the use of lights and the recital of an incantation which is repeated one hundred times.

JAQUIER, NICOLAS Dominican theologian who advanced the principle of the devil's mark. *Flagellum Haereticorum Fascinatorionum*, he tried to defend the actions of the inquisitors in forcing the learned Guillaume Edelin, professor at the Sorbonne, to confess in 1453 that he had traveled to a witches' sabbat on a broom.

JARRY, ALFRED French dramatist and novelist. Alfred Jarry (1873-1907) explored the hidden propensities of evil in *Ubu roi*, a satirical drama which he wrote with a classmate (1888) and expanded for public presentation (1896). Surrealists hailed the author as a precursor of their movement.

JEALOUSY According to some theologians, Satan's rebellion was motivated by jealousy. When he learned that God would create man and love this creature enough to transform himself into man's victim in order to save man, Satan rebelled. This theory assumes that the Devil was one of the angels to whom God communicated the most profound mysteries of the divine idea.

JEANNE DES ANGES, SISTER Jeane de Belcies entered the Ursuline order in 1622 and eventually became the head of their house at Loudun. She confessed that Urbain Grandier, a priest, had made a pact with the Devil and sent demons into the bodies of eight Ursuline nuns. The demons in her own body were named Leviathan, Behemoth, Asmodeus, Isacaaron, Ballam, Gresel, and Aman.

JESUS AND EXORCISM Exorcism had an important place in the life of Jesus. Mark relates (1:32, 34) that many who were sick and possessed came to him and were healed. Matthew (8:16 f.) confirms Jesus' power to drive out evil spirits and interprets it as the fulfillment of Isaiah's prophecy (53:4). Luke (4:40 f.) agrees with Mark. Specific references to Jesus' power to drive out evil demons abound in the Gospels: Luke 4:41, 6:18, 7:21, 13:32; Mark 1:14 f., 3:10 f., 16:17 f.; Matthew 4:23 f., 8:16, 10.1, 8.

JETTATURA The Italian name for the Evil Eye. The superstition is widespread in southern Italy. See Evil Eye.

JETZIRAH The *Sepher Jetzirah* (Book of the Creation) is the most occult of all the extant Cabalistic works. It explains the evolution of the universe in terms of a system of correspondences and numbers. God is said to have created the universe by thirty-two paths of secret wisdom, corresponding with the twenty-two letters of the Hebrew alphabet and the ten fundamental numbers. These ten primordial numbers, from which the whole Universe evolved, are followed by the twenty-two letters divided into three Mothers, seven double consonants, and twelve simple consonants.

JEWISH STONE A stone to which magic properties were attributed. Also called Lapis Iudaicus.

JEWISH AFFLICTIONS Medieval Christians believed that the Jews suffered from characteristic afflictions. Among those were menstruation, hemorrhages, hemorrhoids, quinsy, scrofula, and various mysterious skin diseases. Jews were thought to hide these afflictions or to heal them, sometimes by magical means, sometimes by the use of Christian blood.

JEWS In Christian legend, the Devil and the Jews are Christ's inexorable enemies. The Gospel of John (8.44) says that they are of their 'father the Devil.' The Book of Revelation (2.9 and 3.9) labels a Jewish house of worship a 'synagogue of Satan.' In the Middle Ages the tale of the Wandering Jew, told by Jesus whom he had taunted to 'go on forever until I return,' reinforced the notion of an alliance between the Jews and the Devil. That the Jew was the Devil's creature, fighting the forces of truth, is a notion that permeates medieval literature. The legend of Theophilus, who sold his soul directly to a Jew or (in alternate versions) to the Devil with the help of a Jew, typifies the medieval attitude of Christians toward Jews. It was widely assumed that the Jews would form the spearhead of the Antichrist's legions when he attempted to set himself up as God. Strangely, in Jewish thought the Devil has never had a prominent place as a distinct personality.

JINNI Among the heathen Arabs, a demon representing one of the hostile forces of nature. To Moslems jinn (the plural form of jinni) may be either good or evil supernatural beings. Solomon is supposed to have possessed a magic ring which gave him power over the jinn.

JOAN OF ARC French heroine called the Maid of Orleans (1412-1431). Among the seventy charges made against her were those of invoking evil spirits. The court later struck out all charges of sorcery and condemned her on two main counts: wearing men's dress and refusing to accept the authority of the Church. After being excommunicated and burned as a 'relapsed, heretic, apostate, idolater,' in 1431, she was decreed 'venerable' (1904), beatified (1908), and canonized (1920).

JOB One of the first men to be persecuted by the Devil (Job 1: 6-12).

JOCANNA The name under which the Haitians are reported to have worshiped a supreme evil being.

JOHANNES, DOCTOR Name assumed by Jean-Antoine Boullan, High Priest of Carmel Church in Lyon, France.

JOHN XII Pope from 954 to 964. One of the youngest of all Popes when he ascended the throne of St. Peter, he was accused of having made toasts to the Devil and of having invoked other demons.

JOHN XXII Fourteenth-century pope, author of the bull *Super Illius Specula.* Issued in 1326, the papal bull censured those who worshiped demons and practiced witchcraft.

JOHN XXII Pope, author of bulls and letters attacking witchcraft in the first quarter of the fourteenth century. In 1320 he urged the faithful to

> seek out and otherwise proceed against those who sacrifice to devils or worship them . . ., make an avowed pact with the devils . . ., fashion or cause to be fashioned any waxen image or anything else to bind the devil.

JOHN OF DAMASCUS One of the noted Fathers of the Eastern Church, John of Damascus (700-754) described the demons as dragons flying through the air.

JOHNSON, MARGARET Seventeenth-century English witch. She was accused of having intercourse with the Devil, who appeared in the form of a cat.

JORMUNGAND In Scandinavian mythology, the Midgard serpent.

JUDAS According to the Gospel of St. Luke (22:3) 'Satan entered into Judas surnamed Iscariot, being of the number of the twelve.' Judas took his own life, but the Devil found his soul and tortured it daily. Later, the man who betrayed Christ was reverenced by the Cainites as the emancipator of mankind.

JUDEN BADTUB Jewish bathtub. A sixteenth-century series of prints showing the Devil helping the Jews with the operation of a bathhouse.

JUDENSAU Sow of the Jews. A common medieval caricature of the Jew portrays the sow as the mother suckling her young, often with the Devil supervising the operation.

JU-JU Generic name for African magic practices.

JULIAN THE APOSTATE This Roman Emperor ruled from 360 to 363 A.D. He attempted to reinstate the religion of Mithraism in the West. But after his death it gradually disappeared from Roman territories.

JULIANUS Ancient Roman sorcerer. He is reputed to have used occult practices to banish plague from Rome. He was also known as Theurgus, the Necromancer.

JUNIUS, JOHANNES Mayor of Bamberg. After his wife had been executed as a witch, he was accused of having intercourse with a demon succubus, Fuchsin, and of having been baptized Krix before Belzebuth. He was burned in 1628.

JUSTINE Heroine of a legend recorded in the *Acta Sanctorum*. Cyprian, who had sold his soul to the Devil, tried in vain to seduce her. He became a Christian convert and reached such a high standard of virtue that he was named bishop of Antioch. See St. Cyprian.

JUSTIN MARTYR Second-century church father in Palestine. In his *Dialogue with Triphon* he put forth the theory that Satan became a wicked angel when he tempted Eve.

K

KA See Ba.

KAABA (CAABA, KAABEH) See Baetulus.

KABBALAH See Cabala.

KAHUNA In Hawaii, a sorcerer.

KAIGA'U Among the Trobriand Islanders, a powerful magic designed to bewilder and ward off the *mulukuausi*, or evil sorceresses.

KALI In Hinduism, a goddess, the wife of Shiva, represented with a necklace of human heads and a bloody dripping sword in one of her many hands. She is the personification of cosmic force, the creator of all things, even the gods.

KALKI AVATAR The 'White Horse Avatar' which will be the last incarnation of Vishnu, according to the Brahmins; of Maitreya Buddha, according to certain Buddhists; of Sosiosh, according to the followers of Zoroaster. In his tenth avatar, Vishnu will appear seated on a milk-white steed and with his drawn sword will destroy the wicked and restore purity.

KALLOFALLING In Eskimo religion, he was a terrible creature who dragged brave hunters down beneath the water.

KAMRUSEPA Hittite goddess, skilled in witchcraft. Also known as Katahzipuri.

KARAPS In Zoroastrian sacred literature, the sacrificial priest of the Daevas, who rejected the teachings of Zarathustra.

KARDEC, ALLAN (1804-1869) One of the first French converts to spiritualism (*spiritisme* in France), Léon Denizard Hippolyte Rivail believed that he was the reincarnation of Allan Kardec, an ancient Druid. His numerous works were internationally acclaimed — and condemned by the Bishop of Barcelona. His tomb at Père-Lachaise cemetery is marked by a druidic mehhir.

KARMA A force which works through both evil and good to determine the circumstances and nature of future incarnations.

KARRA-KALF Modern Icelandic magic. The initiate must lick the Devil, who appears in the shape of a newborn calf.

KARSHIPTA In Zoroastrianism, a mystic bird that symbolized the soul.

KASABIAN, LINDA See Manson, Charles.

KASDEYA Name of the 'fifth Satan' who taught men the secrets of destruction (I Enoch 69:12).

KASINA A mystic Yoga rite used to free the mind from agitation.

KATAHZIPURI Hittite goddess, skilled in witchcraft. Also known as Kamrusepa.

KATAKHANES A Singhalese vampire demon.

KATCINAS Among Hopi Indians, supernatural beings identified with the spirits of the dead.

KATOYLLA The Incan god of the underworld. Also known as Illapa.

KATTADIYA In Ceylon, a witch doctor, reputed to be adept in summoning diabolic spirits and performing exorcism.

KELBY Malevolent spirit that appears in the form of a horse, sometimes with a torch.

KEMP, URSULA An Englishwoman whose skeleton is displayed in the Witches' House in Bocastle, England. She was tried and executed for witchcraft in 1589.

KERRIGHED Diabolical spirits feared until the nineteenth century by the inhabitants of Finistère, France.

KETEB Pestilence that strikes at noon. In the words of the psalmist, it is 'the destruction that wasteth not at noonday' (Psalms 91: 6).

KETHER In cabalistic teachings, the first emanation, the power of God as Prime Mover, First Cause, the One. It stands at the apex of the first triangle on the Tree of Life. Guarded by the four 'living creatures of the first chapter of Ezekiel,' according to Alesteir Crowley, in magical image it is a bearded old man, personified by Zeus and Jupiter, supreme gods of Greece and Rome. Its symbols are the crown (kingship) and the point (one). On reaching this sphere, the soul achieves union with God.

KEY OF SOLOMON The most famous grimoire, or handbook of magic, ever written. It exists in many versions in various languages. Josephus referred in the first century A.D. to a book supposedly written by Solomon and containing incantations for summoning evil spirits. Legend holds that the magic manual was composed by devils and hidden under Solomon's throne. A Greek version of the manual, preserved in the British Museum, may date back to the twelfth century. Most versions, in French or Latin, date from the eighteenth century. Aleister Crowley edited, translated, and — unfortunately — bowdlerized the work.

KHADO In popular folklore in Tibet, evil female demons.

KHEM In Egyptian religion, he symbolizes the generative force. He is represented as a figure displaying the itchyphallus. He corresponds to the Roman god Priapus.

KHU See Ba.

KILCROPS Offspring of an incubus and a woman. Bodin calls them 'rocots.'

KINGU In Babylonian religion, god of the forces of darkness and the black arts. In the Mesopotamian epic of creation (*Enuma Elish*), Marduk mixes his blood with earth to produce man.

KISS OF JUDAS (THE) The Evangelists are unanimous in affirming that Judas was possessed by Satan on the evening of the Last Supper, when he betrayed Christ by kissing him.
The Italian poet Ferdinando Tirinnanzi (1879-1940) revived the great vision of Origen and in some of his works, particularly *The Kiss of Judas,* expressed the hope that Satan eventually will be redeemed.

KISS OF SHAME At the Sabbat the kiss of shame (*osculum infame* or *osculum obscoenum*) came after members had completed the ritual of allegiance to Satan. Accusations of the kiss of shame were also made against the Wal-

denses and the Knights Templars. Guazzo described the *osculum infame* in his *Compendium Maleficarum* (1626):
> Then they pay homage to him by kissing him on the rump. Having committed these and similar abominable acts, they proceed to still other infamies.

KLUDDE Flemish sprite. It can be identified by its two small blue flames and by its cry, 'kludde.' It changes into a tree, horse, black dog, or toad.

KNIGHTS TEMPLAR A medieval association of knights, farmers, and monks. During the fourteenth century they were accused of engaging in Satanic practices.

KNIGHTS TEMPLAR See Templars.

KNOTTING See Ligature.

KOBAL One of the demons in charge of infernal pleasures.

KOBOLD In Germany, a familiar spirit who guards buried treasure.

KONGO In Japanese folklore, the sheriff who with his terrible staff of bailiffs, torturers, and executioners carries out the sentences of Emma, chief judge of the underworld tribunal.

KONY-OM-PAX Mystic words used in the Eleusinian mysteries.

KORAH A Hebrew who was destroyed because he rebelled against Moses. He was reverenced by the Cainites.

KOSHAR A Canaanite god. His name means *skilful*. He was also known as Hayin, *dexterous*, and *Hasis*, intelligent. He was the counterpart of the Greek Hephaestus (Vulcan), the craftsman-god. He had a forge in Crete or on the island of Carpathos. Among the Egyptians he was equated with the potter-god Ptah. Koshar was also credited with the invention of magic incantations.

KRAMER, HEINRICH Dominican prior (c. 1430-1505) and co-author (with Jakob Sprenger) of *Malleus Maleficarum*, the source of all subsequent treatises on witchcraft. His name was Latinized as Henricus Institor.

KRIKOIN In Eskimo religion, an evil demon who pursues dogs caught outside when winter storms rage. Dogs died in convulsions when they saw his face.

KRU Cambodian sorcerers and exorcists.

KUANTHROPY Metamorphosis into the shape of a dog.

KUBERA The king of the evil demons in the Hindu pantheon. The god of wealth.

KUEI Malevolent spirits. The Chinese use bonfires and firecrackers to scare them away.

KUMACANGA The name given by the inhabitants of certain regions of Brazil to a werewolf.

KUPLENG Among the Botocudo tribesmen of South America, the ghost-soul of a dead person. Elaborate rituals are used to protect the living against the ghost-souls of the dead.

KUR In Sumerian religion, the realm of the dead.

KURDAITCHA Shoes worn by the Australian aborigines for ceremonial killing by black magic. They are made of emu feathers glued together with human blood.

KURDAITJA A sorcerer and executioner among the Arunta of Australia.

KWEI In Chinese demonology, a spirit akin to the dybbuk. It is capable of taking possession of a human body.

KYTELER, ALICE The first person accused of witchcraft in Ireland. In 1324 she was charged with sacrificing cocks to demons, preparing magic herbs to kill her husband, and having intercourse with a demon named Robert Artisson. She fled to England, but her maid, Petronilla de Meath, was burned alive.

Temptation of St. Anthony
Hieronymus Bosch
(Lugano: Villa Favorita)

L

LABARTU In Assyrian demonology, these are malefic ghosts.

LA-BAS A novel on Satanism by Huysmans (1891). In it Durtal, Huysmans' most characteristic hero, gains insights into Satanism as he writes the life of Gilles de Rais.

LABASSU In Assyrian demonology, these are malefic phantoms.

LACHESIS See Moira.

LACLOS French writer and contemporary of the Marquis de Sade. Pierre Ambroise Francois Choderlos de Laclos (1741-1803) made a woman of Satanic temperament, the Marquise de Marteuil, the central character of his *Liaisons Dangereuses* (1782).

LACTANTIUS FIRMIANUS, LUCIUS CAELIUS Early father of the Latin church, in Africa. Toward the beginning of the fourth century he taught a revolutionary doctrine of Satan's fall. According to him, God created two sons before the creation of the world. Jealousy caused the second son, Satan, to destroy the evidence of his divine origin and to pass from good to evil. Lactantius (c.260-325) made astrology an invention of the demons.

LAMB After the sacrifice of a lamb in the Black Mass, a prayer is intoned:

Lamb, which the priests of Adoni have made a symbol of sterility raised to the rank of a virtue, I sacrifice you to Lucifer. May the Peace of Satan always be with you.

LAMIA A medieval term designating a witch who looks like a woman but has a horse's hoofs. The lamia stole children and sucked their blood. The Greeks considered the lamia bisexual. Philostratus wrote in his *Life of Apollonius of Tyana* (third century A.D.):
> They are wont to lust not for love but for flesh: and they particularly seek human flesh and by arousing sexual desire they seek to devour whom they wish.

LANCASHIRE WITCHES The mass trial of twenty accused witches is described in *The Wonderful Discovery of Witches in the County of Lancaster* (1613). The unusually long chapbook became a textbook on the conduct of trials for witchcraft.

LANCRE, PIERRE DE Author of *Tableau* (1612), based on his experiences in investigating witchcraft among the Basques.

LAODICEA In 360 Canon 26 of the Council of Laodicea ordered the excommunication of 'those who practice witchcraft.'

LARTHY-TYTIRAL Etruscan deity, identified with Pluto, the ruler of the underworld.

LARVA In Roman religion, a malevolent spirit. In medieval occultism, a supernatural monster.

LASAE In Etruscan religion, they were minor demons.

LATERAN COUNCIL The Lateran Council of 1215 embodied the edict of Innocent III against heretics into Canon Law. Frederick II incorporated these principles of excommunication and punishment by death into civil law in order to stamp out heretical practices. The phrase, 'by bell, book, and candle,' had no specific connection with witchcraft but rather with heresy in general.

LAUTREAMONT, COMTE DE Pseudonym of Isidore Ducasse, the epic poet of French Satanism. Ducasse (1846-1870) composed the classic text of Surrealism, his *Chants de Maldoror,* of which the first canto appeared in 1869. Maldoror, a symbolic hero, incarnates the sufferings of humanity. Overwhelmed by despair, he revolts against God and becomes metamorphosed into a Satanic Minotaur.

LAVEY, ANTON The High Priest of the Church of Satan, Doctor of Satanic Theology, lives in San Francisco. He founded the Church of Satan in 1966, the year in which he proclaimed the Satanic Age. In 1969 he published *The Satanic Bible,* which explains the rituals of his church and provides appropriate prayers and invocations.

LA VOISIN, CATHERINE Seventeenth-century French sorceress. With the unscrupulous Abbé Guibourg, she is supposed to have inveigled Madame de Montespan into performing, nude, at a Black Mass attended by members of the French court.

LEEK, SYBIL A woman described by the *New York Times* as 'perhaps the world's best-known witch.' She claims that more than 400 witch covens are active in the United States today. She is the author of *The Sybil Leek Book of Fortune Telling,* an introduction to palmistry, fortune-telling, *I Ching,* and tea-leaf reading.

LEFT In black magic, the left is associated with evil. Leftward motion is executed with the intention of attracting evil influences. 'Sinister' was the Latin word for both left and evil.

LEGBA In Dahoman religion, the name given to the 'joker' who perverts all the rules and hence allows evil to manifest itself in the form of sickness, disasters, etc. His ineptitudes, malice, and carelessness pose a constant threat to society. He may also on occasion propitiate other gods on behalf of men and carry messages to human diviners.

LEGION An 'unclean spirit' exorcised by Jesus. The episode of the demoniac is reported in Chapter 5 of the Gospel of St. Mark:

But when he saw Jesus afar off, he ran and worshiped him. . . . [Jesus] said unto him, Come out of the man, thou unclean spirit. And he asked him, What is thy name? And he answered, saying, My name is Legion: for we are many. . . . And all the devils besought him, saying, Send us into the swine, that we may enter into them. And forthwith Jesus gave them leave. And the unclean spirits went out, and entered into the swine: and the herd ran violently down a steep place into the sea (they were about two thousand) and were choked in the sea.

LEICESTER BOY A seventeenth-century English boy who pretended to be bewitched and succeeded in bringing about the execution of several women. He was exposed by James I. The gullible magistrate and his Sergeant Crew, who had countenanced the ravings of the boy, named John Smith, were satirized by Ben Jonson in *The Devil Is an Ass*.

LELU Among the Nupe (West Africa), the head of all the witches in a town.

LEMEGETON A four-part handbook of magic, also called *Lesser Key of Solomon,* written before 1500. The origin and meaning of the term are obscure. The four parts of the work are Goetia, Theurgia Goetia, the Pauline Art, and the Almadel.

LEMURES In Roman religion, malevolent spirits or souls of the dead. They were conceived as hungry ghosts who roamed by night in search of food. See Lemuria.

LEMURIA Roman festival held on May 9, 11, and 13. Then hungry ghosts from the underworld prowled around houses in search of food. The head of the house made offerings to placate the ravenous spirits.

LEOPARD SOCIETY A native secret organization of West Africa. Among its functions was that of carrying out human sacrifice following the death of a tribal leader. The departed leader's wives and servants were sacrificed in order that they might accompany the leader into Ghost Land.

LEPANTHROPY Metamorphosis into the shape of a hare.

LESHY In Slavic folklore, a wood spirit or sylvan deity possessing both human and animal characteristics.

In classical mythology, the underworld river whose waters brought forgetfulness.

LEVI, ELIPHAS French magician and author of works on the occult. Eliphas Lévi, whose real name was Alphonse Louis Constant, claimed to have summoned up the ghost of Apollonius of Tyana in London in 1854. Born in

Paris about 1810, he is said to have been reincarnated as Aleister Crowley. A. E. Waite, the learned English occultist, said that Lévi's *Doctrine and Ritual* contained the secrets of an occult society into which Lévi had been initiated and from which he had been expelled.

LEVIATHAN The leader of the heretics, according to Balberith's account. He tempts men with sins directly repugnant to the Christian faith. His adversary is Peter the Apostle. In rabbinical tradition he is a demon who appeared in his masculine incarnation as Samuel (Salamiel) and seduced Eve, then in his feminine incarnation as Lilith and seduced Adam.

According to Sister Jeanne des Anges, Leviathan was one of seven demons who possessed her. When he was in her head, she wanted to 'put everything in order,' and she behaved with her sisters 'in a most imperious way.'

LEVITATION A supernatural phenomenon giving rise to the impression that a human being is floating in the air without direct or indirect support. Associated with saints, mediums, fakirs, and those who practice Satanic arts, it is supposed to have been accomplished by Simon the Magician, Apollonius Tyanaeus, and Marie d'Agreda.

LEWIS, MATTHEW GREGORY English author (1775-1818), commonly known as Monk Lewis. *Castle Spectre* (1798) and *Tales of Terror* (1788) won him great popularity among people interested in the occult.

LEYAK A Balinese demon who haunts lonely places and is responsible for the misfortunes of man.

LIBER REVALATIONUM Thirteenth-century work compiled by Richalmus. The *Liber revalationum de insidils et versutiis daemonum adversus homines* reflects contemporary beliefs concerning the wiles of the Devil and records some of Richalmus' personal struggles against him.

LIBER SAMEKH A ritual devised by Crowley to summon up the divine power within himself. It is based on a Graeco-Egyptian magical text.

LIBITINA In Roman mythology, the goddess who presided over funerals.

LIGATURE Impotency resulting from sorcery. It is generally accomplished by administering potions or tying knots in threads. The most common procedure is to tie knots in a strip of leather or cord. The ligature remains in force until the knot is untied. The knot should be tied as the bride and groom are exchanging their vows. Vergil mentions a string with nine knots. Pliny recommends putting wolf-grease on the sill and lintels of the bedroom door to counteract the ligature. During the Middle Ages, urine and salt were used as counteragents. Famous victims of ligature include Philippe Auguste, Theodosius, and Ahmose.
Though not so common as other forms of *maleficia,* it was widely discussed in earlier times and was generally recognized as a just cause for voiding a union about to be made and annulling one already contracted. It was also known by other names *vaecordia* (Latin), *aiguillette* (French), and *ghirlanda delle streghe* (Italian). See Conjunction.

LIGHT AND DARKNESS Primitive men associated darkness with evil forces. Religion helped them to overcome their fears. In early religious symbolism, light stands for good, darkness for evil. Most religions assert that darkness prevailed before life began.

LIGHTNING Many people regard lightning as the invention of the Devil.

LILITH The ancient Jews believed that Lilith bore Adam many children before she abandoned him for the demon Samael. The first she-demon in human history, she is supposed to have hated Eve's children and their descendants. When sons were born, superstitious Jews displayed cards on which was written, 'Adam and Eve, enter here; Lilith, remain outside.'

LILLE NOVICES Thirty-two orphan girls living in a foundling home started in Lille, France, by Antoinette Bourignon (1616-1680) exploited the credulity of their benefactor by declaring

> that they had daily carnal cohabitation with the devil, that they went to the sabbats or meetings, where they ate, drank, danced and committed other illicit acts.

LION Symbol of diabolical perversities and the Antichrist.

LITERATURE AND SATAN The literature of the Middle Ages teems with demons. In modern times, poets and dramatists have kept alive the personality of the Devil. The Don Juan legend has been explored by many writers since its introduction by Tirso de Molina in the seventeenth century. Vondel, Holland's greatest poet, devoted his masterpiece to Lucifer; Milton assigned him the main role in *Paradise Lost* (1667); Goethe made Mephistopheles one of the major figures in his *Faust;* de Vigny (1824) and Lermontov (1840) wrote poems about Lucifer; Leopardi sketched out a hymn to Ahriman (1835); Ibsen called Satan the 'Great Curve' in *Peer Gynt* (1867); one of the manifestoes of German Romanticism, *Die Rauber* (1781) is an apology for Lucifer; Carducci made Satan the symbol of liberty and progress; and Ferdinando Trinnanzi (1879-1940) revived the great vision of Origen and expressed the hope that Satan would find redemption. Among many other writers who have produced significant works related to Satan or Satanism are Huysmans, Baudelaire, the

Marquis de Sade, Laclos, Balzac, Hugo, Byron, Isidore Ducasse, Yeats, Villiers de l'Isle-Adam, Jarry, Rimbaud, Bernanos, Montherlant, Camus, and Gide.

LOA Gods of the Voodoo cult. Their desires are satisfied by acts or offerings of voodoo practitioners. The head of an afflicted family may light a candle, toss water, or place food in a place of worship. If danger threatens, he may consult the *hungan* and arrange for an elaborate ceremony.

LOEW Famous sixteenth-century rabbi of Prague. He attained such power that Death could not touch him. Finally Death hid in a rose and killed the rabbi when he smelled it.

LOKI The Teutonic god of fire. He brought sin and evil into the world. His children are the wolf Fenris, the Midgard serpent, and Hel, the queen of the realm of the dead, Nifelheim. The cunning mischief-maker among the Asas was punished for his crimes, including that of killing Baldur, the god of light and purity. Loki was tied upon three pointed rocks, beneath the mouth of a serpent. Whenever the bowl held by his wife Sigyn is withdrawn, the venom drops into his face, causing him to writhe in pain and the world to tremble.

LOLLARD, WALTER Author of a heretical theory making Satan the protector and patron of mankind. His followers believed that Satan and his angels would be restored to their rightful place in Heaven. They worshiped 'him who had been unjustly disowned and condemned.'

LOLLARDS Fourteenth-century heretical sect. George Sand wrote that the Dutch sect believed that 'Satan was not the enemy of mankind but rather his protector.'

LOMBARD, PETER Italian theologian. Peter Lombard (Petrus Lombardus, c. 1100-1164) surmised that some demons reside in hell and torment the damned. His conjecture was raised to the degree of an absolute thesis by St. Thomas.

LOPT In Norse mythology, Lopt was a variant name for the evil god Loki.

LORAY One of three demons serving Sargatanas, brigadier general of the legions of Hell.

LORD OF THE FLIES One of the names of Satan. These words are the literal translation of the Hebrew word Baalzebub, designating the god of Ekron.

LOTAPES Ancient sorcerer, attached to the court of Pharaoh.

LOUDUN, NUNS OF A group of nuns whose strange behavior is detailed in Aldous Huxley's *The Devils of Loudun* (1952). In 1633 the Ursuline convent established at Loudun in France witnessed an outbreak of diabolical possession. Soon most of the nuns were speaking in tongues and behaving in the most extraordinary and hysterical manner. Jeanne des Anges (Mme. de Belfiel), the Mother Superior of the convent, Sister Claire, and five other nuns were the first to be possessed by evil spirits. The outbreak spread to the neighboring town and created such a stir that Richelieu appointed a commission to deal with it. After attempts at exorcism had failed, Father Urbain Grandier was arrested and charged with using sorcery to give the nuns over to possession of the Devil. The confessor of the convent protested his innocence, but to no avail. A council of judges found the marks of the Devil on his body. Even after he was burned alive at the stake on August 18, 1634, the possession of the hysterical sisters did not cease. The three exorcists who had participated in his condemnation — Lactance, Tranquille, and Surin — also came to a bad end. Lactance died insane one month later, Tranquille followed his example five years later, and Surin experienced diabolical possession for twenty years. The strange behavvior of the nuns made Loudun a tourist attraction until Richelieu refused to provide further financial support for the nuns. Then their possession ceased.

LOUP-GAROU The Haitian werewolf is a red-eyed female. If an old woman suspected of being a loup-garou goes into a house, her escape may be blocked if someone in an adjoining room crosses two brooms and pronounces her name three times.

LOUVIERS, NUNS OF Several nuns and priests were involved in fantastic orgies allegedly committed from 1628 to 1642 in the little convent of the Franciscan Tertiaries at Louviers, France. At least thirty-four books detailed the accusations against Madeleine Bavent and three successive directors of the convent, Father David, Father Picard, and Father Boullé. Madeleine stated in her autobiography that the Devil entered her cell in the form of a huge black cat, dragged her forcibly on the bed, and ravished her. She reported also that the priests said black Mass at midnight Sabbats.

The perverse mingling of sacrilege and sensuality is reported in Madeleine Bavent's confession. She entered the convent in 1625, when she was 18. Father Pierre David, the chaplain of the convent, insisted that God should be worshiped naked. Madeleine was forced to take communion bare-breasted, with Father David caressing her indecently. The chaplain also taught the nuns to fondle each other and to use an artificial penis. His teachings were carried even further by Father Mathurin Picard and his assistant, Father Thomas Boullé. Picard and Boullé may have conducted Satanic rites involving cannibalism, sex orgies, and the Black Mass. These Satanic practices continued until Picard died in 1642.

Many instances of hysterical paroxysms and convulsions were investigated. In 1647 Boullé was burned alive, and with him the exhumed corpse of Picard.

LUBARA Babylonian god of pestilence and disease.

LUCIBEL Name sometimes given to Lucifer before his fall.

LUCIFER The Book of Isaiah (14:12-15) describes Lucifer and foretells his destiny: 'How art thou fallen from Heaven, O Lucifer, who didst rise in the morning? How art thou fallen to the earth, that didst wound the nations? . . . And thou saidst in thy heart: I will . . . exalt my throne above the stars of God. . . . But yet thou shalt be brought down to hell, into the bottom of the pit.' Origen and many of his successors affirmed that Lucifer, once a heavenly spirit, had been cast into the pit of hell because he tried to make himself the equal of God. Thus they identified Satan, the adversary, with Lucifer, 'the bringer of light.'
Christ said (Luke 10: 18): 'I saw Satan like lightning falling from Heaven.' The Latin name Lucifer is a translation of the Greek Hebrew word *Helel*, referring to the morning and evening star and meaning 'light-bearer.' Thus Lucifer is identified with Satan, the archangel who rebelled against God.
In demonology, Lucifer is emperor of the infernal spirits. He tempts men by appealing to their pride and selfish interests. As one of the popular acid rock groups phrases it, 'your love for me [Lucifer] has just got to be real,' for it has endured through time.

LUCIFER A periodical published by Aleister Crowley.

LUCIFERIANS Medieval sects of occultists who mutilated Eucharistic wafers before an idol of Lucifer. The practice of witchcraft may have been initiated by a Luciferian sect in Milan. It was against this sect that Konrad of Marburg, the first German inquisitor, moved zealously in the first part of the thirteenth century. He extorted confessions from them 'proving' that they were out-and-out Satanists who worshiped the Devil as creator and ruler of the world.

LUCIFUGE Prime Minister of the infernal spirits. He commands three subordinate spirits: Baél, Agares, and Marbas. Also known as Lucifuge Rofocale, he has power assigned to him by Lucifer over all the treasures of the world.

LUCIFUGES A class of demons identified by medieval theologians, following the suggestions of John Wier. They shun the light of day. Only by night can they fashion bodies for themselves.

LUG In Celtic mythology, Lug was a god whose functions were similar to those of Mercury. His festival, Lughnasadhm the Feast of Lug, fell in Britain on August 1. The name Lammas is derived from this festival.
One of Lug's centers was the town of Lugdunum, that is, Lug's town. This is now the city of Lyon.

LULLE, RAYMOND Catalan mystic (1235-1315), also known as Raimon Lull. He wrote a treatise on the Cabala. He may have had ties with a secret Muslim sect, The Brothers of Purity. He was said to have practiced alchemy and to have succeeded in changing base metal to gold.

LUTHER, MARTIN Leader of the German Reformation. Martin Luther (1483-1546) reports in his *Table Talks* that he engaged in many struggles with Satan, who 'throws hideous thoughts into the soul — hatred of God, blasphemy, and despair.' Luther is known to have thrown curses at the Devil, but not an inkpot. Although thousands of tourists have been shown a blot of ink on the wall of the castle of the Wartburg where Luther once lived, the account of his hurling an inkpot at the grimacing face of the Devil is probably apocryphal. One proof of his belief in the existence of demons is recorded in his *Colloquia*:

> In many regions there are still dwellings of demons. Prussia is full of demons. Bilappen swarms with witchcraft. In Switzerland near Lucerne on a very high mountain there is a lake where Satan rages. On a lofty mountain, the Procknesberg, there is a lake which, when a stone is cast in, produced a great storm throughout the whole region. These are the dwellings of imprisoned demons.

LYCANTHROPY The changing of a human being into a wolf. The werewolf appears in many cultures throughout the ages. The prevalence of lycanthropy is indicated by statements from Homer, Vergil, Strabo, etc., as well as by royal decrees against the practice in sixteenth-century France.

LYONS, ARTHUR JR. Author of *The Second Coming* (1970), a book on Satanism in America.

M

MA A Cappadocian deity who was equated with Bellona, the Roman goddess of war. As a fertility goddess as well, she exemplified the traits of Cybele and Anahita.

MAA KHERU In Egyptian religion, an expression meaning 'the right word.' When spoken, it permitted the spirit of the dead to enter the halls of the underworld and to assume the powers of the gods.

MACUMBA Magic rituals and dances of Brazil. Macumba involves animism and animal sacrifices.

MADAN Elemental sprite of Hindu origin. He facilitates the malefic operations of sorcerers.

MADELEINE DE DEMANDOLX, SISTER A French nun, one of the famed Aix-en-Provence nuns accused of renouncing God in favor of the Devil. She spent ten years in prison for her crimes.

MAENAD In Greek religion, a nymph who attended Dionysus. Also, a woman who celebrated the orgiastic rites of the god of wine.

MAGA A generic name for witch. The term usually denotes a pleasure-seeking witch.

MAGAS In Zoroastrian religion, master adepts in all things of the Spirit, initiators in the Mysteries, and judges at the Trial by Ordeal.

MAGIC In ancient pagan religions, magic practices played an important role. They were associated with mystery rituals in Rome, Egypt, and in the religions of the Near East. The techniques involved in magic ceremonials included sympathetic magic, the use of amulets and charms, invocations to the infernal deities, necromancy, divination Magic is popularly classed as white, red, and black. White magic is used for good ends; red magic is diabolical (since dark red was characteristic of the Devil during the Middle Ages) and applies also to the use of blood in rites and operations (Macumba and Voodoo); black magic applies to all diabolical operations.
Cornelius Agrippa defines magic as 'the true science, the most elevated and mysterious philosophy, in a word, the perfection and culmination of all the natural sciences. It is a philosophical science of intense, secret power . . . and is based on the study of the planets, elements, and stones. For all the elements of the world contain the soul of the universe.' Collin de Plancy says that magic is 'the art of producing in nature, with the help of demons, things beyond the power of men.' Albert the Great states that 'magic is very dangerous when used to discover the essence of natural things.'

MAGIC CAKE Black millet mixed with the flesh of unbaptized children, served at the Sabbat, was supposed to enable witches to remain silent under torture.

MAGIC CIRCLE A diagram drawn around an object or a person prior to a magic operation. The circle, drawn around the karcist with a new sword, symbolizes the separation of the wizard from the infernal powers. Honi

Ha Me'agel, a first-century Hebrew magician, was known as the circle drawer because he often stood within the magic circle and produced rain. Reginald Scot's *Discoverie of Witchcraft* (1584) offered this advice:
> As for the places of Magical Circles, they are to be chosen melancholy, doleful, dark and lonely; either in Woods or Deserts, or in a place where three ways meet, or amongst ruins of Castles, Abbeys, Monasteries, etc., or upon the Seashore when the Moon shines clear, or else in some large Parlor hung with black . . ., with doors and windows closely shut, and waxen candles lighted.

MAGIC GIRDLES Ferns gathered at midnight on St. John's Eve and arranged to form the magic character HVTY. Magic girdles are supposed to cure diseases.

MAGICIANS Demons collaborate with magicians, according to Tertullian, Origen, and Bossuet. Magicians were excommunicated by the Councils of Agde (506), Orléans (511), Narbonne (589), Reims (625), Tours (813), Paris (829), Angers (1294), Cologne (1357), and Rouen (1445).

MAGICK IN THEORY AND PRACTICE One of the best books ever written on the subject of magic. It was published in 1929 by Aleister Crowley, the self-styled 'Great Beast.'

MAGIC MANUALS Legend holds that the devils composed several handbooks on magic and hid them under Solomon's throne. After his death, they urged his courtiers to dig under his throne to learn how he had secured control over men, spirits, and the wind. According to the Koran:
> And they followed the device which the devils devised against the kingdom of Solomon; and Solomon was not an unbeliever; but the devils believed not, they taught men sorcery.

MAGISTER TEMPLI One of the ten grades in Alesteir Crowley's cabalistic system. It corresponds to sephira 3, Saturn. The Magister Templi tends his garden of disciples and achieves a perfect understanding of the universe.

MAGNET Any body having the power to attract iron. Used in a magic philter, it has the power to draw an affliction from the body.

MAGUS One of the ten grades, corresponding to the sephiroth, in Aleister Crowley's cabalistic system. The magus, in sephira 2, the sphere of the stars, 'attains to wisdom, declares his law and is a Master of all Magick in its greatest and highest sense.'

MALDOROR See Lautréamont.

MALEFICA A witch taught by a demon. Her mission is to inflict injury.

MALEFICIA Mishaps and misfortunes suffered by persons, animals, or property were attributed to evil spirits. Witches, classified as *malefici*, were capable of causing mental as well as physical harm. In his *Discourse of Damned Art of Witchcraft* (1608), William Perkins detailed their powers: raising storms, poisoning the air, blasting corn, killing cattle, annoying people, procuring strange passions in the bodies of creatures, and casting out devils. Nider (1435) compiled an earlier list: inspiring love, inspiring hatred, causing impotence, causing disease, killing, taking away reason, and injuring property or animals. Hex is another term for maleficia.

Martin de Arles (1460) concluded that maleficia involved an implicit pact with Satan. Bernard de Como (1510) decreed in his role as Inquisitor that all incurable and unexplainable diseases were the result of sorcery. Evidence of harm or injury to people was sufficient basis for condemnation as a devil-worshiper.

Exorcistarum (1651) defines maleficia as 'a vicious act directed against the body, through the power of the Devil in a tacit or public pact entered into with the witch. . . .' Accounts of maleficia are still being reported throughout the world.

MALKUTH The tenth sephira, the sphere of earth, in Cabalistic teachings. It contains the force of all the sephiroth within itself. When the Tree of Life is represented as a human body, Malkuth is the union of the whole body.

MALLEUS MALEFICARUM First published in Cologne in 1486. *Malleus Maleficarum* (The Witches' Hammer), by Jacob Sprenger and Heinrich Kramer, has subsequently reappeared in many editions in most of the countries of Europe. Its encyclopedic pages cover every phase of witchcraft. Part I identifies heresy and witchcraft; Part II analyzes evil spells; Part III specifies modes of repression (inquisitorial, episcopal, civil), interrogatories, tortures, and and confessions; Part IV indicates the exorcisms to be applied. The work owes its success to the personalities of its authors, two Dominicans, and to the advice offered to witchhunters.

MALPHAS Grand president of Hell. He commands forty legions. He appears as a crow and often deceives those who make sacrifices to him. He builds impregnable fortresses and easily storms enemy ramparts.

MALUMSECUTUM Any misfortune resulting from a threat of evil (*damnum minatum*). See Maleficia.

MAMAI A pastoral goddess to whom children are ritually sacrificed in India. As recently as September 26, 1970, according to press reports, a four-year-old boy was slaughtered as a sacrifice to Mamai in a small rural community in the Jungadh coastal district of Gujarat.

MAMBO A priestess of the Voodoo cult.

MAMITU (MAMMETUM) Mesopotamian goddess of fate, similar to the Greek Moira.

MANA In Polynesian and Australasian religions, an extraphysical power ascribed to persons or objects behaving in a striking manner. This immaterial power is viewed as the embodiment of the elemental powers which, collectively, constitute the order of the universe. A similar idea is expressed by various words in other languages: *Orenda* in Iroquoian, *Manitu* in Siouan Algonquin, and *Hasina* in Madagascan.

MANASSEH The Biblical king dealt with familiar spirits and used enchantments (II Kings 21:8).

MANDALA A geometric design consisting of an inner circle enclosed in a square with four entrances. Sometimes called a magic circle, its symbolism derives from the yoga doctrine which teaches that the soul can unite with the divine by meditation and concentration. The Tantric sects believe that the mandala is the abode of the deity, who resides in the innermost circle and can be evoked by various incantations. C. G. Jung and others have offered psychological interpretations of the mandala.

MANDEANS Members of a Gnostic sect that makes John the Baptist the central figure and baptism the main rite. John the Baptist is regarded as the Messiah. The ancient texts of the sect, written in a peculiar script and dialect of Aramaic, have recently been studied. The sect arose in southern Iraq some five hundred years B.C., under the influence of Dosithaean, Marcionite, and Manichaean teachings.

The sacred literature was the Great Book. The religious beliefs of the Mandeans were compounded of Jewish, Christian, and pagan elements. Variant names for the Mandeans are Nasoraeans and Sabians.

MANDRAKE A plant of the potato family (*mandragora officinarum*), also known as mandragore. It has often been used as an ingredient in love-philters.

MANES In Roman religion, spirits of the dead. Graves were dedicated to the manes. Their worship was practiced at three major festivals: the Feralia, Parentalia, and Lemuria. Sometimes the term manes is used for the realm of the dead itself. It was also applied to the deities of the underworld: Dis, Orcus, Persephone.

At a later date the manes were identified with the Dii Parentes, the ancestors of the family.

MANI The Persian founder of the religious system of Manicheanism. Born c. 216 A.D., near Ctesiphon in Mesopotamia, he later traveled in Central Asia, India, and China. Mani was subject to visions and revelations, like many religious founders. On his return to Persia, he was persecuted by the Magi, who represented the official religions, and was imprisoned and finally executed.

MANICHEANISM This religion, founded by the Persian Mani in the third century A.D., was a syncretism of Mazdaism, Buddhism, Christianity, Gnosticism. Manicheanism was based on the principle of dualism and taught that Liberation from evil was to be achieved by practicing the virtues taught by Mani. There were two categories in this religious system. The Elect or Perfect lived virtuously, in chastity, and practiced celibacy. They were assured of salvation in the afterlife. The other category consisted of the Imperfect, the Hearers, who might marry but had to confine their sexual indulgence. They might be reborn among the Perfect. The ultimate aim of the Hearers was to attain the status of the Elect. There were twelve chief priests. An annual feast, commemorating the Passion of Mani, was associated with fasting and supplications to Mani for forgiveness of sins.

In spite of hostilities, Manicheanism persisted as an active religion until the fifth century. In the later Middle Ages its tenets infiltrated into areas of Central Europe. In China Manicheanism, in its essence, was adopted into secret cults.

MANILA Philippine city, site of an extraordinary occurrence in 1952. The American evangelist Lester Sumrall freed from a Manila prison a girl who claimed to have been bitten by a demon. On her hands and under her nails she had black hairs. Experts examined her and found that they were neither human nor animal hair. She described the demon as a hairy monster. Her case attracted considerable attention in the press.

MANISM Belief in mana, common to many primitive religions and characteristic of much popular religious thinking today. Manism assumes that the body is inhabited by a spirit which can exist independently as a shade or ghost.

MANITU In Algonquian languages a word used for one of the powers or spirits which inhabit persons or objects and endow them with magical attributes.

MANSON, CHARLES Leader of a 'Satanic family' involved in ritualistic murders in California. In March 1971, the trial that had begun in Los Angeles on June 16, 1970, finally came to an end. Manson and three female members of his hippie 'family' were convicted — largely on the testimony of Linda Kasabian, who had been granted immunity for turning state's evidence — of first degree murder. For the gruesome, ritualistic slaying of actress Sharon Tate and six other victims, they were sentenced to death in the gas chamber.

MANTRA SHASTRA Brahmanical writings on the occult science of incantations.

MANTRIKA SAKTI The occult potency of mystic numbers, sounds, or letters in the Vedic mantras.

MANUAL OF DISCIPLINE This manual contains the tenets of the Essenes, an ancient Jewish sect that explained good and evil in terms of Zoroastrian dualism represented by the beneficent deity Ahura Mazda and his opponent Ahriman, the Spirit of Evil.

MARA The Indian demon of death. The older form of the name was Mrtyu, derived from the root *mr*, meaning 'to die.' Mara is famous for having tried in vain to tempt Buddha on the eve of his enlightenment.
Mara not only kills men, but he also kindles in them the desire for pleasure and carnal love, which perpetuates life and death.
In Buddhism, Mara is the personification of evil. He represents temptation, sin, and death. He is also called Papiyan and Varsavarti. He is identified with Namuche, one of the wicked demons in Indian mythology. His attack upon Buddha under the sacred bo tree is a favorite subject of Buddhist artists. In Buddhistic mythology he holds the wheel of life and death in his hands and is the ruler in the domains of the twelve links of the chain of causation.

MARBAS One of three demons in the service of Lucifuge, prime minister of Lucifer.

MARCION Early Christian teacher (fl. 150 A.D.). His views, similar to those of the Ophites, were rejected as heretical by the Roman church. See Ophites.

MARCOMIR A witch is supposed to have summoned a triple-headed devil to come before Marcomir, king of the Franks.

MARCUS A Gnostic teacher accused by St. Irenaeus in the second century of perverting the Mass to the worship of a deity other than the Christian God.

MARE A demon which sits on the chest, causing a feeling of suffocation. The word derives from an Old Teutonic stem found also in the French word *cauchemar* and often is used interchangeably with incubus. The German word is *alp* or *mara*. The scientific term, ephialtes, derives from the Greek word meaning 'to leap upon.' Robert Macnish gives this picture of the mare in his *Philosophy of Sleep* (1830):

> A monstrous hag squatting upon his breast — mute, motionless and malignant; an incarnation of the evil spirit — whose intolerable weight crushes the breath out of his body. . . .

MARGARET A cat used as a charm to break the spell cast by the enemies of John VI, king of Scotland. See North Berwick Witches.

MARIA See Miriam the Jewess.

MARIKEN VAN NIEUMEGHEN A Dutch miracle play (c. 1500) based on the legend of a female Faust who agreed to live with the Devil for many years, obtaining his favors and presents. The play ends with the salvation of the heroine.

MARK OF THE DEVIL See Devil's Mark.

MARQUISE DE MARTEUIL Perverse, Satanic heroine of Laclos' sensational novel, *Liaisons Dangereuses* (1782).

MARS In Roman religion, the god of war and protector of the fields. The name probably derives from a word meaning 'to destroy.'

MARTEUIL, MARQUISE DE See Marquise de Marteuil.

MARTINET Familiar demon who accompanies sorcerers. Sometimes he helps travelers who have gone astray.

MASCO The Provençal word for witch.

MASCOT An object believed to bring luck. The word derives from the Provençal word for witch. Such a belief is considered superstitious and therefore forbidden to Catholics.

MASKIM Name applied to the seven terrible Babylonian devils, counterparts of the gods of the planets. They lurk in ambush, ready to pounce upon their unsuspecting prey.

MASSALANIANS A heretical sect of the fourth century. They used to expectorate continually in order to rid themselves of demons presumed to be inside them.

MASTEMA In pre-Christian literature Mastema is frequently identified as an evil prince. In apocalyptic writings, the word designates the cosmic power of evil, identified with the evil impulse in man and with death. According to the Book of Jubilees, written before 96 B.C., he is the chief of the evil spirits resulting from the union of the fallen angels and mortals. After God intervened, he remained in control of one-tenth of the fallen angels 'in order that they might continue to serve Satan on Earth.'

He counseled God to test Abraham. In Egypt he aided the sorcerers who opposed Moses.

MASTER JOHN A fourteenth-century English necromancer. He was involved in a plot to kill Edward II by using Black Magic.

MATHER, COTTON New England preacher and writer. He encouraged the Salem witch hunts. He wrote *Memorable Providences Relating to Witchcraft and Possessions* (1689) and *Wonders of the Invisible World* (1693).

MATHERS, SAMUEL LIDDEL Visible Head of the Order of the Golden Dawn. With the help of his wife, a clairvoyant who was the sister of the philosopher Henri Bergson, he deciphered the mysterious manuscript discovered in 1884 by a London clergyman and brought to him by William Winn Westcott. The manuscript dealt with the Cabala and the Tarot. Mrs. Mathers' introduction to the 1938 edition of her husband's *Kabbalah Unveiled* indicates that the Golden Dawn explored 'the intelligent forces behind Nature, the Constitution of man and his relation to God,' and the means by which man may unite with 'the Divine Man latent in himself.' Mathers, who took to calling himself MacGregor Mathers, Chevalier MacGregor, and Comte de Glenstrae, edited and translated magical textbooks: the *Key of Solomon* and the *Sacred Magic of Abramelin the Mage.*
Yeats frequently played chess in the Mathers household in Paris. He and Mrs. Mathers played against Mathers and a spirit. The Order of the Golden Dawn was torn by dissension after Aleister Crowley became a member. When Mathers died in 1918, his friends believed that Crowley had used black magic to cause his death.

MAZATECA The Aztec frog and snake cult.

MAZDAK Fifth-century founder of the Persian cult of Mazdakism. A successor of Mani, he was violently attacked by Zoroastrian priests and warriors, who called him the accursed. He also advocated self-restraint and thereby earned the title of 'the devil who would not eat.' He stressed the two principles of Good and Evil that pervade all life.

MAZZIKIN Mischievous spirits who inhabited the world of the ancient Hebrews. They filled the world, particularly the lower regions of the atmosphere.

MBWIRI In Central Africa, a malefic demon who enters the body of his victim. Exorcism requires some ten days.

MDOKI An evil spirit of the Congo.

MEATH, PETRONILLA DE See Kyteler, Alice.

MEDER In the ancient religion of the Semitic population of Ethiopia, the goddess of the earth and fertility.

MEDICINE-MAN Among Australian aborigines, the medicine-men initiate the tribal members into the mysteries of rituals and myths. They practice meditation, telepathy, and hypnotism. They also act as, seers, treat sickness. and give protection against magic practices.
The term is frequently applied to the priests and shamans of the Indian tribes of North America.

MEDUSA One of the Gorgons. Her frightful appearance turned to stone all those who looked upon her.

MEIFU In Japanese folklore, the dark tribunal, presided over by Emma, the stern judge.

MELANAIGIS The name given to Dionysus at Eleutherai, the village from which his cult spread to Athens. The word means 'he with the black goatskin.'

MELANEPHOROI Sodalities associated with the Egyptian cult of Isis.

MELCHOM One of the demons listed by John Wier. He was worshiped by the Ammonites.

MELCOMBE, GEORGE English politician and member of parliament (1691-1762). He was a leading member of Sir Francis Dashwood's Satanic group. See Friars of Medmenham.

MELEK TAUS The Devil, chief of the angelic hosts, according to the Yezidis.

MELKART Patron deity of Tyre, the Phoenician equivalent of Hermes (Mercury).

MELLIN, HECTOR French magician, inventor of a machine to protect people against evil radiations. See Radiation Machine.

MENAGYRTAE A variant name for the Galli, the priests of the goddess Cybele.

MENAT A magic amulet worn by Egyptian gods, goddesses, kings, priests, and officials. Inscribed with representations of a goddess and a serpent, it was supposed to ensure fertility and was buried with the wearer in order to renew his sex powers in the outer world.

MENSTRUATION Medieval Christians assumed that among the Jews men as well as women experienced the ailment of menstruation. This belief helped to account for the presumed need of Christian blood, the sole therapeutic element available to the Jews.

MEPHISTOPHELES Name of the demon with whom Faust signed a pact. The name may be a faulty Greek rendering of Lucifuge, 'Fly the light.'

MERCURIUS In the writings of the alchemists, Mercurius (or the planetary spirit Mercury) is the god who discloses the secret of the art to the initiates. He is also the soul of bodies, spirit that has become earth, spirit that transforms the material world. Identified with Hermes Trismegistus, he is also symbolized, like *nous* or *pneuma*, by the serpent and called the mediator, the original man, and the Hermaphroditic Adam.

MERLIN Famous magician, born of an incubus and the daughter of King Arthur. He was the wise counselor of four kings and played an important part in the literature of the Middle Ages.

MERODACK Satanic name adopted by Joséphin Péladan. The pseudonym is taken from Assyrian astrology.

MESLAMTAEA (NERGAL) A chthonian god in the Sumerian pantheon. His temple in Cuthah, called 'He Who Issues from Meslam,' indicates that he may have been a tree god originally. The son of Enlil and Ninlil, he appears in hymns as a warrior. As Nergal, he is ruler of the underworld and husband of Ereshkigal.

MESOPOTAMIAN DEMONS The fear of demons perpetually overshadowed the daily lives of the Semitic tribes dwelling in Mesopotamia. Mesopotamian art abounds in representations of terrifying demons, commonly with human bodies and animal heads. Man was regarded as practically defenseless against countless malevolent spirits capable of assuming any shape and moving unseen from place to place. They preferred ruins and desolate places. Some were the ghosts of the unburied and vengeful dead; others emerged from beneath the earth. The one most feared was perhaps the lion-headed fever demon.

MESQET A torture chamber in the Egyptian underworld.

METAMORPHOSIS A change from human to animal form. Zoomorphism dates from the earliest ages of man. Nebuchadnezzar is said to have taken on animal characteristics (growth of hair and the practice of eating grass), Circe changed Ulysses' men into swine, and Ovid reported many examples of metamorphosis. Aeluranthropy (changing into a cat), boanthropy (cow or bull), cynanthropy (dog), lepanthropy (rabbit), and lycanthropy (wolf) are types of metamorphosis. Witches and demons were supposed to be able to assume various shapes.
Isabel Gowdie repeated a number of charms used in effecting transformations:
When we go in the shape of a hare, we say thrice over:
   I shall go into a hare,
   With sorrow and sigh and mickle care;
   And I shall go in the Devil's name
   Ay while I come home again.
And . . . when we would be out of this shape, we will say:
   Hare, hare, God send thee care.
   I am in a hare's likeness just now,
   But I shall be in a woman's likeness even now.

METEMPSYCHOSIS The passing of the soul at death into the body of an animal or a person. Outside of India, the doctrine was held by the ancient Egyptians, the Orphics, and by the later Greek thinkers, Pythagoras, Plato, and Plotinus.

METZ French town, site of several witchcraft trials. The Devil was known there as Persil, and several witches claimed that they had married him.

MEURSAULT Protagonist of Camus' *L'Etranger*. His cynical indifference leads him to commit an absurd crime and to defy all that is human. Papini calls him 'the loathsome personification of existentialist Satanism.'

MEZU In Japanese folklore, a horse-headed demon who assists Kongo, the sheriff of hell.

MIALISM A necromantic offshoot of voodoo practiced in Jamaica and involving intercourse with the spirits of the dead.

MICAELIS, SEBASTIEN In his *Histoire admirable de la possession et conversion d'une penitente* (1613) Father Michaélis lists three hierarchies of demons; (1) Belzebuth, Leviathan, Asmodeus, Balberith, Astaroth, Verrin, Gresil, Sonnillon; (2) Carreau, Carnivean, Oeillet, Rosier, Verrier; and (3) Belial, Olivier, Juvart. He ascribes to these demons the following attributes: Belzebuth tempts through pride; Leviathan tempts one's faith; Asmodeus tempts through luxury; Balberith suggests blasphemy and homicide; Astaroth tempts through vanity or laziness; Verrin through impatience; Gresil through impurity; Sonnillon through hatred; Carreau tempts without pity; Carnivean tempts through obscenity; Oeillet tempts against poverty; Rosier tempts through love; Verrier tempts against obedience; Belial tempts through arrogance; Olivier through cruelty and avarice; and Juvart takes control of different bodies.

MICHAEL Leader of the heavenly hosts in the battle against the Great Dragon who commanded the fallen angels.

MICHAEL PSELLUS Byzantine philosopher and statesman. Michael Psellus (c. 1018-1080) wrote extensively on philosophy, theology, demonology, and Chaldean lore. In a treatise on the works of demons, he declares that they are equipped with everything necessary for procreation.

MICHELET, JULES One of the most brilliant and prolific historians France has produced, Jules Michelet (1798-1874) also wrote one of the classic studies of witchcraft. His *La Sorcière* (published in English as *Satanism and Witchcraft: A Study in Medieval Superstition*) appeared in 1862 and has been called 'a nightmare of the most extraordinary verisimilitude and poetical power.'

MICHTECACUATL Aztec goddess of death, consort of Mictlantecuhtli.

MIDGARD SERPENT In Scandinavian mythology, a sea monster, progeny of Loki and Angerbotha.

MIDWIWIN A secret society of the Ojibway Indians. Initiates progress through several grades with the help of snake-spirits as they learn the mysteries of the group.

MILAN In 1236 Matthew Paris reported that Milan was a refuge for Luciferians.

MILLENNIUM The period of a thousand years during which 'the dragon, the old serpent, which is the Devil, and Satan' will be bound for a thousand years. He will be 'cast into the bottomless pit, and shut up . . . that he should deceive the nations no more' (Rev. 20: 2-3).

MILTON, JOHN The author of *Paradise Lost* initiated the rehabilitation of Satan, attributing heroic qualities to the figure ridiculed and depicted as ugly and evil during the Middle Ages.

MILU In Hawaiian religion, the god who presides over the dead.

MINOAN SNAKE GODDESS The snake goddess of the Minoans was also the ruler of the underworld and one aspect of the Great Nature Goddess of the prehistoric Greeks.

MINOS Judge of the shades in Hades.

MIRACLE OF THEOPHILE Falsely accused of wrong-doing, Theophile turned to a Jewish magician, reputed to be in league with the Devil. Theophile sold his soul to the Devil in order to regain his possessions. Years later, through the intercession of the Virgin, he recovered his soul. The legendary Faustian prototype is supposed to have lived in the sixth century. Theophile, the Virgin, and the Devil figure prominently in the literature and art of the middle ages.

MIRACLES It is widely held that the Devil cannot work miracles but only prodigies which make men marvel. Miracles produce good effects, prodigies only evil. Miracles change the laws of nature, while prodigies are carried out by natural means.

MIRIAM THE JEWESS One of the most famous sorceresses of ancient times. She was the sister of Moses and was said to have been instructed by God himself. Many important works were attributed to her. She was also known as Maria.

MISTLETOE The parasitic plant was sacred to the Druids and is connected with many pagan rites. In Brittany it was hung in stables to protect livestock. In Scandinavian mythology, it killed the god Balder. In Sweden it was said to have the power to reveal the existence of gold. It was cut by the Druids, who may have viewed it as the genitalia of the oak tree. In popular belief, it was supposed to be the source of life. In Frazer's *The Golden Bough,* the Myth of Balder, vulnerable only to an arrow made of mistletoe, is interpreted as a symbolic account of a fertility drama of death and resurrection.

MITHRA In Iranian religion, the Lord of Heavenly Light who battles the forces of evil. In his aspect as a warrior, he is directed by Ahura Mazda to destroy all demons.

MITHRAISM In Roman religion, the cult of Mithra (Mithras). One of the last mystery cults to reach the West, it became the chief rival of Christianity before it was officially suppressed toward the end of the fourth century.

MKHA' SGROMA A frightful demon worshiped by Tibetan Buddhists. The Tibetan goddess, the counterpart of the Hindu goddess Kali, is represented as a lion-headed monster surrounded by a halo of flames.

MOHAWKS Members of a wanton society in London. Toward the end of the seventeenth century and the beginning of the eighteenth, they met in secret places to celebrate Black Masses.

MOI The Vietnamese name for the hill people who have retained pagan cults. They have practiced cannibalism and the ritual eating of human livers.

MOIRA In Greek religion, the fate of a person. Later, one of a group of seven divine powers determining the fate of a person. These include Clotho, who spins the thread of life; Lachesis, who determines the length of a person's life; and Atropos, who cuts the thread. The Romans identified the Moirae with the Parcae — Nona, Decuma, and Morta.

MOLAY, JACQUES DE Conqueror of Jerusalem and Grand Master of the Templars. He confessed under torture (and later recanted) that he had denied Christ and worshiped Baphomet, practiced sodomy, and attended diabolic feasts at which human flesh was served. He was burned on March 18, 1314, along with Guy d'Auvergne.

MOLEK (MOLK) A Hebrew word which probably meant 'offering' and is now used to designate a ritual sacrifice, whether real or a substitute. The practice, mentioned in the Old Testament as 'the abomination of the Ammonites,' is associated particularly with first-born males. Plutarch described the ritual sacrifices practiced in Carthage.

MOLITOR, ULRICH One of the earliest writers on witchcraft, he published his *De Lamiis et Phitonicis Mulieribus* (Concerning Female Sorcerers and Soothsayers) in 1489.

MOLLIES' CLUB A Satanical group that flourished in England in the eighteenth century.

MOLOCH An evil god of the Phoenicians, the counterpart of Baal.

MOMPESSON, JOHN See Drummer of Tedworth.

MONTESPAN, MADAME DE Mistress of Louis XIV, to whom she bore eight children. Mme. de Montespan (1641-1707) is reputed to have taken part in obscene performances at Black Masses attended by members of the French court. Catherine La Voisin, a concocter of love potions, is supposed to have inveigled her into serving, nude, as the central performer on at least one occasion.

MONTHS Demonologists link certain demons with certain months: January and Belial, February and Leviathan, March and Satan, April and Astarte, May and Lucifer, June and Baalberith, July and Belzebuth, August and Astaroth, September and Thamuz, October and Baal, November and Hecate, December and Moloch.

MONTHERLANT, HENRI DE Contemporary French dramatist and novelist, born in 1893. Henri de Montherlant's egotistical cynicism is typical of his times. *Le Démon du bien* is impregnated with Satanism and affirms the superiority of the Devil over God.

MOPSES An esoteric society practicing the occult arts and celebrating the Sabbat.

MORA WITCHES The famous investigation of witchcraft that began at Mora, Sweden, in 1669 was inspired by reports that the Devil had gained control over hundreds of children in the vicinity and had been seen going through the country. Scores of witches were identified. The mania spread to the Swedish-speaking provinces of Finland and to Stockholm. Finally it was stopped by Urban Hjärne, a young doctor who showed that the craze depended on a morbid imagination, malice, and desire for attention.

MORE, HENRY English philosopher (1614-1687). Though he was an earnest champion of the fusion of reason and faith, More had a lifelong interest in the occult. He believed that he had proof that witches and devils with cloven hooves attended Sabbats.

MORMO A ghastly ghoul who served as an emissary of Hecate.

MORS In Roman religion, the personification of Death.

MORTA See Parca.

MORZINE Alpine village, site of an epidemic of diabolic possession in the nineteenth century.

MOSAIC LAW Moses, by divine command, is supposed to have promulgated the law, 'Thou shalt not suffer a witch to live.'

MOSES Medieval Christians linked magic with the Devil, but Jews generally traced magic back to Moses, whom they numbered among the most famous magicians of all time.

MOSES DE LEON Cabalist who revealed the Zohar to the public in 1300.

MOT The Canaanite literature unearthed at Ugarit contains the tale of the struggle between the supreme god Baal and the sea-god Yam. Baal is slain and brought down to the kingdom of the dead, ruled by Mot. Baal's disappearance brings life on earth to a standstill until the warrior-goddess Anat kills Mot, making possible the return upon earth of Baal and, with him, fertility and plenty:
>She seizes the god Mot;
>With sword she cleaves him . . .
>In fields she sows him.

MOTHER GODDESS In pagan religions the Mother Goddess was of supreme importance as the source of fertility. She was Ishtar among the Assyro-Babylonians. In Phoenicia she was known as Astarte. In Syria she was Atargatis. In Phrygia she was Cybele. In Greece, she was Demeter. The Egyptians knew her as Isis.

MOUNTAIN GIANTS See Tornait.

MOUTH Phoenician god of the dead, identified with Pluto.

MRTYU In the age of the Upanishads, Mrtyu was the name of the Indian Satan. Later he was called by the derivative name of Mara.

MULCIBER An epithet of Vulcan, also used to name Satan.

MULUKUAUSI Among the Trobriand Islanders, invisible witches, dangerous on land and water. They feed on the entrails of the dead.

MUMMU The creative utterance or life force mentioned in the Akkadian myth of creation in connection with Apsu. Apsu consults his Mummu and receives advice on how to destroy Nudimmud. Mummu may also be identified as a personification of the Phallus.

MURMUR Demon of music, count of Hell. He appears astride a vulture, shaped like a giant soldier.

MURPHY, BRIDEY Subject of the best seller, *The Search for Bridey Murphy* (1956), written by Morey Bernstein, multimillionaire businessman and amateur hypnotist. Mrs. Virginia Tighe, in a deep hypnotic trance, recalled memories of the childhood of Bridey Murphy, wife of an early nineteenth-century barrister in Belfast. Bernstein concluded that Bridey Murphy was a former reincarnation of Mrs. Tighe.

MURRAY, MARGARET Advocate of the well-known theory that the witch cult is the survival of a pagan religion. In *Witch-Cult in Western Europe,* she tries to prove that 'underlying the Christian religion was a cult practiced by many classes of the community, chiefly, however, by the more ignorant or those in less thickly inhabited parts of the country. It can be traced back to pre-Christian times and appears to be the ancient religion of western Europe.'

MYSTERY RELIGIONS Certain pagan religions received initiates by secret rites that were not publicly divulged. The secret knowledge thus acquired by the aspirant would ensure advantages in his present life and in the life after death.

The most important mystery religions were those of the Greeks, Phrygians, Syrians, Egyptians, Persians.

Among the Greeks the rites celebrated at Eleusis were the most famous. They were associated with Demeter and Persephone and interpreted a vegetation concept.

Other Greek mysteries were celebrated at Andania and on the island of Samothrace. The Dionysiac mysteries were observed in different places. The ceremonies, which were orgiastic, required the drinking of the sacred wine, the eating of the raw flesh of the sacrificed animal, drinking its blood. The ultimate purpose of the cult was an assurance of immortality.

In Phrygia the mysteries were connected with Cybele, the Mother Goddess. As the Nature goddess she mourned the death of her young consort Attis and rejoiced on his return to earth. The mystery similarly involved a vegetation myth.

In Syria the mysteries, again involving a vegetation myth, centered round Adonis, the consort of the Nature Goddess, who dies and is reborn.

The Egyptian mysteries of Isis and Osiris were popular throughout the Graeco-Roman world.

The last mystery religion that was immensely popular in the Roman Empire was Mithraism, the cult of Mithra and his conflict with Ahriman, the Spirit of Evil. Initiation ceremonies were elaborate and demanded a great deal of preparation and austerity. There were sacramental rites, ablutions, sacred meals. In seven stages of advancement, symbolizing the passage of the soul after death through the seven heavens into the abode of the blessed, the initiate reached the ultimate inner mystery. Women were excluded from membership in this cult.

MYTHOLOGY In ancient pagan religions, the relation between man and the gods was interpreted by means of myths. The creation myth of Babylonia is illustrated by the conflict between Marduk and Tiamat. The Egyptian sun myth, the myth of Isis-Osiris, the myth of Orpheus, are all designed to explain man in terms of the cosmic and the creative forces of the universe.

MYTHS The Greek word *mythos* means a tale. Myths were fanciful, imaginative stories that pictured the operations of natural phenomena in terms of anthropomorphic beings. Later, myths evolved into dramatic presentations of these vivid tales of gods and men. Another aspect in the concept of the myth was an attempt to interpret man's activities, his personal longings, his purpose in life, his relation to the divinities who appeared to rule the cosmos. Mystery cults centering on some particular local or universally conceived divinity evolved, with the object of discovering how man could make contacts with such a divinity, how he could commune with him, and how the divinity would help in clarifying the meaning of life, in steering men toward personal salvation, in expounding the possibilities and even the promises of a future life. Votaries of a deity were initiated into secret rituals so that they would comprehend the cosmic scheme. Contacts with the deities were achieved by elaborate ceremonials, liturgies, fastings and ascetic practices, and purifications. There were sacred dancing performances, while magnificent processional parades, led by the priesthood, were a notable feature, together with chants and supplications and temple services.

N

NAAMAH In Jewish tradition, a demoness who smothers newborn children and seduces men in their sleep.

NAASSIANS Devil-worshipers, also called Ophites. The name is derived from the Hebrew word *Nahas*, which means 'serpent.' A branch of the Gnostics, they attached great importance to Satan as the tempter in the biblical account of the temptation of Adam and Eve. They respected the knowledge of good and evil imparted by the serpent and believed that God had withheld this vital knowledge from man. By teaching men to rebel against God, the serpent acted as the emancipator of mankind.

NABATAEANS A sect almost identical with the Mandaeans. They had more reverence for John the Baptist than for Jesus. Maimonides called them astrolaters.

NABERUS Marquis of Hell. He appears in the shape of a crow. He has a hoarse voice and teaches eloquence and the fine arts. Also called Gerberus.

NAGAL A term applied by Mexican Indians to the principal sorcerer of a tribe.

NAGALISM Serpent-worship. The term derives from the Sanskrit *naga*, 'serpent.' Nagalism was practiced in many places, including Burma, Egypt, Greece, and Mexico.

NAGARI The alchemists' dragon. He uttered these words: 'I rise from death, I kill death, and death kills me. I resuscitate the bodies I have created and, alive in death, I destroy myself.'

NAGA In Hindu mythology, a member of a race of semihuman serpents, ruled by Shesha, the sacred serpent of Vishnu. They inhabit Patala, a magnificent subaqueous kingdom.

NAGAS In India, these are snake spirits.

NAGUAL An individual guardian spirit or totem among Central American tribes. A person and his nagual, usually an animal, have the same soul. The notion of the nagual was elaborated into a mystery cult opposed to the religion of the conquerors of these tribes.

NAHAS A Hebrew word meaning 'serpent.' See Naassians.

NAHEMAH A name applied to the princess of all the succubi.

NAILS Like skin, blood, hair, or sperm, nails may be used in casting spells. French children are warned not to bite their nails because the Devil is ready at all times to claim them and use them against the children.

NAKEDNESS Witches regard the human body as a storehouse of energy whose release is hindered by clothing.

NAMES In magic and witchcraft successful invocation or exorcism may depend on exact knowledge of a name. In Egyptian mythology Isis learned by trickery the secret name of Re. Some people (the Hindus, for example) try to conceal the names of their children to protect them against demons.

NAMES OF SATAN *Malleus Maleficarum,* a fifteenth-century treatise by Heinrich Kramer and Jakob Sprenger, indicates that Satan may be invoked under several names, each with a special etymological significance:

As Asmodeus, he is the Creature of Judgement. As Satan, he becomes the Adversary. As Behemoth, he is the Beast. Diabolus, the Devil, signifies two morsels: the body and the soul, both of which he kills. Demon connotes Cunning over Blood. Belial, Without a Master. Beelzebub, Lord of Flies.

Here are the names by which he is generally known in various languages:

Arabic: Sheitan
Biblical: Asmodeus (or Belial or Apollyon)
Egyptian: Set
Japanese: O Yama
Persian: Dev
Russian: Tchort
Syriac: Béherit
Welsh: Pwcca.

NAMTAR (NAMTARU) In the Sumerian version of Ereshkigal's descent to the underworld, Namtar is the offspring and servant of the guardian of the fount of life. He is the evil demon, Death. He uses the sixty diseases under his charge to bring death to mankind. Namtar is also a Sumerian word designating fate, similar to classical Moira.

NAMUCHE In Indian mythology, a wicked demon with whom Indra struggles.

NAPOLEON The French emperor was reputed to have a familiar demon that manifested itself in the corridors of the Tuileries in Paris.

NASTRAND In Nordic mythology, the frozen underworld, where the damned experience the extremes of punishment.

NASU In Zoroastrian religion, a female demon that feeds on the corpses of the dead.

NATS In Burmese demonology, evil spirits that can be exorcised by women.

NATURE According to the Gnostics and the Albigenses, nature is the work of the accursed angels; matter is evil. Medieval Christians considered nature to be under Satan's power, following man's original sin. They assumed that nature was possessed of devils, and that the spirit of Satan pervaded and subjugated the material world.

NATURE WORSHIP In primitive pagan religions, almost all the deities were nature forces, the heavenly bodies, animals, plants. Man had to adjust his needs to his environment in order to secure necessary food for sustenance. Man found that in many manifestations Nature was beneficial but at times also hostile and destructive. Man needed fruits, fresh water, winds, the sun, rain. When he received these aids to his well-being, he expressed his gratitude in mystery rites and appealed to the powers associated with such cults. If the powers responded to his prayers, these powers became manifest divinities, endowed with particular attributes and functions.

NAVAHO GHOSTS The Navahos believed that every human being had an evil portion as well as a good portion. The evil portion, after a person's death, became a dangerous ghost.

NAZAR In Iran, the spell cast by the Evil Eye.

NEBEBKA In Egyptian religion, a judge in the realm of the dead.

NEBIROS Field Marshal of the infernal spirits. He has command over Ayperos, Naberus, and Glasyabolas. He has power to inflict harm on whomever he wishes, to teach the properties of things, and to predict the future.

NEBO Name adopted by Stanislas de Guaita. The founder of the nineteenth-century cabalistic Rosicrucians in France took the pseudonym from Assyrian astrology.

NEBUCHADNEZZAR King of Babylon. God punished him for trying to make his subjects worship him. For seven years he was forced to eat grass and drink dew like an animal.

NECROMANCY Trying to communicate with the spirits of the dead by evocation. The modern form of necromancy is called Spiritism.

NECROMANCY Divination by the dead. Fastidious preparations are required if the necromancer is to communicate with the corpse he intends to disturb. An appropriate incantation must accompany the opening of the grave and the coffin. If the rites involve the body of a suicide, the magician commands the spirit by the flames of Banal and the rites of Hecate to reveal why it took its own life and to answer specific questions. One of the principal aims of the necromancer is to discover the future by communicating with the dead, who are no longer bound by mortal limitations and can foresee events.

NECTANEBUS Egyptian king of the fourth century B.C., renowned as a magician and seer.

NEDU In Sumerian mythology, chief guardian of the entrance to the realm of the dead. He corresponds to the Greek god Charon.

NEEDFIRE In Teutonic folklore, a fire kindled to remove injury from the herd and promote prosperity. Of heathen origin, probably during a time of plague, the practice involved extinguishing hearth fires and relighting them from the new fire. The custom dates back to prehistoric times and survives in some modern settings, particularly in the lighting of fires on St. John's Day.

NEKKER (NIKKER) A Teutonic water sprite whose appearance was linked by sailors to death or drowning. Nekker as a culture god survives both as St. Nicholas (Santa Claus), the beneficent deity who loves children, and as Old Nick, the harbinger of disaster and carrier of souls to the future world.

NEOPHYTE In Aleister Crowley's cabalistic system, the first of the ten ranks or grades designating the spheres through which the student must ascend if he is to wield the magical power accessible to man as the potential God. The tenth sephira is the sphere of earth.

NEPTUNI Another name for aquatic demons.

NERGAL The Sumerian god of the Lower Regions, husband of Ereshkigal. He may be equated with the Greek god Pluto, who ruled the Underworld. Nergal, like the Biblical Satan, originally dwelt in heaven.

NESHAMAN In the Cabala, as taught by the Rosicrucian order, one of the three highest essences of the human soul. It corresponds to the Sephira Binah.

NETSAH The seventh sephira, the sphere of Venus, in Cabalistic teachings. It stands for animal drives, instinct, impulse. It stands opposite Hod on the Tree of Life.

NEWBURY, WITCH OF In 1642 a soldier shot a woman who was reputed to have the ability to walk on water. The 'witch' was killed by his bullet.

NEW SATANIC AGE The New Satanic Age was proclaimed in 1966 by Anton LaVey, High Priest of the San Francisco Church of Satan.

NICHUSCH In Cabalistic teachings, a prophetic indication.

NIDER, JOHANNES (c. 1380-1438) Professor of theology and author of the second book ever printed on witchcraft. He wrote *Formicarius* (The Anthill) in 1435. The fifth part of the book, a discussion of the evil powers of witches, was sometimes appended to the *Malleus Maleficarium*.

NIFELHEIM (NIFLHEIM) In Norse mythology, the northern region of cold and darkness. The ash of Yggdrasill extended its roots into Niflheim, the deepest cavern of darkness.

NIGHTMARE The word commonly designates either the mare (demon) believed to cause a frightful dream or the dream itself. All nightmares share certain characteristics: intense fear, the feeling that something is pressing down on the chest and interfering with normal breathing, and a feeling of utter helplessness. See Mare.

NIGHT-RIDERS The ancient Teutons thought that the souls of the dead returned to the world of the living by night or during storms to harass sleepers. The belief in such demonic spirits is the foundation of the medieval belief in terrifying night-rides or night-mares. Many stories circulated about hordes of night-flying demons and dead souls. The ninth-century Canon Episcopi states that some women were under the illusion that they rode by night 'upon certain beasts with Diana, the goddess of pagans, and an innumerable multitude of women, and in the silence of night' traversed great distances and obeyed her commands 'as their mistress.' These evil incubi pressed down on the breasts of women, sucked their milk and the milk of cows, and disturbed the dreams of mortals. Part of a group of *hexen* ('witches) responsible for much mischief and capable of assuming many forms, they were the female counterparts of the werewolves of European legend.

NIGHT SPELL A charm to protect the sleeper against harm, especially the mare. Guazzo's *Compendium Maleficarum* (1626) states that reciting holy psalms and prayer 'are the safest protection and rampart against all the wiles of the prince of darkness.'

NINAZU Sumerian underworld deity.

NINE MYSTIC NAMES The medieval grimoire *Key of Solomon* lists nine mystic names to be used in summoning demons: Ehieh, Iod, Tetragrammaton Elohim, El, Elohim Gibor, Eloah Va-Daath, El Adonai Tzabaoth, Elohim Tzabaoth, Shaddai.

NINGISHZIDA In Sumerian religion, an underworld deity.

NINHARSAG Sumerian goddess, known by many other names (Ninhursag, Ninhursag, Ninhursaga, Ninmah, Nintu) and having the attributes of the Minoan Great Goddess. As Nin-Khursag, she is 'the one who gives life to the dead.'

NIRRITI In Hindu mythology, goddess of death.

NITHHOGG In Norse mythology, a dragon living in Nifelheim. He gnaws at the root of Yggdrasill, the great ash tree that symbolizes the universe.

NIX In Teutonic folklore, demons that lived in or near streams.

NONA See Parca.

NORNS In Teutonic mythology, demigoddesses or divine giantesses who determine the fates of men and gods. The original Norn was probably called Wyrd by the Anglo-Saxons and Urth by the Norse. Two other Norns were added later, forming the Norse trio of Urth, Verthandi, and Skuld. These three Norns represent the past, present, and future.

NORTH BERWICK WITCHES The trials of witches in North Berwick, Scotland, began with seemingly miraculous cures effected by Gilly Duncan, a young servant who confessed her ties with the Devil and named her accomplices. The trials took place between 1590 and 1592 and may have inspired King James to write his *Demonology* (1597). In 1590 David Ceaton tortured his young servant Gilly Duncan, forcing her to confess that she was possessed by the Devil and to name her accomplices. Among those named were Dr. John Fian, who was charged with practicing levitation and using cadavers to make charms, and Agnes Sampson, who accused scores of men and women of attending the Sabbat and of conspiring to raise a storm and sink the ship bearing James VI from Oslo to Leith. The king survived, thanks to the power of Margaret, a cat that had been thrown into the sea, but he had Fian, Sampson, and others put to death 'for witchcraft and sorcery.' The North Berwick trials were the most famous ever held in Scotland.

NORTON, THOMAS English alchemist who flourished in the fifteenth century. He wrote a treatise on alchemy and hermetics.

NOSTRADAMUS French physician, astrologer, and seer whose real name was Michel de Notre-Dame (1503-1566). His book of predictions, titled *The Centuries,* has been remarkably accurate.

NOVIKH, GREGORI Notorious Russian monk and cultist, known to millions as Rasputin (1871-1916). He mingled dancing and debauchery with mystical seances, gaining power over the royal family of imperial Russia.

NUMA POMPILIUS Second king of Rome. He was supposed to have practiced magic and to have had as his adviser Egeria, a fountain nymph whose worship was associated with that of Diana at Nemi.

NUMBER OF DEMONS According to Talmudic tradition, there are 7,405,926 demons.

NUMBER OF THE BEAST The Number of the Beast, mentioned in the Book of Revelation (13:18), is associated with the Antichrist. According to the Biblical account, a beast emerged from the sea. 'Let him that hath understanding count the number of the beast, for it is the number of man; and his number is six hundred threescore and six.' Modern scholars assume that the seven-headed beast was meant to represent the Roman Empire and its seven emperors. Less scholarly speculations make the Beast Napoleon, the Pope, Luther, Hitler, etc. Jehovah's witnesses hold that the Beast stands for whatever political organization prevails at a given time. Now it is the United Nations. See Crowley, Aleister.

NYBRAS One of the demons in charge of infernal pleasures.

NYSROCK Chief cook in the kitchen of Hell. He presides over the pleasures of the table.

O

OBEAH A cult originated by the Ashanti, who predominated among the African natives brought to the West Indies. The chief center of the cult is Jamaica. Claude McKay, the twentieth-century Jamaican poet, wrote: 'Obeah is black people's evil God. Of the thousands of native families, illiterate and literate . . . there were few indeed that did not worship and pay tribute to Obi, the god of Evil. . . .' Its practitioners, called obeah men or women, rely on sorcery, magic ritual, poisonous herbs, and fear, in casting spells, locating missing items, and causing sickness or accidents.

Among the items used by the obeah man are blood, feathers, teeth, grave dirt, rum, egg-shells, cards, mirrors, camphor, sulphur, myrrh, incense, asafoetida, shells, wooden images, and strangely shaped sticks. The obeah man is engaged to make love philters, exorcise evil spirits, inflict harm on a disliked person, prevent theft, etc. An obeah man who uses incantation at home may appear in court to influence witnesses, jury, and judge.

OBELISK An upright monolithic pillar. Like many other elements of the Egyptian religion, it may have been a phallic symbol.

OBI The deity brought to the New World by the Ashanti. The 'God of Evil' was worshipped by many Jamaican families, literate and illiterate.

OBSESSION In cases of obsession, the tormented subject is unable to identify the presence of a persecuting spirit. Possession occurs when this spirit manifests itself clearly.

OCCULTISM A name given to a group of rejected sciences: astrology, horoscopy, palmistry, alchemy, etc.

OCCULT PHILOSOPHY Title of Agrippa von Nettesheim's defense of magic as a composite of religious doctrine, occultism, and scientific knowledge.

OCHER The widespread practice of coating corpses with red ocher seems to have existed since the beginning of the Paleolithic period. Perhaps the red color is associated with life-supporting blood and represents an attempt by survivors to make the body of the deceased again serviceable for its owner's use. The red powder is found in almost all Paleolithic graves, yet its use was in no way necessary for burying a corpse. It was also scattered on the floors of caves, such as the Lascaux caves, in southern France. Though its exact significance remains a mystery, it clearly was linked with religious rites.

OCHNOTINOS A demon named in an ancient Hebraic incantation, used to banish fever. The fever subsided as the demon's name was uttered in diminishing size:
Ochnotinos
Chnotinos
Notinos
Tinos
Inos
Nos
Os.

ODACON A Syrian deity, identified with Dagon.

ODD The souls of the damned are supposed to appear at odd-numbered hours during the night.

ODIN In Norse mythology, the supreme god.

OERA LINDA BOEK A Frisian manuscript that putatively contains esoteric knowledge.

OKEE A word used by Captain John Smith to designate the chief god of the Indians of Virginia. 'Their chiefe God they worship is the Deuell,' he wrote. 'Him they call *Oke*, and serue him more of ea feare than loue.'

OKI A North American sky demon.

OLD GENTLEMAN One of the names of Satan.

OLD HORNY One of the names of the Devil.

OLD NICK Colloquial name for the Devil, derived ultimately from Nikker (Nekker), a Teutonic water sprite whose appearance was supposed by sailors to forebode death. As a harbinger of death, he is closely related to the banshee of Irish and Scottish folklore. Names similarly used for the Devil are Old Harry, Old Scratch, and Old One.

OLD ONE In many primitive religions the Old One is an epithet of the chief deity, who is generally a creator. In English the term designates the Devil.

OLD SCRATCH A sobriquet of the Devil. It derives from an old Germanic word meaning goblin or wizard.

OLIVER, JOSEPH Swedenborgian and apostle of magnetism. In 1849 he wrote in *Magnétiseur spiritualiste*, journal of the French magneto-Swedenborgian association, 'The god of the real force, the true force, is SATAN.'

OM (AUM) A mystic syllable used in Hinduism, occultism, primitive masonry, and syncretic cults practiced in modern youth communes which have recently sprung up all across the United States. The Hindu syllable originally denoted assent but is now the most solemn of all words heard in India. A mantra representing the triple constitution of the universe, it is used as an invocation, a benediction, an affirmation, and a promise. It is generally placed at the beginning of sacred scriptures and prefixed to prayers. The three component parts of the syllable are the Absolute (Agni or Fire), the Relative (Varuna or Water), and the relation between them (Maruts or Air). The mystic syllable is called the Udgitta and is sacred with both Buddhists and Brahmins. It is chanted each evening before dinner by members of youth communes after they have joined hands and stood for two or three minutes in silent meditation.

ONI-NO-NEMBUTZU In Japanese folklore, a grotesque devil who exemplifies greed and hypocrisy, The name means 'the devil as a monk.'

OPENING OF THE MOUTH A ceremony which originated among the early inhabitants of the valley of the Nile. Ancient formulas were recited during the performance of ceremonial rites to reconstitute the body of a person who had died and restore to it its *ba* and *ka*, its living soul and the ghostly double of this soul, given to the person at birth. Originally, the ceremony was performed on a statue and consisted in using holy water and other substances to purify the statue, presenting the foreleg of a slain ox to the statue, touching its eyes, nose and ears with various magical instruments, and pronouncing a formula which ended, 'the mouth of every god is opened.' Finally, the statue was invested with royal insignia and a sacred meal was served on the altar. The king had the sacred duty to perform the reanimation rites for his deceased father.

OPHIOLATRY The cult of the serpent. This cult was prevalent in ancient Greece where the serpent was regarded as a domestic deity.

In Egypt the serpent was sometimes a god of evil. As such he was crushed by Horus. Among the Romans too both Jupiter and Apollo destroyed the serpent.

In many primitive religions the serpent is an object of tabu and is associated with magic rites.

In another aspect the serpent was revered for his healing attributes. Among the Gnostics, he was the Master of Wisdom. In pre-Columbian America, he was the plumed serpent Quetzalcoatl.

The cult of the serpent was prevalent among the Ashanti in Africa and was introduced by them to the Western World. It survives in the Voodoo rituals of the West Indies.

OPHITES A Gnostic sect that originated in the second century. The name of the sect derives from the Greek word for serpent.

The members of the sect were also called Naassians, from the Hebrew word for serpent. Their great respect for the knowledge (*gnosis*) of good and evil which the serpent had enabled men to obtain drew them to Satan the tempter. The serpent was seen as their liberator since he had taught them to rebel against God, who withheld knowledge from them.

ORACLE HEAD In the alchemical tradition, the oracle head seems to point to an original human sacrifice. Such sacrifices may have been made for the purpose of summoning up familiar spirits. A severed head, prepared according to prescribed rites, was supposed to reveal to people their inmost thoughts and to answer questions addressed to it. Gerbert of Reims, who later became Pope Sylvester II, was believed to have a golden head with oracular powers. The alchemical head may be connected with the teraphim, considered by Rabbinic tradition to have been a decapitated skull or a dummy head.

The oracle head was also known in ancient Greece and

may go back to the severed head of Osiris, which was linked with the notion of resurrection. Aelian swore that the head of Archonides was preserved in a jar of honey by his friend Cleomenes of Sparta, who consulted it as an oracle. Similar powers were attributed to the head of Orpheus.

ORCUS In Greek religion, he was the god of the underworld. He is identified with the Roman Dis.

ORDEAL BY CORPSE At the end of the twelfth century courts began using a test based on an ancient superstition: that the corpse of a murdered victim bled if touched by the murderer. Del Rio explained the phenomenon by the victim's accumulated hatred for his assassin.

ORDEAL BY IMMERSION See Swimming.

ORDEALS Various tests were employed by tribunals established to try those accused of witchcraft. These included the ordeal by corpse, cold water, boiling water, fire, and the cross. In the ordeal by water the right hand of the accused was tied to the left foot, the left hand to the right foot, and the victim was thrown into a vat of cold water to determine whether he would sink. When hot water was used, the hand of the accused was plunged into the container in search of a ring, then bound for three days. If no injuries were discovered, the accused was presumed to be innocent. In the ordeal by fire, the accused had to carry a red-hot bar several steps. In the ordeal by the cross, the accused had to stand before a cross with outstretched arms.

ORDER OF KNIGHTS TEMPLAR See Templars.

ORDER OF TEMPLARS OF THE ORIENT A German occult society specializing in sex-magic. In 1912, the society accused Aleister Crowley of publishing its secrets in *The*

Equinox. When they learned that he had discovered these secrets independently, he was invited to join the society.

He became head of the British branch of the society, acquiring the title of Supreme and Holy King of Ireland, Iona, and all the Britains that are in the Sanctuary of the Gnosis.

ORDER OF THE GOLDEN DAWN Occult society whose members included W. R. Yeats, Algernon Blackwood, Arthur Machen, the Astronomer Royal of Scotland, and Allan Bennett, an eccentric who renounced his Catholic faith when he discovered the mechanism of childbirth. Founded in England, the society at its peak had lodges in London, Edinburgh, Bradford, and Weston-super-Mare. Its most precious possession was a mysterious manuscript discovered on a London bookstall in 1884. It was deciphered by Samuel Liddell Mathers, who replaced William Wynn Westcott, an authority on the Cabala, as Visible Head of the Order of the Golden Dawn.

ORDIN Corsican name for the Evil Eye.

ORENDA Among American Indians, a term applied to occult spirit-forces.

ORGEUIL A demon who possessed Elisabeth Allier, a seventeenth-century French nun.

ORI Among the Lugbara, ghosts and shrines erected by children for their deceased parents.

ORIAS Count of Hell. He is an expert in astrology and in metamorphoses. He carries a serpent in each hand.

ORIGEN Christian writer and teacher of Alexander. Origenes Adamantius (c. 185-254) believed that demons were able to predict the future by observing the aspects and movements of the heavenly bodies.

ORLEANS In 533 the Council of Orléans proscribed the excommunication of Catholics 'who fail to preserve intact the faith into which they have been received and return to the worship of idols.'
In 1022 a whole chapter of canons from Orléans in France were burned at the stake because 'they worshiped the Devil.'

ORNIAS In Solomonic legend, a vampire demon.

ORPHIC MYSTERIES These mysteries, founded by Orpheus, were secret rituals associated with the cult of Dionysus. Orphism taught morality, a pure life, and promised reincarnation in the life after death. Details of rituals are obscure, but it is known that initiates were required to abstain from meat, beans, and sexual intercourse.

ORTHON Familiar demon of Raymond, Count of Corasse, and later of his friend Foix.

OSCULUM INFAME Also called *osculum obscoenum*. See Kiss of Shame.

OSIRIS In Egyptian religion, the great god of the underworld, sun god, and judge of the dead. The son of Jeb and Nut, he was the brother and husband of Isis. The Greeks identified Osiris with Dionysus, the symbol of fertility and life.

OSTRICH The Arabs link the ostrich with demons. Sometimes a demon takes the shape of an ostrich; sometimes he sits astride an ostrich.

OUTWITTING THE DEVIL Medieval literature contains many legends in which the Devil is outwitted by his foes. The episode of Buonconte in *The Divine Comedy* echoes the theme of the deluded Devil. Similar motifs are found in Ben Jonson's *The Devil Is an Ass,* William Haughton's *The Devil and His Dame,* and Thomas Dekker's *The Devil Is in It.* The most famous example of deception in all literature is Goethe's Mephistopheles. In *Faust* the Devil labors many years to fulfill his part of the bargain, yet loses the soul of the old doctor to a host of angels.

OVID Roman poet. (43 B.C. - 17 A.D.) In *Metamorphoses* he attributes this invocation to Medea, the most famous magician of Greek mythology:
O night, faithful preserver of mysteries. . . . With your help I stir up the calm seas by my spell; I break the jaws of serpents with my incantations. I bid ghosts to come forth from their tombs.

O YAMA The Japanese name of Satan.

OZARK WITCHCRAFT According to Vance Randolph (*Ozark Superstitions*), the hill people of the Ozarks practice a form of witchcraft in which a key element of the initiation ceremony involves sexual intercourse between a neophyte and a male member of the cult, who acts as the Devil's representative. For three nights in succession, the initiate and the cult member, meet at midnight, in the dark of the moon, in the family burying-ground of the woman seeking admission. There she formally renounces her faith, learns the secrets of the cult, and recites the Lord's Prayer backwards. Cultists report that 'the witch's initiation is a much more moving spiritual crisis than that which the Christians call conversion.'

Devils cast out of Arezzo detail
Fresco by Giotto
(Assisi: Upper Church of San Francesco)

P

PACTUM EXPRESSUM A pact entered into by a witch and a demon in writing, verbally, or by signs.

PACTUM TACITUM An assumption on the part of a witch that Satan collaborates in an undertaking.

PACT WITH THE DEVIL A medieval Grimoire describes the manner of making a pact with the Devil:
> The magician cut a bough of wild hazel that had not yet produced fruit, with a new knife, at sunrise. Then he brought a bloodstone and two wax candles to some secluded spot. . . . With the bloodstone he traced a triangle on the floor, and placed the candles by the triangle. A circle was now made around the triangle. Within the triangle, holding a hazel wand, the magician uttered his conjuration:
> Aglon Tetragram Vaycheon Stimulathon
> Erohares Retragsammathon Clyoran Icion
> Esistion Existien Eryona Onera Erasyn Moyn
> Meffias Soter Emmanuel Saboth Adonai, I call you.
> Amen. See Conjuration.

According to the *Great Key* attributed to Solomon, to command the forces of nature one must first learn the names, qualities, and jurisdiction of the six demons empowered to make pacts. Each of the six is served by three lesser demons: Lucifuge by Baël, Agares, and Marbas; Satanachia by Pruslas, Aamon, and Barbatos; Agaliarept by Buer, Guseyn, and Botis; Fleuretty by Bathym, Pursan, and Aligar; Sarganas Sargatanas by

Loray, Valefar, and Forau; and Nebitos by Ayphos, Naberus, and Glasyalabolas.

PADERBORN In 785 the Synod of Paderborn decreed that 'anyone, blinded by the Devil and believing as the pagans do that a certain person is a witch who eats men, and for this reason burns this person and eats his flesh or has others eat his flesh, will be punished by death.'

PAIGOELS Hindu devils, created as such or expelled from heaven for their sin. They tempt men, enter their bodies, and welcome into their ranks the souls of the wicked.

PALAS ARON AZINOMAS An ancient formula for invoking a demon.

PALENGENESIA The Greek mystery religions consisted of symbolic rites whose meaning was esoteric and whose aim was to inspire the initiate with a mystic experience that led him to palengenesia or regeneration.

PALEOLITHIC CULT OF THE DEAD Available evidence concerning the disposal of the dead suggests that a cult of the dead existed from the beginning of the Pleistocene period and that it became associated with the cult of the Great Mother. Preservation of the skull and extraction of the brain, ceremonial interment, the presence of flint implements, animal bones, ochreous powder, shells and other ornaments at burial sites, all available data point to the existence of religious rites and beliefs.

Scores of sepulchers dating from the age of the reindeer have been discovered in Europe. The deceased usually was interred in a pit, with a few stones to protect his head Ornaments included shell hairnets, necklaces, and delicately carved objects of bone or ivory. At Laugerie-Basse, Dordogne, cowries were placed in pairs on the forehead, feet, etc. The shape of the shells suggests a connection with the female principle and their employment as fertility charms. Thus the distribution of these shells may have been for the purpose of giving life to the deceased. Firm trussing of the body immediately after death may have been a cautionary measure, intended to protect the living against the dead, but the care taken in the ritual disposal of the body indicates that respect and concern for the dead went beyond fear. See Ocher, Blood.

PALLADISM Cult of Satan, ascribed to certain Masonic lodges in the last part of the nineteenth century.

PALMISTRY CHURCH Gipsies arrested in October, 1964, by the Los Angeles police on charges of fortune-telling, claimed that their civil rights had been violated. 'Gipsies are born with the power to look into the future,' they argued. 'It's part of our religion. We are members of the Palmistry Church.'

PALOU, JEAN French historian (1918-1967). In his study of Witchcraft (*La Sorcellerie*), he follows Michelet in ascribing the origins of witchcraft to economic and social forces.

PAMYLIA An ancient phallic ceremony, observed in honor of the birth of Osiris.

PAN A lustful, energetic god whose cult spread throughout the Hellenic world. Pan was half man and half goat. A leader of satyrs, he is said to have participated in celebrations of the witches' Sabbat.

PANDEMONIUM Capital of the infernal empire where Milton placed Satan's palace.

PAPA GUEDE The voodoo deity evoked by cultists on the Day of the Dead. Dr. François Duvalier, who was elected ruler of Haiti in 1957 on a program of 'Africanism,' is called Papa Guédé by his back-country supporters.

PAPINI, GIOVANNI Italian philosopher and historian. Giovanni Papini (b. 1881) was at first a severe critic of Christianity but was converted to Catholicism in 1920. His many books include *The Devil: Notes for a Future Diabology* (first published in English in 1955).

PAPIYAN Another name for Mara, the Buddhist Devil.

PAPUS See Encausse, Gerard.

PARACELSUS The name adopted by Theophrastus Bombastus von Hohenheim (c. 1490-1514), one of the most famous physicians and occultists of the Middle Ages. He regarded the life of man as inseparable from that of the universe and disease as the result of a separation of the three mystic elements of which man is compounded — salt, sulfur, and mercury.

PARCA In Roman religion, the fate of a person, identified with the Greek concept of Moira. The three *Parcae* or fates determining the life of a man are Nona, Documa, and Morta. Nona spins the thread of a person's life, Documa determines its length, and Morta cuts it.

PARE, AMBROISE The sixteenth-century 'Father of Modern Surgery' believed that demons could transform themselves quickly into any desired shape, into 'serpents, toads, screechowls, hoopoes, crows, goats, donkeys, dogs, cats, wolves, bulls. . . . They even take on human bodies, alive or dead.'

PARIS WITCH TRIAL The first secular trial in Europe for witchcraft took place in Paris in 1390. Jehenne de Brigue, called La Cordière, confessed that she had practiced witchcraft, and she implicated Macette de Ruilly. Both were burned alive at the Pig Market on August 19, 1391.

PATRON OF WITCHCRAFT Among the Greeks and Romans, Hecate was the goddess most often invoked by witches. Represented with three heads or three bodies corresponding to the three phases of the moon — new, full, and old — she ruled the night and darkness, ghosts, tombs, and dogs. As Luna, the moon, she appeared in the sky; as Diana she stalked the earth; and as Proserpine she ruled over the underworld. Hecate seems to have been forgotten in early Christian times, but memories of Diana survived and gave rise to the belief that mortals could ride with her at night. See Night-Riders.

PAUT In Egyptian religion, the gods who helped Osiris as judge in the realm of the dead.

PAYMON Powerful demon. He appears as a robust man with the face of a woman, mounted on a camel.

PAZUZU Assyrian demon, son of Hanpa, the king of the evil spirits of the air.

PEACE SYMBOL A circle bisected by a straight line which in turn bisects an inverted V. Now worn by pacifists throughout the world, the peace symbol is of ancient and obscure origin. Opponents of the wearing of the peace symbol claim that it has always been displayed by the enemies of Christianity, and they cite Nero, Titus, and Hitler. Nero is supposed to have used a broken cross as the sign of the Broken Jew. Titus' troops are said to have carried shields bearing the symbol when they destroyed Jerusalem in 70 A.D. Fifth-century illustrations of the peace symbol are reproduced in the dictionary compiled by the Grimm brothers. Hitler used the symbol to mark the death notices and tombstones of his officers. In 1958 a demonstration group led by Bertrand Russell (1872-1970) adopted it as symbol of modern pacifism. Lord Russell, hailed, by some, the greatest logician since Aristotle and censured by others for his failure to stand firm against Communism, established the Peace Foundation that bears his name.

PEACOCK The peacock is used by the Yezidis to represent the Devil, known to the masses as Melek Taus.

PELADAN, JOSEPHIN Grand Master of Parisian Rosicrucians, esthete, and avowed Satanist.

PENDRAGON, UTHER A warlock in Welsh legend.

PENTACLE A five-pointed figure used as a magic symbol. A medieval grimoire known as the *Key of Solomon* tells how to make and consecrate pentacles:
> The pentacles are to be made on the day of Mercury, and in its hour. The Moon is to be in a sign of air earth, and waxing, and her days shall be the same as those of the Sun. Retire to a specially prepared room or other place, set aside for this purpose, with your companions. It is to be censed and perfumed with magical incense and fragrances. . . .
> We with humility beg and implore thee, Majestic and Holiest One, to cause the consecration of these Pentacles, through thy power: that they may be made potent against all the Spirits, through thee, Adonai, Most Holy, for ever and ever.

PENTALPHA A design formed by five interlacing A's and used in divination and the conjuration of spirits.

PERIS Sprites similar to Sylphs in Iranian mythology.

PERKINS, WILLIAM Puritan preacher (1555-1602). His *Discourse on the Damned Art of Witchcraft* (1608) supplanted the *Demonology* of James VI.

PERSEPHONE In Greek religion, the daughter of Demeter, the earth-mother, and Zeus. Abducted by Hades (Pluto), she was allowed to spend only the summer months with her mother, becoming the symbol of the vegetation powers of nature.

PERT EM HRU The Egyptian Book of the Dead, a guide to the Nether Regions for the souls of the dead and a kind of manual of instructions.

PETER OF ALBANO A thirteenth-century Italian philosopher and astrologer who wrote on magic. He was reputed to have had associations with Satanic forces.

PETERSON, JOAN Called the 'Witch of Wapping,' she was accused of possessing familiar demons (a black dog and a squirrel) and of casting spells. She was hanged in London on April 12, 1652.

PETRO In Voodoo, the dispenser of magic powers.

PEYOTISM In the old, Pre-Colombian peyote cult, a spineless cactus plant called peyote (*peyotl* in Nahuatl) was used by Indians in Mexico and the United States to obtain visions and induce supernatural revelation. It was widely used to induce trances during tribal dancing rites. The modern peyote cult, which probably originated out of an Apache peyote rite, spread rapidly during the last half of the nineteenth century and became the most widespread indigenous religion of North America. It is a syncretistic cult stressing prayer, quiet contemplation, and peyote as a symbol of spirits and a sacrament. Peyotist doctrine is based on belief in the existence of power (mana, the Holy Spirit or Holy Ghost), spirits or personifications of power (the Christian trinity and Indian spirits such as the Indian thunderbird or the Christian dove), and incarnations or material embodiments of power in the form of peyote, water, and the foods used in the morning communion breakfast. The main features of the peyotist ethic are brotherly love, concern for the family, self-reliance, and avoidance of strong drink. The peyote rite has four major components: prayer, singing, eating the sacred plant, and contemplation. It is through contemplation that the worshiper rises to the level of spiritual sublimity and communes with God.

PHALLICISM A form of nature worship in which the generative principle in nature is symbolized by the male organ or phallus. The custom is characteristic not only of primitive religions but also of sophisticated cultures. Anciently prevalent among the Semites, it was later adopted by the Greeks. Often occurring as a form of sympathetic magic, it may assume an orgiastic character in ceremonies, as in the *Sakti puja* of the Indians.

PHANTOM An immaterial semblance, apparition, or ghost.

PHILOSOPHUS In the cabalistic system of Aleister Crowley, the Philosophus must ascend through sephira 7, corresponding to Venus, before he can reach the highest rank or grade and wield the magical power belonging to man as the potential God. Here he completes his moral training and is tested in 'Devotion to the Order.'

PHILOTANUS A lesser demon who helps Beliel to turn humans to pederasty and sodomy.

PHRYGIAN MYSTERIES A ritualistic cult that was practiced in the Mediterranean littoral. It centered around Cybele, the Great Mother of the Gods, her lament on her lover Attis' death, and her jubilation on his rebirth in spring. The cult symbolized a vegetation myth.

PICO DELLA MIRANDOLA Italian sage (1463-1494). He is supposed to have advanced the study of magic, which he called 'the noblest part of the natural sciences.' His *Strige* was the first important work on witchcraft to be published in Italy.

PIETRO D'ABANO Famous physician and astrologer. Pietro d'Abano (Petrus Aponus, d. 1316) is said to have kept seven devils locked in a vial.

PIKE, ALBERT Leading figure in the Scottish Rite of Freemasonry and author of a Masonic classic, *Morals and Dogma of the Ancient and Accepted Scottish Rite of Freemasonry* (1872). Sensational reports attributed to Dr. Bataille made Pike the founder of a diabolic order of Freemasonry and possessor of a bracelet used to summon Lucifer.

PILATE'S POOL According to Martin Luther, 'In Switzerland . . . there is a lake which is called Pilate's Pool. There the Devil gives himself up to all kinds of infamous practices.'

PILLIWINKS See Thumbscrews.

PIPI A witch who serves as cup-bearer at the Sabbat.

PISACHAS In India, demons that haunt scenes of violent death.

PISTIS SOPHIA The secret writings of the Gnostic sect.

PITRIS In mysticism, the ancestors of mankind.

PITS Pits were dug in mystery cults and in other religious ceremonies. Liquids were poured into these pits as offerings to the gods of the Lower Regions.

PLUTO A euphemistic name for the Greek god of the underworld. He was the son of Cronus and Rhea, husband of Proserpine, and brother of Zeus and Poseidon. Black victims were sacrificed to him, particularly at Elis, where he was Hades, god of the dead.

PODOVNE VILE Slavonic water sprites.

POIMANDRES The book on which all Hermetic literature is based. See Hermes Trismegistus.

POLITI, LANCELOT Author of a treatise setting forth the theory that Satan did not aspire to replace God but to be the future Christ (*De gloria bonorum angelorum et lapsu malorum,* 1552). Lancelot Politi (1483-1553), an Italian from Siena, changed his name to Ambrosius Catharinus when he became a Dominican in 1535. His theory was elaborated by Francisco Suarez.

POLTERGEIST A spirit assumed to create disturbances and otherwise unexplained noises. The word means 'noisy ghost.' A seventeenth-century manual gives a formula for exorcising a poltergeist:
> I adjure you, ancient serpent, by the Judge of the living and the dead, by the Creator of the universe, who has power to send you to Gehenna, that you depart forthwith from this house. He orders you to do so, cursed devil, who ordered the winds and the sea and the tempests. He orders you who ordered you to go back. Hearken, therefore, Satan, and be afraid, and withdraw, subdued and prostrate.

POLTERSBERG According to Martin Luther, on a high mountain in Germany called Poltersberg, there is a pool. 'If one throws a stone into it, instantly a storm arises. . . . . This lake is full of demons. Satan holds them captive there.'

POLYDAEMONISM Worship of many local deities linked with trees, plants, and other objects. Characteristic of ancient Semitic populations, it is typical of the nomadic way of life. Tribal deities had no fixed abode and were unlikely to spread beyond the region occupied by a tribe. The prestige of local deities varied with the ascendancy of the tribes to which they belonged.

POLYGLOT INVOCATION A powerful spell uttered in Greek, Hebrew, and Syriac is binding on the spirit invoked. It is found in a Graeco-Egyptian magical manuscript.

I call upon thee that didst create the earth and bones, and all flesh and all spirit, that didst establish the sea and that shakest the heavens, that didst divide the light from darkness, the great regulative mind, that disposeth everything, eye of the world, spirit of spirits, god of gods, the lord of the spirits, the immovable Aeon, Iaoouei, hear my voice.

I call upon thee, the ruler of the gods, high-thundering Zeus, Zeus, King. Adonaid, lord, Iaoouee. I am he that invokes thee in the Syrian tongue, the great god, Zaalaer, Iphphou, do thou not disregard the Hebrew appellation, Ablanchanalb, Abrasiloa.

For I am Silthakhookh, Lailam, Blasaloth, Iao, Ieo, Nebouth, Sabiothar, Both, Arbathiao, Iaoth, Sabaoth, Patoure, Zagoure, Baroukh Adonai, Eloai, Iabraam, Barbarauo, Nau, Siph.

PONTICA A stone, marked by blood-like stains, used to compel demons to answer questions.

PORPHYRIA A class of inherited diseases characterized by the production of an excessive amount of pigments called porphyrins. One of its rare forms is marked by excessive growth of hair on the arms and face. Medical authorities speculate that the disease may have led to the execution of many persons identified by their accusers as werewolves. The practice of putting suspected werewolves to death ceased in the seventeenth century.

PORPHYRY Neoplatonic philosopher (c. 232-305). He believed in demons and in the use of secret rites, invocations, and conjurations to dispel them. Among his works is a mystical treatise *On the Return of the Soul*.

POST, SARAH The last witchcraft trial in the United States was held at Ipswich, Massachusetts, in 1693. Sarah Post of Andover was freed after standing trial on the charge of signing a pact with the Devil.

POTET, BARON Founder (1826) of the school of magnetism in France. 'Belief in the Devil,' he wrote, 'has been weakened considerably over the past two centuries. . . . All those who wish to learn something about the evil spirits have only to invoke them.'

POZEMNE VILE Slavonic earth-dwelling spirits.

PRACTICUS The third grade or rank in Aleister Crowley's cabalistic system. The student completes his intellectual training in sephira 8, corresponding to mercury, and studies the Cabala.

PRELATI, FRANCOIS Florentine 'expert in the prohibited art of geomancy,' he helped Gilles de Rais (1404-1440) to invoke evil spirits.

PRETAS In Hindu mythology, the pretas are malefic ghosts.

PRIAPUS In classical mythology, he was the god of procreation and fertility. He is represented as a deformed figure in an ichthyphallic pose.

PRICE, HARRY British researcher who died in 1948. He reported that 'in all the districts of London, hundreds of men and women of high education and belonging to the best families, worship Satan. . . .'

PRICKING Persons suspected of being witches were examined for signs that they had been branded by Satan's mark. If no such mark was visible, they were stuck with long pins. It was assumed that they would feel no pain when the pin was stuck into the invisible devil's mark.

PRIDE Origen and his successors in the East, Basil and Athanasius, rejected the theory based on the Book of Enoch and held that pride caused the Devil's fall from heaven. Augustine also believed that the Devil's fall was occasioned by pride.

PRIESTESS The officiating priestess at a Black Mass was commonly known as 'The Ancient One' even though she usually was young. Her opening words were:

I will come to the altar. Save me Lord Satan from the treacherous and the violent.

PRIMITIVE RELIGION A term applied to the supernatural elements within the whole complex of life. Belief in spirits and associated patterns of behavior have been called *animism*. Spirits may inhabit objects or bodies and may control the well-being of individuals and groups. Specialists (shamans) may communicate with the spirit world. An interesting feature of American religion is the development of the notion of guardian spirits. Preanimistic religion, sometimes called animatism, stresses *mana*, or supernatural power as conceived by the Melanesians.

Worship of a 'high god' or supreme being has been observed among primitives as well as among advanced cultures.

Primitive people often have complicated theories about the origin of the universe and divine powers. These mythologies vary widely. Ritual, sacrifice, exorcism, and prayer are essential elements of many primitive religions. Magic is important in the lives of primitive people, but most of them make a distinction between natural means of achieving goals and magical means. Finally, tabu is an important element of most primitive religions.

Outstanding among the many theories of primitive religion is that of Emile Durkheim, who thinks that from the psychological point of view, society is the real god. The most distinctively religious behavior is a part of group activities, such as religious festivals. The totem animal is the symbolic representation of the true object of religion, which is too abstract for the primitive mind.

PRINCE OF THIS WORLD An expression used by Jesus to designate Satan.

PROCREATION The demons regularly copulate with each other and reproduce their own kind, according to certain Cabalists. Sammael, a prominent figure in rabbinical demonology, personifies the principle of evil. His four wives are said to have given birth to countless demons. St. Thomas Aquinas and other theologians affirm that devils have no seed of their own but become succubi, receive the seed of a man, then transform themselves into incubi and impregnate the women with whom they copulate.

PROMETHEUS One of the primeval deities of Greek mythology. A Titan, he sided with the Olympians in the Titanomachy, but his sorrow over their neglect of mankind caused him to steal fire from heaven for man's use. Zeus chained him to Mount Caucasus and caused a vulture daily to consume his liver in a vain attempt to wrest knowledge of the future from him. The fall of Prometheus and Tityus, both hurled from on high and bound in torment, is the Hellenic transfiguration of the rebel archangels in the Bible.

PROSTITUTION Sacred prostitution of both sexes was practiced by the Syrians and Anatolians. In the second millennium B.C. the Syrian goddess was commonly represented as a naked woman holding fertility symbols, such as snakes and lily stalks. The name applied to eunuchs by the Western Semites also meant 'male prostitute.'

PROTERIUS One of the main figures in an ancient legend based on the signing of a pact with the Devil. The Devil caused Proterius' daughter to marry a servant who had signed a pact with him. Proterius had intended for his daughter to enter a convent. St. Basilius gained possession of the pact, enabling Proterius' daughter and her husband to live happily.

PRUDENTIUS Latin Christian writer. Aurelius Clemens Prudentius (c. 348-410). 'Psychomachia,' one of his poems, is an allegory depicting the struggle between good and evil in the human soul. Another, 'Hamartigenia,' is perhaps the first statement of the Devil's claim to be independent of God. See Hamartigenia.

PRUSLAS One of three demons in the service of Satanachia, grand general of Satan's legions.

PSELLUS, MICHAEL Byzantine author, scholar, and statesman of the eleventh century. He was also one of the first demonologists.

PSYCHAGOGUES A Greek expression denoting a conjurer of the spirits of the dead.

PSYCHOPOMPOS In classical mythology, a conductor of the souls of the dead to Hades. Hermes (Mercury) carried out this assignment.

PSYLLI A class of persons thought in ancient times to have had the power to charm snakes.

PTOLEMY (CLAUDIUS PTOLEMAEUS) Alexandrian astronomer (c. 100-170), mathematician, and author of the thirteen-volume work familiarly known as the Almagest.

PUNISHMENT Those who made Satanic pacts generally were burned alive. An eighteenth-century Teutonic Law states: If anyone is convicted of having made a pact with Satan . . . it is decreed that he be burned alive and driven from our midst in the avenging flames.

PUNISHMENT OF THE DEMONS Prior to the reform launched by Peter Lombard in the twelfth century, the demons were held to be exempt from sensible pains. Tertullian wrote (*Apologeticus*, 27): 'Condemned without hope, their consolation is the evil they do while awaiting the torture reserved for them.' After Lombard, the Devil and his demons were believed to be undergoing the torture of fire in the depths of hell.

PURIFICATION Purification rites were performed in ancient pagan religions for various purposes. Sometimes the objective was to avert an evil influence. Then the cleansing procedure entailed baptism in water, in blood, a change of garments — all directed to a spiritual purification achieved during the mystery rites.

PURSAN One of three demons in the service of Fleuretty, lieutenant general of the legions of Hell.

PWCCA The Welsh name of Satan.

PYRAMID TESTS Beginning in the Fifth Dynasty (c. 2400 B.C.), the Egyptians covered the walls of the interior chambers of pyramids with hymns and magic spells to be used by the deceased king as he ascended to heaven. Magic spells were also used by each new ruler to achieve identification with Osiris.

PYTHAGOREANISM A system of mystical philosophy founded by Pythagoras of Samos in the sixth century B.C. It includes the concept of number, soul, metempsychosis, and the eternal repetition of all things.

PYTHON In Greek mythology, a monstrous serpent slain by Apollo in the caves of Mount Parnassus. The Revised Version of the New Testament identifies him in the margin as a soothsaying demon.

Temptation of St. Anthony
Nikolaus Manuel Deutsch

Q

QENNA In Egyptian religion, she was the goddess of matter that has been revivified.

QUEEN OF ELFAME (ELFIN) In some of the Scottish witchcraft trials, the Queen of Elfame or Elfin was mentioned as the presiding deity of the witches' Sabbat. She was said to copulate with male witches.

QUEEN OF HEAVEN A presiding deity worshiped by modern witches. Also known as the Queen of Heaven and All Living.

QUEEN OF NIGHT In the twelfth century John Salisbury wrote that a few ignorant men and women believed that the Queen of Night, or Herodias, summoned them to nightly meetings. Children were eaten, vomited up whole, and returned to their cradles by the presiding goddess.

QUEEN OF THE SABBAT Although most Sabbats were presided over by a male, in the early seventeenth century Basque witches had a Queen of the Sabbat who was the Devil's principal bride.

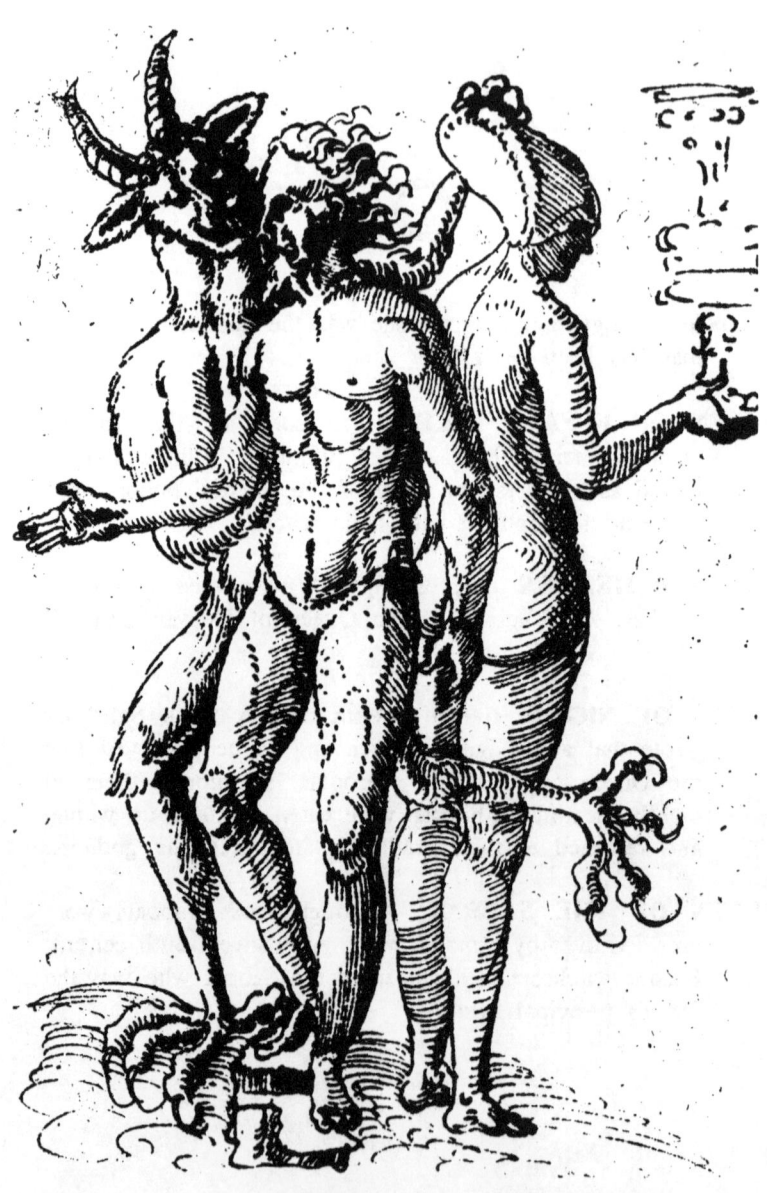

The Devil With Nude Couple
Pen drawing
(Erlangen: Library)

R

RABDOS A demon, said to have been a wise man at one time. Known as the strangler, he personifies the *rhabdos* or wand, one of the supreme emblems of magical power. The wand or rod is also a phallic symbol.

RABINU One of the most horrible demons of ancient Mesopotamia. He hid in the shadows and leaped forth to overpower his victims.

RADIATION TRAP The French weekly newspaper *Quatre et Trois* reported recently (July 30, 1947) that Hector Mellin, a magician and inventor, had perfected a machine 'to capture and return evil radiations.'

RAGNAROK In Scandinavian mythology, the final destruction of the world in the great battle between the Aesir, led by Odin, and the powers of Hel, under the leadership of Loki. The Ragnarok combines three versions of the 'Twilight of the Gods': destruction by flood, freezing, and fire. Odin is slain by Fenir, who in turn is slain by Vitharr. Other gods are slain, the sun is devoured by a monster, the earth sinks into the sea, and flames reach the sky. Later the earth emerges from the sea and some gods who escaped death return with two mortals, Lif and Lifthraser (Life and Vitality). The human pair become the progenitors of a new race.

RAHAB A raging monster, the dragon of darkness, the 'crooked serpent' formed by the hand of God (Job 26:13).

RAHU Hindu demon snake. He was thought to be on the point of swallowing the sun god during a solar eclipse.

RAIS, GILLES DE LAVAL DE French nobleman and soldier (1404-1440). He fought beside Joan of Arc and was named Marshal of France at the age of twenty-three. He delved into alchemy, invoked evil spirits, and signed a pact with the demon Baron. He sacrificed children to obtain favors from Satan and was arrested by the Inquisition. He was hanged and burned at Nantes on October 6, 1440.

RAKSHASAS In Hindu mythology, rakshasas are huge vampires who endanger the lives of men.

RAKSHASAS Multiheaded goblins or ogres who torment the people of India.

RALARATRI A Hindu demon and vampire.

RAMMON See Adad.

RAMUEL One of the leaders of the angels who rebelled against God and swore allegiance to Samiaza. The story is recorded in the Book of Enoch.

RASHNU In Zoroastrian religion, Rashnu symbolizes justice and forms a triad, with Mithra and Sraosha, to judge the dead.

RASPUTIN See Novikh, Gregori.

RATHFARNHAM CLUB A blasphemous group, famous in eighteenth-century England for its mock crucifixions.

RAUM One of the seventy-two demons described in the *Lemegeton*. He reconciles enemies but is always ready to destroy cities.

RAVANA Hindu demon who ravished Sita, wife of Rama, in the *Ramayana*.

RAYS In Akkadian literature, the undefined but elemental power or force possessed by all gods. One god might deprive another of his supernatural functions by stealing his Rays. Similar notions are expressed by Mana in Melanesia and by Ton as the word is used by the Dakotas.

RED BOOK The Sabbat opened with a ritual of allegiance to Satan, who then opened his red book and called the roster of those present.

RED DRAGON Handbook on magic. It is based on the *Grand Grimoire*.

REDEMPTION Pope Gregory the great (c. 540-604) advocates in his *Moralia* (38: 13-14) a theory of redemption in which God used Christ as bait to ensnare the Devil and redeem mankind: 'Our Lord . . . assumed a body in order to induce this Behemoth to kill the flesh that in this way became for him a fishhook. Wrongly desiring the death of the body, he let us, whom he legitimately held, slip from his grasp. He was caught by the bait of the Incarnation.'

RELATIO A confession of guilt based on affirmative answers to a list of prepared questions. The questions were generally put to those accused of witchcraft while they were undergoing torture.

REPTILES In the Gilgamesh epic, the serpent stole the magic plant that conferred immortality. Because of its ability to shed its skin, the snake was widely considered to be inmortal. The Zulus believed that two lizards were entrusted with messages concerning immortality; the second lizard, arriving last, canceled the immortality which had been conferred by the first. In East Africa, a snake stole the secret from a bird.

RESHEF An important Phoenician deity. In a cuneiform text from Ugarit, he is identified with Nergal, the Babylonian god of Hell.

RESURRECTION BODY According to the Cabala, an inner fundamental spiritual type remaining after death.

RE-THEURGISTES-OPTIMATES An association described in Huysman's *Là-Bas*. It was supposed to have been founded for the purpose of converting people to the worship of Satan.

RETROVERSION Turning backward. In Satanic rites, prayers, supplications, and formulas were delivered backward. The Lord's Prayer was recited backward, words were written backward, and mystical names and invocations were written in reverse order.

REUCHLIN, JOHANN German scholar (1455-1522), author of *The Kabalistic Art* and *The Mirific Word*. His writings profoundly influenced Agrippa von Nettesheim.

REVELATION, BOOK OF See Satan's Fall.

RICHALMUS Latinized name of Abbé Richaume, author of *Liber Revelationum*, written about the middle of the thirteenth century. Many of the Cistercian saint's personal encounters with the Devil are recorded in the book, which reflects the naive faith of his century, together with contemporary beliefs concerning the Devil.

RIMBAUD, ARTHUR French poet, author of *Une Saison en enfer* (1873). Arthur Rimbaud (1854-1891) cultivated hallucination, disorder, and the irrational. The 'Season in Hell,' a psychologically autobiographical creation, was his last poem.

RIMMON A demon who served as ambassador to Russia, according to medieval demonologists. He was a Syrian god whose temple was at Damascus.

RITUALE ROMANUM A liturgical book ('The Roman Ritual') contains all the rites normally administered by a priest, including the rite of exorcism. See Exorcism, the Rite of.

ROCOTS Name given by Bodin to the offspring of an incubus and a woman.

RO-LANG In Tibet, a corpse that roams the plains.

ROMAN RELIGION Primitively, Roman religion was animistic, that is, it acknowledged the existence of spirits indwelling in trees, rivers, springs. There were also spirits associated with the home and the farm. With the development of the state, the spirits assumed new functions. For instance, Jupiter god of the sky, became a god of justice. Etruscan and Greek influences brought an anthropomorphic conception of the deities. The old Roman gods were frequently identified with Greek gods, with regard to functions and attributes.

Roman religion was extremely ritualistic. It stressed the formal and ceremonial features of all religious acts in which the Romans participated.

During the Empire, the old indigenous religious beliefs were gradually abandoned. The mystery cults of the East became influential, particularly among the common people but in time among the ruling classes as well and even in the Imperial court.

These Oriental cults appealed strongly to the emotions

in the afterlife. Furthermore they brought an assurance of happiness. The cults included the Eleusinian Mysteries, the cult of Cybele, of Isis and Osiris, of Mithra, and of Sabazius.

RONWE   A lesser demon who commands nineteen legions.

ROSENKREUZ, CHRISTIAN   Reputed founder of the Rosicrucian order.

ROSES   Some occultists maintain that demoniacs and witches cannot touch or smell roses. The same applies to vampires and werewolves. Apuleius' ass turned back into his human shape when he ate roses.

ROSICRUCIAN SOCIETY   Secret society devoted to occult studies. Known since the beginning of the seventeenth century through *Fama Fraternitas* and another anonymous pamphlet, the society did not exist as an organized body until the nineteenth century. There are now four organized sects of Rosicrucians in the United States.

RUILLY, MACETTE DE   See Paris Witch Trial.

RULE, MARGARET   In 1693, Margaret Rule confessed that she was possessed by the Devil and by a 'white Spirit.' Cotton Mather studied her case.

RUNES (FUTHARK)   The word 'rune' means 'mystery' in its earliest usage in English and related languages. From the outset, runes were associated with magic, divination, and other rites. The runic alphabet later became the storehouse of pagan Germanic rites. The twenty-four runes of the common Germanic *futhark* (alphabet) were used to evoke or ward off the power contained in their names. In Germanic mythology, Woden hung upon the world-ash Yggdrasil for nine nights, tormented by hunger and pain, until finally he glimpsed the runes which he then seized and passed on to men. Runes are credited with the power of resurrecting the dead and are associated with health, fertility, love, etc. Belief in rune-magic survived until the seventeenth century.

RUPERT VON DEUTZ An eleventh-century writer who revived the notion that Satan was the creator of himself. In his treatise *De victoria verbi Dei* he restated the notion set forth in the fourth century by Prudentius.

RUSALKAS Slavic demons who hide in plants, kidnap children, cast spells, and bring bad luck to men.

The Prince of Darkness
After a Miniature of the "Holy Grail"
15th Century Manuscript
(Paris: National Library)

S

SABAZIUS He was a Thraco-Phrygian deity, who was sometimes identified in Greek mythology with Dionysus and in Roman religion with Jupiter. His cult was predominant in Lydia and Phrygia. In the late fifth century B.C. Sabazius was also worshipped at Athens. His cult was linked with that of Cybele. Symbolically, he was represented by a snake. The snake was also a central feature in the mystery cult of Sabazius. Sculpturally, he was depicted in Phrygian costume, bearing the eagle and the thunderbolt of Zeus. His Greek designation as *kurios Sabazios*, Lord Sabazius, has led some scholars to consider him as the Jewish God, the Lord Zebaoth.

SABBAT A periodic gathering of witches and warlocks wonderworkers and necromancers in dark forests, secluded caves, abandoned ruins, or even in sanctified places such as the Blokula Church in Sweden. Throughout the continent of Europe and in the British Isles, the adepts gathered to celebrate their lascivious devotion to the infernal demons, indulging in frenzied orgies, back-to-back dancing in the dark, demonic conjurations, and obscene sacrifices.

The Latin and French spelling of the word sabbath, may have been used to designate witches' assemblies because of its association with the Jews, who were constantly persecuted by medieval Christians.

Special meetings were held on certain evenings each year, but the dates are somewhat uncertain. In some regions the great feasts were held on February 2 (Candlemas), the

Eve of May 1 (Walpurgis Night), August 1 (Lammas), and October 1 (Hallowe'en). These days recall the old Celtic divisions of the year, May 1 (Beltane) and November 1 (Samhain), and the two subdivisions, beginning on February 1 and August 1.

SABELLICUS, GEORGIUS Fifteenth-century necromancer. He called himself a second Faustus.

SACRED GROVES In ancient pagan religions, in addition to temples, altars, and 'high places,' groves served as sanctuaries for the worship of the gods. They were also meeting-places for the initiates in the mystery cults. Here they performed their rituals and ceremonies. Such groves were considered to be the special haunts of divinities and thus acquired a particular sanctity.
Notable among such religious retreats were the groves associated with the Druidic worship and sacrifices held annually in Central Gaul.

SACRED LITERATURE OF EGYPT The sacred writings of Egyptian religion consist of the Book of the Dead, the Pyramid Texts, the Litanies of Seker, the Festival Songs and Lamentations of Isis and Nephthys.

SACRIFICES Sacrifice, whether in the form of a human victim, an animal, or an object, was prevalent in ancient rituals. It was practiced by the Assyro-Babylonians, the Egyptians, the Greeks and Romans, the Zoroastrians, the Aztecs, Mayans, Incas and many tribal communities in Asia and in the Pacific Islands.
In Greek and Roman religion, offerings to the gods in very ancient times consisted of cereals, vegetables, fruit, milk, honey, cheese, oil.
The most popular offering was a blood sacrifice of animals, birds, sows, dogs, horses, asses, and occasionally fish.

Human sacrifices belong to primitive practices. They were associated too with cannibalistic features.

Among American Indians sacrifices often assumed a more or less innocuous form. Objects were thrown into a fire, or rocks were placed at certain assigned spots, or wounds were self-inflicted. During the Sun Dance all such practices constituted 'sacrifices.'

SACROCANNIBALISM The custom of partaking piously of the flesh of the deceased is considered to be a sacred duty among the Melanesians of New Guinea. A variety of this custom may be exemplified by the Australians and Papuasians, who smear the body with the fat of the deceased.

SADE, MARQUIS DE The notorious eighteenth-century atheist and nature-worshiper described in his works Satanic orgies involving the use of consecrated hosts.

SADRIPU According to the Balinese, the evil in human nature. Many rituals are intended to protect people against sadripu.

SAGA According to Michelet, the Saga or Wise Woman was the sole healer of the people of Europe for a thousand years. If her cure failed, she was called a witch. Generally, she was called Bella Donna ('Beautiful Lady'). She gathered plants to heal and save, yet was often looked upon as the Devil's bride, 'the mistress of the Incarnate Evil One.' Paracelsus declared when he burned the whole pharmacopoeia of his time, in 1527, at Bayle, that the sorceresses had taught him all he knew.

ST. ALBANS A member of a witch coven of St. Albans, naked except for a string of beads, justified her participation in the celebration of one of the great annual festivals of the British witches, All-Hallows Eve, by saying, 'We are not anti-Christian. We just have other means of spiritual satisfaction.' She was referring to a celebration that occurred in 1963, involving incantations, nudity, and frenzied dances.

ST. ANTHONY Egyptian founder of monachism. St. Anthony (c. 251-356) had to combat the Devil at each stage of his conversion. His temptations, interpreted by various artists and writers, had a strong influence on fashioning popular notions of the Devil.

ST. ATHANASIUS Greek church father (c. 296-373). His biography of St. Anthony records many of the Christian hero's temptations and is the source of inspiration of many artists and writers whose works are responsible for many of the popular notions about the Devil.

ST. AUGUSTINE Numidian bishop of Hippo. St. Augustine (354-430) believed that the demons knew the future, not through direct vision, but through the acuteness of their intellect and their ability to move with lightning speed from place to place.

ST. BONAVENTURA Italian scholastic theologian. St. Bonaventura (1221-1274) maintained that the demons knew only future things that follow fixed laws, not future things that are contingent. He reasoned that the demons fully understood the course of nature.

SAINT-CLAUDE Village in the Jura Mountains in France. Four members of the Gandillon family, two sisters, the brother, and his son, were accused of lycanthropy and of attending the Sabbat. Perrenette Gandillon was lynched by peasants. The three other members of the family were found guilty and burned.

ST. CYPRIAN Hero of a legend recorded in the *Acta Sanctorum* (Lives of Saints). At an early age he had sold his soul to the Devil. After trying in vain to seduce Justine, a virgin who had become a Christian convert and taken a vow of chastity, he renounced the worship of the Devil. Named bishop of Antioch, he placed Justine in charge of a convent. Together they effected many conversions. In 304 they were seized by the agents of Diocletian, thrown into boiling oil and, when the flames miraculously spared them, beheaded.

ST. DUNSTAN The Abbot of Glaston and later Archbishop of Canterbury. St. Dunstan (c. 925-988) is reputed to have been visited by the Devil while fashioning a Eucharist cup. The saint took his pincers out of the fire, and applied them to the nose of the Devil. An old rhyme recalls the incident:

> St. Dunstan, as the story goes,
> Once pulled the Devil by the nose
> With red-hot tongs, which made him roar
> That he was heard three miles or more.

SAINT-GERMAIN Eighteenth-century French occultist. The Count of Saint-Germain was attached to the court of Louis XV. He claimed to be two thousand years old, to speak and write many Oriental and Western languages, and to have achieved invisibility. He wrote an occult book entitled *La Très Saint Trinosophie* (The Most Holy Triple Philosophy).

Of disputed origin, he claimed to have known Christ and the apostles. He also claimed extraordinary powers of alchemy, including the ability to transmute metals and make diamonds from pure carbon. He lived in France, England, and Russia before moving to Schleswig, where he engaged in magical practices with the landgrave Karl of Hesse. He died about 1784.

ST. IRENAEUS Second-century Greek bishop of Lyon. He taught that the Devil became an apostate and rebel against God through jealousy of man.

ST. JOHN'S EVE Midsummer, June 23. The traditional day in European folklore for seeing Satan, not in one of his many disguises, but in his own true form.

ST. NICHOLAS A bishop of Myra, Asia Minor (died c. 345). In medieval folklore, he acquired the attributes of Nekker, the Teutonic culture god beloved and respected by the pagan people as a lover of children. The same beneficent deity, in an opposite role, also survives as Old Nick, harbinger of disaster.

ST. TERESA Carmelite nun and mystic. St. Teresa (1515-1582) reports in her autobiography that she was repeatedly assailed by the Devil. She used the sign of the cross and holy water to put him to flight.

SALAMANCA Medieval center of occultism. The Spanish city had institutions where the occult arts were taught.

SALAMANDERS In the medieval theory of elementals, particularly as formulated by Paracelsus, salamanders were associated with fire and were assumed to be composed of the most subtle parts of the sphere of fire (in contrast to sylphs, formed of air particles, and nymphs, formed of water particles). Some demonographers make Romulus the offspring of a salamander and an incubus.

SALEM WITCHES Much has been written concerning the most famous witchcraft trials in North America. Among the best works are Charles Wentworth Upham's *Salem Witchcraft* (1867), Marion Lena Starkey's *The Devil in Massachusetts* (1949), and Arthur Miller's play *The Crucible* (1953), in which a link is established between the Salem witch hunters and McCarthyism. The affair began when two young girls, influenced perhaps by Indian tales, became hysterical. Collective hysteria spread until it had assumed frightening proportions. More than three hundred persons were arrested. In 1692, thirty-one persons, including six men, were convicted. Three died in prison, nineteen were hanged, and one (Sarah Dustin), though exonerated, died in prison because she was unable to provide for her upkeep.

SALIC LAW The ancient law of the Franks, revised by Clovis and Dagobert, covered diabolical practices. For example, any woman who used sorcery to prevent another woman from giving birth to a child was subject to a heavy fine, and anyone who falsely accused another person of carrying a brass caldron to a witches' feast was subject to lesser fine.

SALT In magic, salt is used to ward off demons. All devils are supposed to detest salt. As a preservative, it is contrary to their nature.

SAMAEL (SALAMIEL) In rabbinical tradition, the incarnation of Leviathan, the demon seducer of Eve.

SAMAN The Druidic god of death. He assembled the souls of evil men, condemned to inhabit animal bodies, annually on the evening preceding All Saints' Day. All Hallows Eve (Halloween) recalls the ancient festival.

SAMIAZA The chief of the fallen angels, according to the Book of Enoch.

SAMOVILE See Vile.

SAMPSON, AGNES See North Berwick Witches.

SAMRU The Persian bird of immortality, akin to the phoenix and the Egyptian bennu.

SAMSAVAEL According to the Book of Enoch, one of the leaders of the two hundred angels who rebelled against God and swore allegiance to Samiaza.

SANASEL A sacred musical intrument, used in Ethiopia to exorcise demons.

SANBENITO A cloak worn by impenitent heretics in Spain. It bore a red cross surrounded by flames, devils, and serpents.

SANTERIA A Cuban ritual based on Yoruba traditions. The mystic rite is conducted by the *santeno* (priest) when a person is near death. The object of the rite is to persuade Icú, the god of death, to transfer the sickness to another person. If the santero fails to persuade Icú to make the transfer, he may make a puppet, dress it or have a close relative dress it in the patient's clothes, bury it at midnight, and grieve loudly to convince Icú that the patient has died. A third device used to deceive the god of death is to give the patient the pallor of death by applying powdered eggshell to his face.

SANTERO In Cuba, an adept who conducts the *santeria*, a mystic rite designed to protect a patient near death against Icú, the god of death.

SAOSHYANT In Zoroastrian religion, he is the last savior of mankind. On the final day he will help to purify and regenerate the universe, eliminating all evil. The souls of the righteous will arise, while the souls of the wicked will be purified. The Resurrection will then be consummated.

SARAKMYAL One of the leaders of the two hundred fallen angels, according to the Book of Enoch. He rebelled against God and swore allegiance to Samiaza.

SARAPEUM A temple dedicated to Sarapis. It was one of the wonders of the ancient world.

SARAPIASTAI Greek votaries of the Egyptian god Sarapis.

SARAPIS Egyptian god of the underworld and healing. In Rome he was called Serapis.

SARGATANAS Brigadier of the infernal spirits. He controls Loray, Valafar, and Foraü. He has the power to confer invisibility, to transport people everywhere, to open any lock, and to teach every trick. He commands many demonic brigades.

SATAN The name by which the Devil is commonly called in the Bible, popular legends, and poetry is the English transliteration of a Hebrew word meaning 'adversary.' The Talmud states that he was once an archangel but lost his place in Heaven because of pride and disobedience. With the definite article in Hebrew, the word denotes the supreme adversary of man. Also called the Prince of Darkness, the Devil, Lucifer, and the Archfiend, he belongs to the world of the supernatural. He is identified with the serpent in the Garden of Eden and with Beelzebul in New Testament references to demoniac possession. In later Judaism, under the influence of Persian dualism, he is identified with the cosmic power of evil.

SATANACHIA Grand General of the infernal spirits. He commands Pruslas, Aamon, and Barbatos. He can make women completely submissive to his will. He commands the great legion of demons.

SATANAS The Greek transliteration of the word Satan. It is used throughout the New Testament.

SATANIC BIBLE A paperback book published by Anton LaVey, High Priest of the Church of Satan, in 1966. It codifies the philosophy of the Church of Satan, supplies prayers and invocations in both English and Enochian, a language said by the founder of the sect to be 'older than Sanskrit,' and tries to dispel mistaken notions about the movement.

SATANIC SCHOOL A group of writers identified by Southey as being 'characterized by a satanic spirit of pride and audacious impiety.' Byron, Shelley, and their followers are among those named in Southey's preface to his *Vision of Judgment*.

SATANAEL See Sammael.

SATAN IN ART Artists have treated the theme of the Devil variously. Hieronymus Bosch portrays him as the ape of God, supreme master of disorder. Albrecht Durer depicts him as a pig waiting to snatch a human soul. Goya shows him as a goat. He often appears in medieval art and sculpture as a grotesque figure with horns and tail.

SATANIS A film shown to interested outsiders by San Francisco's Church of Satan. It shows black-robed men and women conducting a Black Mass, using a nude woman as an altar. Worshippers proclaim their lust and hate, receiving encouragement from the priest who says, 'May all your lustful thoughts reach fruition. Hail Satan!'

SATANISM The cult of Satanism with its necromantic rites, hierarchy of demoniac powers, and monstrous distortions of orthodox beliefs, is rooted in the Manichaean cult of ancient Persia and has endured, overtly or covertly, through the centuries. A revival of interest in a material Arch Fiend in the post-medieval period resulted in many ecclesiastical and secular prohibitions against Satanism, and in the condemnation and killing of hundreds of sorcerers. Satanism was popularized in the earlier decades of this century by Aleister Crowley and has flourished in seclusive drawing rooms and in secretive clubs throughout Europe and the Americas. Contemporary interest in Satanism, now at its peak, has been ascribed to various causes: the urbanization of society with a break-down of social controls, the failure of the modern church to appeal to the mind of the young and to satisfy their spiritual needs, the anxieties and uncertainties that result from the presence of a great number of conflicting forces, ideals, etc.

First used in 1896 in connection with the Black Mass, the term Satanism today is used in both a narrow and a broad sense. In a narrow sense, it designates the cult which defiles or travesties Christian rites. In a broad sense, it designates Satan's dominion over the world and man's tendency to imitate him in his behavior toward God.

SATAN'S ATTRIBUTES Numerous figures out of Western mythologies have contributed to the evolution of a composite set of characteristics now attributed to Satan. The classical mythologies embraced a whole race of maleficent genii, monsters, and evil demons of every sort: Typhon, Medusa, Geryon, Python, lemures, larvae, Febris, etc. In contact with northern barbarians, Satan became Germanized. Loki, the dark god Tiw, the death goddess Wyrd, the wolf Fenris, elves, sylphs, and gnomes all conferred new attributes on Satan.

SATAN'S CHARIOTS A nickname given to early locomotives. Inventions and scientific innovations have often been ascribed to the Devil. Pope Gregory XVI called steam Satan's invention.

SATAN'S DAUGHTERS   A group offering instruction in occult practices, including the fabrication of voodoo figures, ritual candles, etc.

SATAN'S FALL   The Book of Revelation, also called the Apocalypse, is the source of various accounts of Satan's fall. Chapter 12 depicts the great struggle between the heavenly hosts under the command of Michael and the Devil:
> And there was a war in heaven: Michael and his angels fought against the dragon; and the dragon fought against his angels. And prevailed not; neither was their place found any more in heaven. And the great dragon was cast out, that old serpent, called the Devil, and Satan, which deceiveth the whole world; he was cast out into the earth, and his angels were cast out with him. . . . Therefore rejoice, ye heavens, and ye that dwell in them. Woe to the inhabiters of the earth and of the sea! For the Devil is come down unto you, having great wrath, because he knoweth that he hath but a short time.

SATARAN   In late Sumerian liturgies, the name given to Tammuz. The word means 'The Serpent Goddess.'

SATOR FORMULA   The most famous of all magic squares. It has been found inscribed on ancient walls, drinking vessels, etc. It is recommended for finding witches, extinguishing fires, fulfilling wishes, and many other purposes. It may be an anagram of *Pater noster* and the first letters, repeated, of Alpha and Omega:

```
S A T O R
A R E P O
T E N E T
O P E R A
R O T A S
```

SATURN SQUARE A magic square used to attract Saturn's influence. It is the oldest magic square known and appears in *I Ching*. It consists of three rows of three figures because Saturn is the third sephira, or agency through which God manifested himself in the production of the universe:

```
4 9 2
3 5 7
8 1 6
```

SAUNDERS, ALEX The leading witch of Great Britain. His biography, *King of the Witches,* was written by June Johns.

SCALINGER A familiar demon who belonged to Jerome Cardan.

SCARABAEUS The dung beetle, symbolic in Egyptian religion of the male generative principle and of resurrection.

SCARLET WOMAN One of the mistresses of Aleister Crowley. She helped him to establish his Sacred Abbey of Thelema at Cefalu in Sicily.

SCHEMHAMPRORAS Seventy-two divine names discussed in the Cabala.

SCHONENBURG, JOHANN VON Prince-Archbishop (1581-1599) who initiated the campaign against witchcraft at Treves. See Treves.

SCHROPFER, JOHANN GEORG (1730-1774) German necromancer who initiated many followers into occultism.

SCHWAGEL, ANNA MARIA The last person officially executed for witchcraft in Germany. She was put to death on April 11, 1775, after confessing that she had copulated with the Devil.

SCOT, MICHAEL Scottish sorcerer (c. 1175-1232), attached to the court of Emperor Frederick II. He acquired a legendary reputation and was mentioned by Dante.

SCOX Duke of Hell. Deceitful, he steals money and keeps it for two centuries before returning it.

SCRAPFAGGOT GREEN (WITCH OF) In 1944 an American bulldozer pushed aside a stone that had imprisoned the Witch of Scrapfaggot Green, in Essex County, England, and released a malicious poltergeist. According to press reports, many strange events occurred — bells rang, haystacks were scattered, and huge stones were carried considerable distances.

SCREWS See Thumbscrews.

SCRYING Using a crystal ball, glass of water, or a shiny surface to foretell the future.

SEANCE A meeting of votaries of Spiritism. The purpose of a séance is to communicate with the dead.

SEATON, DAVID A deputy bailiff who prosecuted Gilly Duncan. See North Berwick Witches.

SEBAU In Egyptian religion, the name of a host of demons in the underworld.

SECRET NAMES In many societies people believe that to discover the name of a person or supernatural being is to gain power over him. Hence the use of hidden or secret names. The hidden name of the Egyptian god Re was known only to Isis. Marduk, the Babylonian god, had fifty secret names.

SECRET OF SECRETS (THE) Handbook of magic. *The Secret of Secrets,* also called *True Black Magic,* is a French version of the *Key of Solomon.* It was published in 1750.

SEDDIM Demon of destruction.

SEERE A demon described in the *Lemegeton* as 'indifferently good or bad' and ready to 'do the will of the operator.'

SEFER YEZIRAH (SEPHIR YETZIRAH)
See Book of Formation.

SEIRIM The Israelites believed in evil spirits dwelling in wastelands and darkness. Among these spirits were the seirim and the shedim. Seirim are chimeras or goat-demons. Azazel was the leader of the *seirim,* mentioned several times in the Old Testament. The goat-demons were worshiped by some of the Jews. The cult seems to have involved copulation between women and he-goats. Plutarch describes a similar cult in Egypt. The most beautiful women were chosen to copulate with the divine he-goat at Mendes.

SEKTET The Egyptian boat of the setting sun, steered by the souls of the dead.

SEMJAZA An evil prince mentioned frequently in pre-Christian literature.

SEPA In Egyptian religion, a name given to the god Osiris.

SEPHIROTH Ten successive emanations from God, each of them containing less of the divine substance. The cabalists teach that God is the total of all things, the sum of all ideas, and that man is God in miniature. The soul can climb the hierarchy of the sephiroth and man can become God on earth. Occult groups which teach the theory of the soul's descent and ascent through the ten spheres may have ten corresponding grades. In Crowley's system, the student begins as a Neophyte (Sephira 10, or the earth), moves on to become a Zelator (9, the moon), Practicus (8, Mercury), Philosophus (7, Venus), Adeptus Minor (6, the sun), Adeptus Major (5, Mars), Adeptus Exemptus (4, Jupiter), Magister Templi (3, Saturn), Magus (2, sphere of the stars), and Ipsissimus (1, sphere of God). *Sepher Yetzirah* teaches that the 'Ten ineffable Sephiroth have ten vast regions bound to them,' following the Pythagorean concept of the importance of the numbers from 1 to 10, the basis of all things. A complicated system of correspondences was worked out by Crowley. Traditionally, the ten Sephiroth are arranged to form the Tree of Life, illustrating the underlying pattern of the universe and its essential unity. Number 1, Kether (Supreme Crown), is the first emanation, the force of God as Prime Mover or First cause. Then come 2, Hokmah (Wisdom); 3, Binah (Understanding); 4, Hesed (Love); 5, Geburah (Power); 6, Tiphereth (Beauty); 7, Netsah (Endurance); 8, Hod (Majesty); 9, Yesod (Foundation); and 10, Malkuth (Kingdom). When the Tree is shown as a human body, Malkuth is the union of the whole body. It contains the forces of all the Sephiroth. The kingdom of the earth, which is its sphere, is also the kingdom of God. See also Ten Evil Sephiroth.

SEPTERIUM A religious festival held every ninth year at Delphi in honor of Helios (Apollo) to commemorate his triumph over Python or darkness.

SERAPIS See Sarapis.

SETHIANI A pre-Christian Gnostic sect described by Hippolytus as a society whose life was based on three principles: Light, Darkness, and Spirit. The sect probably tried to reconcile Judaism with Hellenism.

SET The god of darkness and the sworn enemy of the gods of light originated in the Egyptian desert and represents drought and storm, the two arch enemies of agrarian tribes. The enemy of gods and men, he stands for everything that can be destroyed by fire. More ancient than the Hebraic Satan or the Greek Typhon, he was identified with the supreme god of the Hyksos. Set killed his brother by tricking him into lying down inside a coffin, then closing the lid throwing the coffin into the Nile. Thus Set became the patriarch and patron of fratricide.

SEVEN DEADLY SINS Peter Binsfield lists the demons credited with the power to provoke people to commit the seven deadly sins:

Lucifer:	Pride
Mammon:	Avarice
Asmodeus:	Lechery
Satan:	Anger
Beelzebub:	Gluttony
Leviathan:	Envy
Belphegor:	Sloth

SEXUAL UNION Sexual union with the Devil is an essential element of witchcraft. According to Vance Randolph's *Ozark Superstitions,* a Devil's representative, a man who is already a member of the cult, has intercourse with a woman initiate for three nights in succession. The rite occurs at midnight, in the dark of the moon, at the family burying-ground of the would-be witch. Women who have been initiated into a cult report that the initiation 'is a much more moving spiritual crisis than that which the Christians call conversion.'

SHADDAI One of the Nine Mystic Names used to summon demons.

SHAI In Egyptian religion, the god of destiny or fate. He has a part in the weighing of the souls of the dead.

SHAMAN Among Siberian tribes, the shaman is a healer and conductor of souls. He descends into the Lower Regions to capture the soul of a patient, or to accompany the soul of the deceased into the Infernal Realms. To bring back the soul, three routes are possible for the shaman: a subterranean descent into Hell; immersion into the Ocean depths; ascent to Heaven.

SHAVING Those suspected of having relations with Satan were shaven. The reasons deduced were mainly these: the suspect might conceal charms in the hair; the hair might conceal devil's marks; and a demon might be hiding in the suspect's hair, advising her what to say and do.

SHEDIM A class of demons having the claws of a cock. They are mentioned in the Old Testament (Psalms 106:37).

SHEITAN The Arabic name of Satan.

SHENIU In Egyptian religion, an underworld chamber where the enemies of Re are tortured.

SHEPHERD, THE A book written by Hermas in the middle of the second century A.D. It sets forth the theory that every man has as his constant companions two angels, an evil angel and a guardian angel.

SHESMU The henchman of the Egyptian god Osiris. His nightly duty was to dismember the bodies of the wicked dead.

SHIELD OF DAVID A six-pointed figure used to control demons.

SHIVA The first or highest of the three members of the Hindu trinity is often called 'the destroyer.' He is often depicted as dancing. Worship of Shiva is a response to his call for men to put away or destroy desire and all else that binds them to their material incarnation and to seek the freedom of pure being — the divine kingdom that lies beyond the manifestations of form.

SIGILLUM DIABOLI See Devil's Mark.

SIGNORA In the early sixteenth-century Italian witches were said to be presided over by *la Signora* ('the Lady'), who wore a golden robe at the Sabbat.

SIGN OF TANIT See Tanit, Sign of.

SI GYN In Norse mythology, the wife of Loki. She catches the venom dropped by the serpents who hang over him in the cavern in which he is chained.

SILCHARDE One of the demons who may be summoned by a necromancer. Bread will induce him to appear between three and four o'clock on Thursday morning.

SIMON MAGUS Simon the Magician is mentioned in Acts 8:5-24 and is frequently referred to by early Christian writers. A sorcerer who had been converted to Christianity, he was reputed to have had a companion, Helena, who had become enslaved to matter. Having fallen under the power of evil angels, she had occupied, successively, a number of mortal bodies, including that of Helen of Troy. Simon is said to have promulgated an Oriental doctrine in which he was the first Aeon or Emanation, the first manifestation of the primal deity, the Word, the Paraclete, the Almighty.

SIMURGH In Persian mythology, the 'all-knowing bird of ages,' said to possess oracular powers. The half-phoenix, half-lion creature was the guardian of the ancient Persian mysteries.

SIN In the Mesopotamian pantheon, the wise moon god who revealed the future to the adept. Identified by the Sumerians with Nanna.

In Mesopotamian religion, sin was the most natural way for a demon to enter the body of a man. Moral and ritual offenses were put in the same category. A man who sinned was abandoned by the gods, whereupon demons entered his body and made their presence felt in disagreeable ways. Priests used specific exorcisms to drive out the invading demons.

SINCLAIR, GEORGE Author of *Satan's Invisible World Discovered* (1685). His fabulous collection of witch stories perpetuated a belief in witchcraft long after witch-burning had been discontinued. It was said to have a place in every cottage library in Scotland.

SINISTRARI, LUDOVICO MARIA Professor of theology at Pavia University and author of *De Daemonialitate* (On Demoniality), discovered in 1875. He concentrated on the problems that arise from relations between devils and humans. He was born in 1622 and died in 1701.

SIRENS According to the Book of Enoch (I Enoch 19:2), sirens are the wives of the angels who went astray on the earth.

SISYPHUS In Greek mythology, an avaricious king of Corinth. His punishment in Hades was extreme. He was condemned to be engaged forever in the task of rolling a huge stone to the top of a hill only to have it roll back down the hill again.

SKULD See Norns.

SKULL WORSHIP Skulls play an important role as sacred relics and as objects of worship among primitives. Among Polynesians and Melanesians, skulls of ancestors are worshiped in order to establish connections with the spirits of the dead. Like the head of Osiris in Egypt, the skulls of ancestors may also serve as tutelary deities. The head or its parts, each of which may stand for the whole, can be used as magical food or as a means of increasing the fertility of the soil.

SMARAGDINE TABLE The *Tabula Smaragdina*, a work on alchemy published in the sixteenth century and attributed to Hermes Trismegistus, is said to condense the whole of magic on a single page. Certain Masons and Cabalists allege that it was found by Abraham's wife on the body of Hermes.

SMITH, CHRISTOPHER NEIL One of perhaps a dozen exorcists now practicing in England. He is the vicar of St. Saviour's in Hampstead, London. He casts out spirits by laying his hands on the victim. He is kept busy the year round, according to the *London Sunday Times*.

SMITH, JOHN Called the 'Leicester Boy,' in 1607, at the age of five, accused several women of bewitching him. Later, in 1616, he caused nine other victims to be hanged. He was finally exposed by James VI, king of Scotland.

SMOKE The liver and heart of a fish when burned produce smoke that will drive away the demon Asmodeus.

SNAKE GODDESS In ancient Greece, the Minoan snake goddess was a chthonic deity.

SNEEZE Popular belief holds that a sneeze is bad in the morning but good in the afternoon. Some people are convinced that a sneeze rids the body of a demon, justifying the use of the phrase, 'God bless you.'

SOCIETY FOR THE REPARATION OF SOULS An occult sect founded by Abbé Boullan and Adèle Chevalier in 1859. It was centered around sex-magic. On at least one occasion, ritual murder was practiced.

SOCRATES The Greek philosopher claimed to have a kind of guardian angel, an inner voice that warned him of impending danger.

SODOMY Like all other forms of sexual aberration, sodomy is cultivated by Satan and his followers. Divine sodomy involves the use of the Eucharist in satisfying sexual passions.

SOKER In Egyptian religion, a funerary god, often identified with Osiris.

SOLOMON King Solomon, traditionally known as an arch magician, used a spell to banish the infernal beings sent by the king of demons to extract human hearts:
Lofaham,
Solomon,
Iyouel,
Iyosenaoui.

SOLOMON'S RING Solomon is said to have possessed a magic ring enabling him to command the angels and all the forces of nature.

SOLOMON'S THRONE Devils are reputed to have hidden magic manuals under Solomon's throne. See Magic Manuals.

SONS OF MIDNIGHT Members of an occult society in London. In the last decades of the seventeenth century and on into the eighteenth, they engaged in sinister, demoniac activities.

SORCERER An adept in the occult, bound to Satan in return for knowledge and skill in magic. Traditionally, he is represented as having a fixed stare. He keeps his occult power only so long as his feet touch the ground.
In 1591 J. G. Godelman defined sorcerers as those who by evil spells, dire curses, etc. harm and destroy the lives and health of men and beasts. See *De Magis*.

SORCERY The use of power gained through control of supernatural forces. In a strict sense, sorcery is universal and timeless, whereas witchcraft is limited for the most part to the period between 1450 and 1750 and to the Christian nations.

SORTILEGA Medieval designation of a diviner.

SOUBERET French sorcerer who summoned two demons, Avarus and Superbus. He was burned in 1437.

SOULIS, WILLIAM Fourteenth-century Scottish noble, professed Satanist, and reputed performer of human sacrifices. Known as the Black Lord of Hermitage, he was also credited with having made a pact with the Devil.

SOUTHWEST WIND, DEMON OF THE In Assyrian demonology, a horrible demon with the head of a dog, the feet of an eagle, the paws of a lion, and the tail of a scorpion.

A statue in the Louvre shows him with the flesh missing.

SOVIJ A Baltic god of the dead.

SPECTER A visible disembodied spirit. An apparition, phantom, or ghost.

SPECTRAL EVIDENCE The Devil who made a pact with a witch could not be subpoenaed to provide evidence against the accused. Evidence of association with the Devil therefore had to be supplied by the accused, by other confessed witches, or by innocent victims of the accused. Torture was used to induce the accused and confessed witches to provide evidence. Innocent victims claimed that they could see the spirit or specter of the accused torturing them. This evidence was accepted by the courts.

SPEE, FRIEDRICH VON Professor of theology at Wurzburg (1591-1635). He was the author of *Cautio Criminalis,* an attempt to put an end to the unjust persecution of those accused of witchcraft.

SPELLS Victims or intended victims of spells include Ramses III, John XXII, Louis X, Charles VI, Enguerrand de Marigny, and Leonora Galigai.

SPENTA MZINYU In early Zoroastrianism, one of the names of Ahura Mazda (Ormazd). The Holy Spirit is seen as the cosmic rival of Ahriman (Angra Mainyu), the Evil Spirit.

SPICES Like other preservatives, spices have the power to ward off demons.

SPINA, ALFONSO DE Fifteenth-century Spanish theologian. He used Jewish sources to prove 'according to the doctrine of the Talmud' that the Jews are the children of the Devil. He was the author of the first book on witchcraft to be printed in Strasbourg. His *Fortalicium Fidei* ('Fortress of Faith'), written in 1460, identifies ten kinds of demons.

SPINA, BARTOLOMMEO Theologian and author of *Quaestio de Strigibus* (On Witches), published in 1523. He advocated spectral evidence and expressed his belief in transvection, sexual intercourse with demons, and metamorphosis.

SPIRITISM The French form of spiritualism, particularly as developed from the doctrines of Allan Kardec. It stresses reincarnation.

SPIRITUALISM Recently there has been a revival of spiritualism, based on nineteenth-century theosophy and Rosicrucianism, and relying heavily on communication with the dead. According to the National Council of Churches, some four hundred churches have been established to serve at least 150,000 members who have turned seriously to the occult for comfort and companionship.

SPRENGER, JAKOB Fifteenth-century Dominican. With Heinrich Kramer he wrote *Malleus Maleficarum* (The Witches' Hammer), a guide for discovering and punishing witches.

SQUASSATION Torture designed to make those accused of witchcraft name their accomplices. Philip Limborch's *History of the Inquisition* (1692) gives a detailed description:

> The prisoner hath his hands bound behind his back, and weights tied to his feet, and then he is drawn up high on high, till his head reaches the very pulley. He is kept hanging in this manner for some time . . ., and on a sudden he is let down with a jerk, by slacking the rope, but kept from coming quite to the ground, by which terrible shake his arms and legs

are all disjointed, whereby he is put to the most exquisite pain.

SRADDHADEVA An epithet of Yama, the god of death and king of the underworld.

SRAOSHA A Zoroastrian deity who protects the souls of the faithful against demons.

SRIYANTRA The double triangle known as the seal of Vishnu and also as Solomon's seal.

STAKE With the exception of England and New England, witches were burned at the stake: alive in Italy and Spain, often after strangulation in France, Scotland, and Germany. Jean Bodin recommended the use of green wood to prolong the suffering of recalcitrant witches.

STARS The Koran teaches that the stars are the sentinels of Heaven, preventing the Devil from approaching and learning the secrets of God.

STAVROGIN The most important character in Dostoevski's *The Possessed*. Katkov refused to publish the chapter of the novel cataloguing Stavrogin's sins, holding that the public was not ready for an account of such debauchery. The 'unwritten masterpiece' referred to in Dostoevski's notes as *The Life of a Great Sinner* would have explored Stavrogin's character.

STEVENOTE DE AUDEBERT French witch. At her trial in 1616 she produced a pact she had made with Satan.

STIGMATI DIABOLI Devil's marks. Cotton Mather believed that witches were branded by the Devil:
I add, why should not witch marks be searched for?

The properties, the qualities of those marks are described by divers weighty writers.

The Devil's mark or seal (*sigillum diaboli*) was frequently confused with the witch's mark, and these terms came to be used interchangeably by many people. See Devil's Marks, Witch's Marks.

STILL-HEART Epithet of the Egyptian god Osiris.

STOLEN CHILDREN In the Middle Ages fairies were thought to steal children and substitute for them little monsters to which they had given birth. These children were given over to the Devil or sacrificed at the Sabbat.

STONEHENGE There have been attempts to connect the mysterious formation of rock monoliths in the British Isles with a stone age cult that still survives in the secret rites of modern covens. Modern scientists believe that the monoliths were an observatory that existed almost two thousand years B.C. The circular monument on the Salisbury Plain in southern England probably was built in three waves. Started by people who were just beginning to domesticate cattle, it was enlarged a century later by the Beaker folk, who erected a circle of five-ton bluestones, and completed by 1600 B.C., when an entire nation moved giant boulders from twenty miles away.

STORM-RAISING A power attributed to witches. As early as the eighth century, the Archbishop of Canterbury admitted that sorcerers had the power to cause storms. In 1489 Ulrich Molitor reported that witches were commonly thought to have the power to provoke lightning and hail.

STRANGLER In the sixteenth century the Devil was called 'The Strangler.' He was said to strangle people dying of apoplexy.

STRANGULATION Method of killing witches before burning them, provided they did not retract their confessions. Strangulation was accomplished by garroting or hanging.

STRAPPADO A form of torture commonly used to make witches name their accomplices. It was less severe than squassation. In both forms of torture the victim was bound and hoisted in the air. In squassation he was suddenly dropped to within a few inches of the floor. The German word for strappado is *Zug*. In Italian the expression *tratti di corde* is also used.

STREET OF GOLD A street in medieval Prague noted as an occult center where witches and alchemists plied their trade. In Czech, the name is Zlata Ulicka.

STREGA The name by which a witch is known in Corsica.

STRIX Medieval designation of a sorceress. The word is associated etymologically with 'screech-owl.' Its plural form is striges. The strix was believed to suck the blood of children.

STROUP, HARRY See Baker, Stanley.

STUBB, PETER A sixteenth-century German convicted of lycanthropy and put to death in the town of Bedburg, near Cologne. He confessed that he was able to change his shape by means of a magic belt. He became 'a greedy devouring wolf' and committed many murders. Sentence was pronounced on October 28, 1589. He was
> to have his body laid on a wheel, and with red-hot burning pincers in ten several places to have the flesh pulled off from the bones . . .; afterward to have his head struck off from his body; then to have his carcass burned to ashes.

STYX In Greek mythology, a river which encircled the underworld seven times and had to be crossed by those who passed to the regions of the dead.

SUAREZ, FRANCISCO Spanish theologian and philosopher. Suarez (1548-1617) suggested that when God revealed his plan for the Incarnation, some of the angels, knowing that they would have to humble themselves before a creature lower than themselves (the Son of God), rebelled against the Creator.

SUBTERRANEAN DEMONS A class of demons identified by medieval theologians, following the suggestions of Jean Wier. They live in caves, are spiteful by nature, and work to bring about the ruin of the human race.

SUCCOR-BENOTH Chief of the eunuchs in the palace of the princes of Hell. The favorite of Proserpine, he is the demon of jealousy.

SUCCUBUS An evil spirit thought to assume the shape of a female for the purpose of having intercourse with a man. See Incubus.

SUCELLUS In Celtic religion, he was a chthonic god identified with Pluto. He was the god of the dead. In another aspect, he was a deity who presided over fertility.

SUKIAS In parts of Central America, these are witches.

SUMMIS DESIDERANTES A papal bull, promulgated by Innocent VIII on December 5, 1484, containing the theory of magic and demonology. It ordered Kramer and Sprenger, two inquisitors of the Order of the Preaching Friars, to proceed with firmness in the suppression of heresy.

SUN DANCE A ceremony, usually lasting eight days, that is characteristic of the Plains tribes of the American Indians. Smoking, fasting, and secret rites constituted part of the celebration. The underlying significance of the dance was an act of penance.

SUNYA A Sanskrit word meaning illusion, in the sense that all existence is but a dream or shadow.

SUOYATOR In the Finnish epic poem, the *Kalevala*, the name of the Spirit of Evil whose saliva produced the serpent of sin.

SUPERBUS A demon summoned by the French sorcerer Soubert.

SUPER ILLIUS SPECULA A bull issued in 1326 by Pope John XXII. 'There are people,' it states, 'who are Christians only in name. . . . They make sacrifices to demons and worship them, fashioning or procuring images [to be used in] executing their evil designs.'

SURGAT A demon who may be summoned on Sunday and commanded to bring the magic stone. He will appear between eleven p.m. and one a.m. and will ask for a hair from any conjurer's head. He will accept a hair from any animal.

SURIN, FATHER JEAN-JOSEPH Seventeenth-century exorcist. The learned Jesuit was called to exorcise the famous Ursulines of Loudon. He succeeded in his mission but was possessed by demons who dominated his life for twenty years.

SURSUNABU In Babylonian mythology, the ferryman who rows passengers across the waters of death. His functions are similar to those of Charon.

SURT In Norse religion, the fire god who is destined to destroy the universe.

SUSANOWO In ancient Japanese religion, the storm god, representing all that is dark, violent, or evil.

SUTECH A Hittite god, identified with the Egyptian god Set.

SUTI In Egyptian religion, another name of Set, god of darkness.

SWASTIKA The name given by Brahmin priests to the pramantha, a lighting stick which was turned in a small hollow formed at the intersection of two pieces of wood. The tips of the cross were bent at right angles and secured by four nails. It is found not only in ancient Persia and the ruins of Troy but also in China and Japan. It was used in the sun worship of the Kickapoos, and Pottawatomies. It is also called a fylfot.

SWAWMX A Burmese vampire demon.

SWEDENBORG, EMANUEL Swedish engineer, savant, and theologian (1688-1772). Balzac called him the 'Northern Buddha.' He became interested in the occult and claimed that a purple-clad seer had revealed to him all the secrets of the universe. He conversed frequently with Vergil and Luther, to cite only two luminaries. His voluminous writings affected German romantic philosophy and led to the foundation of the Church of the New Jerusalem, or New Church. He correctly foretold the date of his own death.

SWIMMING Trial by water (*iudicium aquae*), an ancient means of determining innocence or guilt, was incorporated in witchcraft trials. The witch's thumb was tied to her toe. If she floated and failed to sink, she was deemed guilty.

King James I approved of ordeal by immersion:

> So it appears that God hath appointed, for a supernatural sign of the monstrous impiety of the witches, that the water shall refuse to receive them in her bosom, that have shaken off them the sacred water of baptism.

SWINE Demons frequently are associated with swine. Two thousand demons asked Jesus to allow them to enter a herd of swine. 'And the unclean spirits went out, and entered into the swine; and the herd ran violently down a steep place into the sea' (Mark 5:13).

SWORD Separation by the sword is a recurrent theme in alchemical literature. The sword is used to divide the philosophical egg, to separate the elements, and to restore the primitive state of chaos in order to produce a perfect body. It is prefigured in the flaming sword of the angel guarding paradise.

SYBACCO Familiar demon of Adriano Lemmi, according to Margiotta's *Le Palladisme*.

SYLPHS Spirits made of the purest atoms of the air that they inhabit.

SYMPATHETIC MAGIC The ancient view of the underlying unity of all things, summed up in the expression 'as below, so above,' is at the heart of sympathetic magic. Sympathetic magic is based on the principle that like affects like, that a desired result may be achieved by mimicry, imitation, incantation, etc.

SYSTEM OF CORRESPONDENCES Necromancers use a system of correspondences to control the occult forces of the universe. Planets, metals and colors are linked in this manner: Sun, gold, yellow; Moon, silver, white; Mercury, quicksilver, grey or neutral; Venus, copper, green; Mars, iron, red; Jupiter, tin, blue; Saturn, lead, black.

T

TAGES An Etruscan god of the underworld.

TAIGHEIRM A magical sacrifice of cats to the devils of the underworld, formerly practiced in Scotland. In the seventeenth century two exorcists, Allan and Lachlain Maclean, were supposed to have held a Taigheirm in Mull and to have received the gift of second sight. In Celtic demonology, the practice might also involve the slaughter of a bull in the vicinity of a waterfall or precipice.

TALAPOIN In Thailand, a Buddhist ascetic, frequently credited with magic powers.

TAMIEL One of the leaders of the angels who rebelled against God, according to the Book of Enoch, and swore allegiance to Samiaza.

TANIT, SIGN OF Symbol used for more than a thousand years to express the hopes and beliefs of the Punic civilization. Its primitive form was that of a trapezium closed by a horizontal line at the top extending beyond its adjacent sides like the extended arms of a human body and surmounted in the middle by a head-like circle. It appears as a good-luck symbol in many buildings and on stelae.

TANTALUS In Greek mythology, a wealthy king who was punished in the underworld for some atrocious sin. He was placed in a lake whose waters rose to his chin but receded when he tried to quench his thirst. Fruit-laden branches receded beyond his reach when he tried to grasp them.

TAROT The oldest surviving card game. The curious pack of cards that make up the Tarot are still used in a game called *tarocchini* in Italy and *tarot* in France. The pack is used in fortune-telling and is believed by many occultists to have originated in Egypt, as a storehouse of ancient lore. An alternate hypothesis attributes its invention to a committee of learned Cabalists who met in Fez in the year 1200. The modern Tarot pack contains four suits of fourteen cards each and twenty-two trumps. The suits are Swords (Spades), Cups (Hearts), Coins or Pentacles (Diamonds), and Wands or Staffs (Clubs). The cards in each suit are the King, Queen, Knight, Page (Knave or Jack), Ten, Nine, Eight, Seven, Six, Five, Four, Three, Two, and Ace. The trumps are usually placed in this order, beginning with zero and continuing through twenty-one: Fool, Juggler, Female Pope, Empress, Emperor, Pope, Lovers, Chariot, Strength, Hermit, Wheel of Fortune, Justice, Hanged Man, Death, Temperance, Devil, Falling Tower, Stars, Moon, Sun, Day of Judgment, World. The cards are rich in symbolism and lend themselves to a variety of interpretations, particularly when studied as elements in a system of correspondences based on the *Sepher Yetzirah*.

TARTARUS In Greek mythology, the infernal regions described by Homer as being as far below Hades as heaven is above the earth.

TARTINI, GIUSEPPE Italian violinist (1692-1770) whose *The Devil's Sonata* is supposed to have been dictated by the Devil in a dream.

TA-TCHESEHT In Egyptian religion, a name for the underworld.

TATE, SHARON Victim of a ritualistic slaying carried out in August 1969 by members of a hippie 'family' headed by Charles Manson. Manson and three of the self-styled new Messiah's followers — Leslie Van Houten, Susan Atkins, and Patricia Krenwinkel — were convicted by a Los Angeles jury of the brutal murder of the actress and six other persons. See Manson, Charles.

TAU CROSS A cross shaped like a T. It was used by the ancient Phoenicians as a magic symbol.

TAUROBOLIUM The sacrifice of a bull and baptism of a worshiper with its blood. The rite probably originated in the worship of Anahita, the Great Mother in the ancient Persian religion, and was adopted in the cults of Cybele, Attis, and Mithras. The initiate was supposed to secure the magic potency of a powerful animal by contact with its blood. Later the rite symbolized death and rebirth.

TAUVA'U Among the Trobriand Islanders, these are malignant beings. Invisible to ordinary human beings, they walk at night through villages, rattling gourds and clanking lethal wooden sword clubs. They sometimes change into reptiles, when injured or ill-treated, and revenge themselves by death.

TAXIL, LEO Author of many sensational revelations concerning occult and satanic practices. See Bataille, Doctor.

TCHORT The Russian name of Satan.

TEARS At witchcraft trials the condemned never shed tears. Their behavior, caused by terror and hysteria, was universally attributed to demoniacal forces.

TEDWORTH See Drummer of Tedworth.

TELCHINES A variant name for the Galli.

TEMPLARS Members of the Order of Knights Templar confessed in 1307, under torture or the threat of torture, to charges of worshiping idols, worshiping the Devil, renouncing Christ, practicing homosexual vice, and omitting from the canon of Mass the sacred words *Hoc est corpus meum,* 'This is my body.'

TEMPTATION The Devil never misses an opportunity to merit his title, 'The Tempter.' From the medieval point of view, worldliness, with all its deceptions, allurements and lusts, was nothing other than Satan. During its earthly pilgrimage every soul had an angelic companion and a diabolic one, a guardian angel and the tempter.

TEMPTATION OF ADAM Theologians have speculated that the Devil tempted Adam before he tempted Eve. After he failed to convince Adam, the Devil settled for Eve. This theory was echoed in *Adamus exul,* a tragedy written by Hugo Grotius before he reached the age of eighteen.

TEN EVIL SEPHIROTH Ten evil sephiroth ruled by archdemons commanded by Sammael, are listed by Samuel Mathers: Satan and Moloch, Beelzebub, Lucifuge, Ashtaroth, Asmodeus, Belphegor, Baal, Adrammelech, Lilith, and Naamah.

TERAPHIM Idols, images, or other objects representing the primitive household gods of the ancient Semites. Their cult survived into the early centuries of Christianity. They may once have been associated with ancestor worship. Later they were used in divination and as talismanic figures in cabalist practices. According to a legend from a collection of twelfth-century midrashim (exegeses), they were idols made from the head of a firstborn male whose hair had been plucked out. The head was sprinkled with salt, rubbed with oil, and set up in a room behind lighted candles. A small plaque, inscribed with the name of an idol and placed under the tongue, enabled the head to speak.

TERRAGON Henri III was charged with having a familiar spirit named Terragon. D'Aubigné, the great Protestant poet, accused the king of conducting black masses at the Louvre.

TERRESTRIAL DEMONS Hurled from Heaven for their sins, they dwell in the forests, where they set snares for the unwary, or in the open country, where they lead travelers astray.

TERRIBLE ONE The heart of the Egyptian god Osiris. It devours all things that have been slaughtered.

TERTULLIAN Early Latin church father. Quintus Septimius Florens Tertullianus (c. 160-230) in *De Patientia* taught that the most perfect of the angels was overcome by anguish and rage when he observed that man, created in the image of God, was to dominate all the creatures of the earth. He studied the question of devil worship and concluded that those who traffic with the Devil must renounce their baptism.

TESTAMENT OF SOLOMON A grimoire written in Greek, 100-400 A.D.

TETRAGRAMMATON ELOHIM One of the Nine Mystic Names used to summon demons.

TEZCATLIPOCA In Aztec religion, the god of the upper air who watched over the affairs of men. Originally the chief god of the Nahuas, he was later identified with many gods of conquered tribes. Each year a youth who had imitated him was sacrificed on his altar at Tenochtitlan. He was also known as Yaotzin ('The Enemy'), and was worshiped by the Mexican witches at their sabbat.

THAUMATURGY The opposite of black magic or theurgy. The thaumaturge performs miracles with the help of divine or beneficent forces.

THEATRUM DIABOLARUM A voluminous collection of the views of Luther and his followers concerning the existence, power, and nature of devils. The work was edited by Sigmund Feyerabend.

THEODORIS OF LEMNOS Greek witch mentioned by Demosthenes and Herodotus. Notorious for sorcery, she was condemned to death for her acts.

THEODORUS Archbishop of Canterbury (668-690). His *Liber Poenitentialis* is the first legislative document on witchcraft. Fasting was the only punishment prescribed.

THEOPHAGY In ancient mystery cults, theophagy denoted the eating of a sacred animal or a god in animal form.

THEOSOPHY Knowledge of God and the universe achieved by direct mystical insight, philosophical speculation, or both. A modern Theosophical Society was founded in New York in 1875 by Mme. H. P. Blavatsky and others, with the avowed aims of promoting the brotherhood of man, advancing the study of the ancient world-religions, and developing the latent divine powers in man. A second theosophical organization was established in the United States after the death of Madame Blavatsky (1891).

THERIOLATRY The cult of animals.

THEURGY The art of persuading a supernatural power to act in one's favor. The occult art was practiced by certain

Neoplatonists who relied on self-purification, sacred rites, and knowledge of divine indications in nature (signatures) to invoke beneficent spirits.

THIASOI In ancient Greece these were brotherhoods composed of initiates in the Orphic mystery cult.

THIBAULT, MME. High Priestess of the satanic sect who founded Carmel Church in Lyon, France.

THIRD EYE Often identified with the pineal gland, the third eye is an organ used to observe the astral world.

THOTH Egyptian god of wisdom, learning, and literature. Neoplatonic philosophers regarded Egypt as a source of ancient secret knowledge. See Hermes Trismegistus.

THRACIAN RITES Early Thracian cults were marked by human sacrifices, orgiastic practices, and magic. Dionysus, who symbolized fertility, was virtually identified with Sabazius.

THRAETAONA The Persian Michael. He struggled with Zohak, the destroying serpent.

THREAD A red thread or cord was considered in medieval times to be the mark of a witch. The belief springs from the Jewish ritual mentioned in Leviticus and in Isaiah 1:18. Aaron is told to select a goat for Azazel, to put all the sins of Israel on the head of the goat, and to send the goat into the wilderness. The Jews performed the ritual until 70 A.D. They tied to the head of the scapegoat a scarlet thread, recalling the words of the prophet, 'though your sins be as scarlet, they shall be white as snow.'

THROCKMORTON, ROBERT See Warboys Witches.

THUMBIKINS See Thumbscrews.

THUMBSCREWS A common and effective method of extracting confessions from those accused of witchcraft. A small vise was used to crush the tip of the finger to a pulp. A simpler method involved the application of pressure on the thumb or toe by means of a piece of string. Also known as pilliwinks, the screws, thumbikins, and (in French) *grésillons*.

THYADES See Bacchantes.

TIAMAT In Semitic-Babylonian religion, the primal Mother, symbol of darkness and chaos. She is represented as chaotic waters, a raging serpent, a monstrous dragon.

TIBETAN BOOK OF THE DEAD The *Bardo Thodol* is a guide for the dead man who must spend forty-nine days awaiting his rebirth. The first part of text (Chikhai Bardo) describes the psychic aspect of the moment of death. The second part (Chönyid Bardo) describes the dream state that follows death. The third part (Sidpa Bardo) reveals the secrets of the birth instinct and prenatal events. Instructions are intended to fix the dying man's attention on the nature of his visions. The book is said by some interpreters to cloak the mystical teachings of the ancient gurus. Seen as a guide to the death and rebirth of the ego, it stresses the attainment of freedom by remembrance of certain teachings. The Tibetan title of the book means 'Liberation by hearing on the after-death plane.'

TIBETAN WITCHCRAFT The indigenous animistic Bon cult of Tibet is based on ancestor-worship, superstition, and witchcraft.

TIPHERETH The balancing force between Hesed and Geburah the vital energy of the life-force, and the sixth sephira, representing the sphere of the sun, in Cabalistic teachings.

TIRESIAS Ancient Greek necromancer, afflicted by the gods with blindness but endowed with the gift of prophecy.

TIRINNANZI, FERDINANDO Modern Italian poet. Ferdinando Tirinnanzi (1879-1940) in *The Kiss of Judas* and other works, revives the great vision of Origen and expresses the hope that Satan's redemption will eventually be accomplished.

TITANOMACHY The great event of Titan history. The war between the Titans and the Olympian gods in Thessaly resulted in the overthrow of the Titan dynasty. It corresponds to the Hebraic account of the revolt of the angels against Jehovah.

TITANS Primeval deities of Greek mythology. They were the children of Uranus and Gaea. Their revolt against Zeus (the Titanomachy) is the Hellenic version of the rebellion of the archangels against Jehovah.

TITYUS A Titan, son of Zeus or Gaea. Because he offered violence to Leto, he was slain by her son Apollo. He lies bound in Hades, where two vultures gnaw at his liver. The fall of Tityus and Prometheus is the Hellenic transfiguration of the fall of the rebel archangels in the Bible.

TIU (TIW, TIWAZ) In Teutonic mythology, a god of war and destruction. His attributes were later transferred to Satan.

TLINGIT INDIANS As recently as 1957 several members of the Tlingit tribe of Indians living at Angoon, on Admiralty Island off the coast of Alaska, were accused of practicing witchcraft. A child's death was the occasion for a sequence of magic rites. Cats and dogs were burned in sacrificial ceremonies, while two young Indian girls were beaten with 'devil clubs.'

TOADS Witches were especially fond of toads, pampering them as if they were children and dressing them in scarlet silk and green velvet capes for the celebration of the Sabbat. They wore bells around their necks and were baptized at the Sabbat. They were supposed to have in their heads stones which changed color in the presence of poison and could be used as an antidote against it. Pierre Delancre says that a witch ordinarily was attended by several demons. These demons sat on her left shoulder. Having assumed the shape of a two-horned toad, they were visible only to those familiar with witchcraft.

TOBO In Gnostic writings, a mysterious being who carries the soul of Adam from Orcus to the place of life.

TOIA An evil spirit worshiped by the Indians of Florida.

TOLEDO According to Michelet, Toledo was the Holy City of sorcerers and sorceresses. Their association with highly civilized Jews and Moors enabled them to form at Toledo a sort of university of their own.

TO MEGA THERION Greek words meaning 'The Great Beast.' Aleister Crowley, who claimed to be the Beast, often signed himself 'The Beast 666' or TO MEGA THERION.

TORNAIT Among the Eskimos of Greenland, various spirits who help the medicine man. In Alaska, they are usually evil and harmful; there they are known also as the Half-People, the Wanderers, or the Mountain Giants. They are controlled by more powerful agents.

TORTURE A witch generally could not be executed unless she confessed her guilt under torture. The first stage of torture, called preparatory torture (*question préparatoire*), was designed to force a confession. It consisted mainly of threats, including the viewing of the torture chamber. Final torture (*question définitive*) consisted of the ordinary torture followed by the extraordinary torture (*question extraordinaire*). The strappado generally was employed for the ordinary torture, and squassation for the extraordinary torture. The purpose of the final torture was to force the accused to name accomplices.

Other methods of torture included piercing the tongue of the accused, forcible feeding on herrings cooked in salt, thrusting knotted clouts down the throat of the victim and pulling them up again with a string, denial of water, immersion in hot salt water containing lime; the wooden horse, many kinds of racks, the wheel, the heated iron chair, leg vises, and thumbscrews; and pouring hot water or molten lead into the boots of the accused.

TOVODUN The gods of the ancient Dahomeans. The name contains the root of the word *vodun* (voodoo).

TRANSMIGRATION The belief that the soul passes at death into another body figures prominently not only in Buddhism, Jainism, Ajivikas, and the great sects, but also in the Orphic mysteries.

One of the basic tenets of the mystery cult of Orpheus was a belief in the transmigration of the soul. The Orphic cult promised union with the divine agent and a permanent liberation from the prison-house of the body. See Metempsychosis.

TRANSVECTION The flight by night with the aid of a broomstick, a cleft stick, a distaff, or even a shovel, was a salient feature of witchcraft. Transvection was first illustrated in Ulrich Molitor's *De Lamiis* (1489). Here three witches are shown riding through the air on a long forked stick. One has the head of an ass, another that of a bird, and the third that of a calf.

TRATTI DI CORDE See Strappado.

TREE OF LIFE In cabalistic teachings, the Tree of Life represents the underlying pattern of the universe and its fundamental unity. It is a model of God, the universe, and man. It consists of three triangles containing two opposing forces together with a third force which balances and reconciles them, plus one remaining sephira at the bottom.

TRENT, COUNCIL OF Called in 1545 to define the teaching of the Catholic Church on a number of issues that Protestantism had raised, the Council of Trent affirmed that the Devil has dominion over death:
> Let him be anathema who does not admit that the first man, Adam, after having transgressed God's commandment, in the earthly paradise, immediately lost his holiness and the justice in which it had been established, and incurred . . . death, with which God had previously threatened him, and with death, captivity under the dominion of him who, from that instant ever after, had dominion over death, that is to say the Devil.

TREVES Site of several witchcraft trials. Five witches were burned by Father St. Maximim in 1572. Johann von Schonenburg persecuted Protestants and witches there between 1581 and 1589. Flade, the civil judge, was too lax and was put to death as a witch. Father C. Loos protested Flade's execution and was exiled. Peter Binsfeld was in full control during the climactic years of the witch hunters (1587-1594), when fifteen hundred persons were brought to trial.

TRIAL BY WATER See Swimming.

TRIBULAT BONHOMET See Villiers de l'Isle-Adam.

TRICKSTER In many primitive societies the supreme god is generally assumed to have created a world without regard to good or evil, then to have withdrawn and left its operation dependent on spiritual energy supplied by human effort. Evil enters the world through human effort. Evil enters the world through human selfishness or through a trickster who perverts the system bequeathed to man by the supreme god. Only a trickster, or fate as he is often called, can explain disaster in the absence of selfishness.

TRIGLAV The triune deity of the Slavs. He was the chief god of the Slavs inhabiting the Elbe and Oder regions. He seems to fit Dante's portrayal of Dis.

TRITHEMIUS, JOHANNES German abbot (1462-1516) and author of *Liber Octo Quaestionum*, which classifies demons. He is supposed to have exorcised the wife of Emperor Maximilian.

TROBRIAND ISLANDERS The natives of Kiriwina, in the Trobriand Islands, believe that when an individual dies, his *baloma* (soul) leaves the body and leads a shadowy existence in another world. The baloma, which is the main form of the dead man's spirit, goes to a neighboring island; but the *kosi*, an offshoot of the spirit, remains near the usual haunts of the dead man and may be seen or heard for a few days after his death. The kosi soon vanishes forever, but the baloma confronts and pays the Topileta or headman of the villages of the dead, and enters the village where he will live forever.

TROLL In teutonic religion, an earth demon or a personified nonhuman power.

TRUE BLACK MAGIC See Secret of Secrets.

TUCHULCHA The Etruscan demon of infernal tortures.

TUNRAQS Spirits controlled by an Eskimo shaman. If dispatched on an aggressive mission, they may turn against the shaman in case of failure.

TUREL According to the Book of Enoch, one of the leaders of the rebellious angels who swore allegiance to Samaiza.

TWARDOWSKY The Polish Faust. He had written the fateful pact with his own blood on an ox-hide. One day while he was astounding others with his feats, he was reminded by the Devil that the appointed hour had come. He first sought protection by approaching a sleeping infant, then surrendered when reminded that a gentleman cannot break his word.

TWIN MAINYU Twin Spirits used by Zarathustra to explain the origin of evil and the dual nature of the human mind.

TYPHON In Classical mythology, a hideous monster, father of Cerberus, the Chimera, the Sphinx, and other monsters. Later he is identified by the Greeks with the Egyptian Set.

TYPHON (TYPHOEUS) The most terrible of the Titans. In Greek mythology, he assumes the role of Satan. A powerful, wrathful symbol of evil, he used his forces to combat Zeus. Though he was struck by thunderbolts and imprisoned beneath a mountain, he continues to try to overturn the cosmos and destroy the hosts of heaven.
Like Satan, Typhon is associated with the serpent. He chose as his bride a half-woman, half-serpent, and he fathered many monsters — the Chimera, Cerberus and the Hydra.

TZITZIMITL Aztec deities who preside over evil. They descend as monsters from the sky to devour mankind whenever an eclipse of the sun occurs.

TZURUH In the Cabala, the divine prototype.

U

UBASTI Feline goddess, represented as a cat-headed woman in an Egyptian bronze statue.

UBU ROI A satirical drama (1896) in which Alfred Jarry explored the hidden propensities of evil.

UGLINESS The ugliness of witches is proverbial. Only Hans Baldung Grien and Albert Dürer painted attractive witches.

UKOBACK Lesser demon who keeps the fires of Hell burning.

UPUSAUT Wolf-headed or jackal-headed Egyptian god of the dead.

URAEUS In Egyptian religion, the sacred asp, symbol of immortality.

URAKABARAMEEL One of the leaders of the fallen angels, according to the Book of Enoch.

URIAN Satan or Leonard. In Germany he presides at the Sabbat on Brocken. He appears in this role in Goethe's *Faust*.

UROBOROS The tail-eating serpent, used by Greek alchemists to symbolize the unity of the sacrificer and sacrificed.

URTH See Norns.

USHEBTIS Egyptian figurines placed in the tomb of the deceased.

UTCHAT Amulet worn by Egyptians as a protection against evil forces. It is commonly called the Eye of Horus.

UTUKKU In ancient Mesopotamia, the spirit of one who had died. The utukku preferred ruins, graveyards, and desolate places. He was feared by the living.

V

VAECORDIA The Latin name for ligature. Guazzo's *Compendium Maleficarum* (1608) classifies this form of *maleficia* under seven headings:
1. When one partner is made hateful to the other.
2. When there is a physical separation of the partners.
3. When the emission of semen is prevented.
4. When the semen is infertile.
5. When a man's penis remains flabby.
6. When natural drugs prevent conception.
7. When the female genitals contract or the male organ retracts.

VALAFAR Duke of Hell. On good terms with robbers, he has the head of a thief and the body of a lion. He is one of three demons in the service of Sargatanas, brigadier general.

VALHALLA In Norse mythology, the abode of the slain. Dead warriors are served by the Valkyries.

VALKYRIES In Norse mythology, the beautiful daughters of Odin. They hover over the field of battle, choosing those to be slain and conducted to Valhalla. They were originally demons.

VALLIN, PIERRE A French witch who confessed on March 15, 1438, that he had surrendered himself to the Devil, dedicated to the Devil a six-months old child, caused storms, attended Sabbats, eaten the flesh of children, and had intercourse with a young succubus. He named ten living accomplices and four dead ones.

VAMPIRE A creature, sometimes a human being, that drinks human blood. The vampire may be the soul or reanimated body of a dead person risen from the grave. It roams by night, sucking the blood of sleepers.

VAMPIRISM In 1949, in London, a man was accused of vampirism. He confessed that he had murdered nine persons and drunk their blood. He was executed.

VARSAVARTI One of the favorite names of the Buddhist Devil. The name means 'he who fulfils desires.' In his capacity as Varsavarti, Mara personifies fulfilment of the triple thirst: the thirst for existence, pleasure, and power.

VASUS In Hindu mythology, the eight evil deities who attend Indra. They are personifications of cosmic phenomena.

VAUDERIE (VAULDERIE) A term derived from the Waldensian cult and used to designate the witches' Sabbat.

VAUDOISIE A term derived from the Waldensian cult and used to designate witchcraft in general.

VAUGHAN, DIANA An American woman credited by Dr. Bataille with revealing the secrets of a palladian triangle (women's Masonic lodge) in New York. See Bataille.

VAUTRIN Satanic character in Balzac's *Old Goriot*.

VELLADA Ancient German priestess, mentioned by Tacitus.

VENFICA A witch who uses philtres and poisons.

VERNON Town in Normandy where women were burned in 1566, charged with having changed themselves into cats.

VERRINE One of the demons who possessed Louise Capeau. See Aix-en-Provence.

VERTHANDI See Norns.

VERVAIN A common plant which is widely supposed to have the power to ward off demons.

VERVER Occult signs made with cornmeal by the voodoo priest. The verver are made on the ground in sacred places where tables are set up, heaped with food for the *loa*.

VETALA In India, a special class of demons or vampires.

VIDUUS A Roman deity who separated the soul from the body at the instant of death.

VIGNY, ALFRED DE French Romantic poet who sought to rehabilitate Satan. In 1824, according to his *Journal*, he planned to write a poem describing the redemption of Satan.

VIKODLAK A Slavic expression for vampire.

VILE (SAMOVILE) Slavonic spirits that control the destinies of man. *Zracne vile* are evil spirits; *pozemme vile* are earth-dwelling spirits that give good advice; and *dopovne vile* are water-spirits.

VILLIERS DE L'ISLE-ADAM French writer, author of a collection of Satanic tales, *Les contes cruels*. (1883). Jean Marie Marthas Philippe Auguste, comte de Villiers de l'Isle-Adam (1838-1889) created the despicable hero of evil for evil's sake. *Tribulat Bonhomet* (1887) personifies the sadistic enemy of beauty, liberty, and life itself. 'The killer of swans' is the predecessor of Jarry's bestial drama, *King Ubu*.

VINTRAS, PIERRE Nineteenth-century French occultist. He announced that he was a reincarnation of Elijah and founded a mysterious sect, the Work of Mercy, which boasted a collection of miraculous communion wafers. Eliphas Levi examined the bloody hosts and concluded that they bore the markings of the Devil. After Vintras died in 1875, the sect was led by a defrocked priest, Abbé Boullan.

VISCONTI, GIROLAMO Fifteenth-century Italian professor and Dominican provincial of Lombardy. He wrote his *Little Book of Witches* about 1460, preparing the ground for acceptance of the *Malleus Maleficarum*.

VISHAVASU In Hinduism, a mystic fire. It is linked to the beginning of the dissolution of the universe.

VJESHITZA Female sprite with flaming wings. She crawls over the bellies of sleepers, suffocating them or driving them out of their minds by her lascivious caresses.

VOODOO A cult originating in African religious practices and popularly identified with witchcraft in the West Indies and parts of the United States. Voodoo ceremonies, derived from Dahomey, center around the idea of propitiating the *loa*. Offerings to the loa, gods whose desires must be satisfied by the cultists, may take the form of a lighted candle, food, or water. They may be made by an individual or, if more elaborate ceremonies are required by the *hungan* (voodoo priest). Despite persistent efforts to eradicate it, voodoo has survived for three centuries in its New World setting.

VRITRA In Vedic mythology, the leader of the demons, generally represented as a serpent or dragon.

Three Old Wives in Battle with the Devil
Daniel Hopfer

WAGNER, RICHARD The German composer who created the modern musical drama also brought back to life the forgotten world of dragons and demons that constituted an important part of the racial mythos of the Third Reich. Inspired by the Siegfried legend and the Norse myths, Richard Wagner (1813-1883) created works designed to promote a social and aesthetic revolution.

WALDER, SOPHIE Dr. Bataille claimed that Sophie Walder had been commissioned to spread Satanic Freemasonry in Switzerland. He revealed the details of her conversion to Christianity and of her account of the secrets of Freemasonry. See Bataille.

WALHALLA See Valhalle.

WALKYRIES See Valkyries.

WALPURGA (ST.) The chief festival of witches in Germany was celebrated on the Eve of St. Walpurga, or Walpurgis Night. St. Walpurga moved from England to Germany in the eighth century. There she was an abbess.

WALPURGIS NIGHT One of two main festivals of the Druids, celebrated on the night of April 30 in honor of Walpurga. It became the night of the witches' Sabbat par excellence. The great celebration was supposed to take place on the Brocken or some other high mountain.

WANDERERS See Tornait.

WANDERING JEW Sometimes associated with the Devil and the Antichrist, the Wandering Jew of medieval legend was credited with visiting the major cities of Europe in the sixteenth century. The legend teaches that he had taunted Jesus on the way to the crucifixion and been told to 'go on forever till I return.' In 1228 an Armenian archbishop had brought to England the report that the Wandering Jew, who was named Joseph Cartaphilus, was living in the Orient. In 1599 a rumor spread through Europe that the Antichrist had been born at Babylon. The Wandering Jew, now known as Ahasuerus, was supposed to die when Christ returned at last to the earth.

WARBOYS WITCHES Three persons were convicted of witchcraft at the conclusion of the most widely discussed trial in England before 1600. The convictions were based on charges made by the five daughters of a prominent resident of Warboys, Robert Throckmorton. The case is reported in *The Most Strange and Admirable Discovery of the Three Witches of Warboys*, a pamphlet published in London in 1593.

WATCHERS The legend of the heavenly Watchers, or 'Sons of God' who married the daughters of men, has its source in the Book of Enoch (3:3):

. . . The Watchers called me, Enoch the Scribe, and said to me: Enoch, thou scribe of righteousness, go, declare to the Watchers of heaven, who have left the high heaven and defiled themselves with women. . . .
'Ye shall have no peace nor forgiveness of sin.'

Thus the former prince of the heavenly spirits used his power to engender evil demons.

WAXEN IMAGES Small figures made of wax or clay, used by necromancers to inflict harm on the body of an enemy.

Belief in *maleficia* by means of waxen images is both primitive and universal.

WEALTH According to Nicholas Remy's *Demonolatria* (1595), demons guard vast treasures that lie hidden, yet cannot possess wealth in their own right.

WEIR, THOMAS Famous Scottish wizard, executed in 1670. His sister, Jane, was charged with him, for incest, sorcery, and consulting 'witches, necromancers, and devils.'

WEISHAUPT, ADAM Eighteenth-century German necromancer.

WEKUFE Evil spirits to whom the Mapuche Indians attribute the deaths of their kinsmen.

WENGWA In Gabon, a corpse that walks about like a living person.

WENHAM, JANE (d. 1730) The last woman to trial for witchcraft in England occurred in 1712. Jane Wenham, known as 'the wise woman of Walkerne,' was convicted by a jury of 'conversing familiarly with the devil in the form of a cat.' The judge obtained a reprieve, and the accused was pardoned.

WERET HEKAU An Egyptian expression used in magic. It means 'great' and applies to Isis in her aspect as goddess of magic.

WEREWOLF Among the many names given to the werewolf are these: Ghin-Grelin, Gerulg, Neure, Versipelle, and Ganipote.

WEST The ancient Egyptians considered the West to be the abode of the dead, whom they called Westerners. Isis was called the First of the Westerners.

WESTAM English village dating from the twelfth century. According to press reports, four persons celebrated a Black Mass in the local church in 1963.

WESTCOTT, WILLIAM MYNN Founder of the Order of the Golden Dawn, physician, authority on the Cabala, and Supreme Magus of the Rosicrucian Society in England. He resigned as Visible Head of the Order of the Golden Dawn in 1897.

WEYER, JOHAN See Wier, John.

WHEATLEY, DENNIS Contemporary English novelist whose books on occult and Satanic themes include: *The Ka of Gifford Hillary, Strange Conflict, The Devil Rides Out,* and *To the Devil — a Daughter.*

WHITE, JOHN Name given to the host in the Black Mass.

WHITE, MOLL An eighteenth-century English witch. She had a cat which was believed to have talked in English.

WHITE WITCHES Leaders of covens of suburban housewives consider witchcraft a pre-Christian faith. Some of them claim to be versed in ancient Celtic lore and to use their powers for good ends only. Like Louise Huebner of Los Angeles, they are contemptuous of satanic rites 'based on sexual perversions.'

WIER, JOHN Physician and tutor to the sons of François I. John Wier (1515-1588) wrote *De Praestigiis* (On Magic), published in 1563 and later revised and abridged as *De Lamiis* (On Witches). He made a distinction between harmless witches who worked no evil and wicked magicians who actually conspired with Satan. Also Johan or Johann Vierus or Weyer.

WILLIAMSON, CECIL A practicing sorcerer living in Bocastle, England. He is the proprietor of the Witches' House, said to be Europe's most extensive museum of black magic. He claims to have produced spirits by ritual magic. He describes their initial appearance as
> a little globular moisture, like a frog blowing bubbles. The globule keeps growing up to the size of a football. . . . As it expands, it takes on a glasslike, luminously blue appearance, and you see a human head forming inside.
> Eventually . . . , the head is full sized, and sometimes you even get speech from it. Often, the light becomes too dazzling for the eyes; then, suddenly, the globe is gone.

WISHART, JANET An Aberdeen witch, burned alive after she had been indicted for casting a spell on Alexander Thompson and performing other Satanic acts.

WITCH In England a witch is defined as 'a person who hath conference with the Devil to consult with him or to do some act.'

Now applied to a female magician, the term stems from the Old English word *wicca,* designating a male magician. A witch may appear to be young and beautiful but is actually old, repulsive, branded with the Devil's Mark and clothed in the Devil's Girdle. She eats human flesh, drinks human blood, fashions mannikins to represent humans, disrupts the forces of nature, is responsible for changelings, wreaks vengeance on those who scorn her, copulates with those she desires, summons the infernal hosts, and has recourse to a vast array of formulas, implements, and agents in conducting her goetic operations. Since witchcraft reached its apogee during the Middle Ages, many designations for witches are in Latin, the common literary vehicle: incantatrix, lamia, maga, malefica, saga, sortilega, strix, venefica.

WITCH-BURNING Throughout the Middle Ages and later, witch-burning was prevalent in Europe and America. Official records show that the practice was widespread until the eighteenth century.

Seven thousand witches were burned at Trèves, five hundred within three months at Geneva (1513), eight hundred at Wurzburg, fifteen hundred at Bamberg. During the reign of terror that encompassed all of Europe between 1300 and 1600, according to Michelet, everywhere the administration of justice was the same. Men were blinded and turned into cruel savages 'by the poison of their first principle, the doctrine of Original Sin.' If the innocent die, they die justly, by reason of original sin. Thus 'the judge is always sure of doing justice. . . . In every case the decision is a foregone conclusion.'

WITCHCRAFT, BOOKS ON See Books on Witchcraft.

WITCHCRAFT COVENS Circles of thirteen witches. According to a recent news item: witchcraft covens — circles of thirteen worshipping witches — exist in many major U. S. cities.

WITCH ELM The leaves of the witch elm, said to resemble a lightning flash, are used as talismans to locate hidden treasures.

WITCHES' BATH Ordeal by water, prescribed for those suspected of practicing witchcraft.

WITCHES' BROTH Made from the flesh of infants and men who had died by hanging, frogs, black millet, and magic powder, witches' broth enabled those who drank it to fly through the air.

WITCHES' HOUSE A museum housing an extensive collection of items associated with witchcraft and black magic. It is located in Bocastle, England. The proprietor is Cecil Williamson.

WITCHES' LADDER A knot used by witches to cause the death of a hated enemy. The string has nine knots and is hidden somewhere near the intended victim.

WITCH-HUNTING During the sixteenth and seventeenth centuries witch-hunting was prevalent in Europe and the United States. Lancashire was the locale of many investigations and trials in England. Salem became notorious as a result of campaigns against witchcraft in New England.

WITCH OF ENDOR King Saul, attacked by a Philistine army, sought advice from the Witch of Endor (I Samuel 28). She summoned the spirit of Samuel, his predecessor:
> And Saul perceived that it was Samuel, and he stooped with his face to the ground, and bowed himself.

The episode was widely discussed by seventeenth-century believers in witchcraft.

WITCH'S BRIDLE An iron instrument with four sharp prongs. Two prongs pressed against the tongue, two against the cheeks.

WITCH'S MARKS Protuberances for familiars to suck. Technically, they are the extra breasts or nipples possessed by rare individuals.

WIZARD A male witch.

WORK OF MERCY A mysterious sect founded by Pierre Vintras and led, after 1875, by Abbé Boullan. Members of the sect performed ceremonious Unions of Life, or ritual copulations. They believed that the sex act could be humanity's pathway to God.

WORLD Satan is referred to as the Prince of this World and as the God of this World. The Church Fathers, recognizing the close ties between sinners and Satan, regarded the world as the 'mystical body' of Satan.

WORSHIP OF SATAN According to William of Paris' twelfth-century *De Legibus*, Satan appears in the form of a black cat or a toad and demands kisses from his adherents: 'one abominable kiss, under the cat's tail, the other, a horrifying one, in the toad's mouth.'

WRAITH An apparition or double closely resembling its prototype and supposed to be an omen of death.

WROUBEL, MICHAEL ALEXANDER Russian artist. The image of Satan as a defeated hero obsessed Michael Alexander Wroubel (1856-1910). Before he began to be persecuted by this image, he had completed important works, inspired by ancient Byzantine art. After he started drawing and painting Lucifer against various backgrounds, his creative powers left him.

WYRD In Teutonic mythology, the goddess of death.

XAPHAN Lesser demon. At the time of the rebellion of the angels, he suggested setting fire to Heaven. He kindles the fires of Hell.

XEZBETH Demon of lies, miraculous tales, and fanciful prodigies.

XIBALBA Among the Quiché Indians, the realm of the dead.

XILKA The first word in an ancient formula used to invoke malefic demons. The complete formula is *Xilka, Xilka, Besa, Besa.*

XIUHCOATL Aztec fire serpent. He accompanies Xiuhtecuhtli, the god of fire. He is the object of the Plumed Serpent cult.

XIUHTECUHTLI Aztec god of fire. Also called Ixcozauhqui.

XYLOMANCY Divination by casting sticks or twigs on the ground and interpreting their positions. Milfoil stalks were used by the Chinese in divination, giving rise to the elaborate system presented in I Ching.

Satan on His Throne
(N. Y. Public Library Picture Collection)

Y

YAMA See Yima.

YACHU A deity of the Apa Tanis. Himalayan tribesmen sacrifice a fowl to Yachu and Pila, expecting in return the release or escape of a prisoner of war.

YAKSHA In popular Indian folklore, a class of demons who devour men.

YAKU In the shamanistic religion of the Vedas, a diminutive Stone Age group living on the island of Ceylon, the *yaku* or spirits were considered to be dangerous. A yaka could possess a shaman during a dance and cause him to fall to the ground.

YAM In Canaanite religion, Yam is the Sea. He is in charge of the ocean, rivers, lakes, springs. His variant names are Ruler of the Stream and Leviathan. He is depicted as a dragon of hydra form.

YAWN The yawn is considered to be dangerous since it allows demons to enter the body. Danger may be averted by making the sign of the cross on the mouth with the thumb, just as one feels the desire to yawn.

Y CHING Chinese compilation of divinatory interpretations. Begun in prehistoric times, the collection was completed in the third century B.C. Also, I Ching.

YEATS, WILLIAM BUTLER Irish poet. William Butler Yeats (1865-1939) was a member of the Order of the Golden Dawn. His magical name was Daemon est Deus Inversus ('The Devil is God Reversed'). He was a frequent visitor in the Parisian household of Samuel and Moina Mathers.

YEKUM Demon who 'seduced all the sons of the holy angels' and persuaded them to descend to the earth to copulate with mortals (Enoch 68:4).

YESOD The balancing force between Netsah and Hod in Cabalistic teachings. It is the ninth sephira, the sphere of the moon, and is associated with the aphrodisiac mandrake. When the sephiroth are shown as a human body, Yesod is the genitals. It is the dark depths of the personality in which the true self lies buried.

YEZIDIS (YEZEEDEES) A sect comprising a number of Kurdish-speaking tribes in Armenia and the Caucasus who worship the Devil, known as Melek Taus and represented as a peacock. F. Nau collected and translated their sacred books into French (*Recueil de textes et de documents sur les Yézidis*, 1918). Also known as Yezdi. See Devil Worshipers.

YGGDRASILL (YGDRASIL) In Norse mythology, the giant ash tree which spread its branches over the whole world and above the heavens. Its roots extended into Niflheim, the deepest cavern of darkness, presided over by Hel, the queen of the dead.

YGGR In Norse religion, a variant name for the supreme god Odin.

YIDAMS In Tibetan mysticism, occult agents with diabolical associations.

YIMA In Persian mythology, the king of the dead. Also called Yama.

YIN The negative, female principle in Chinese speculative thought, magic, and divination. It is associated with darkness and evil.

YOMAEL According to the Book of Enoch, one of the leaders of the rebellious angels who swore allegiance to Samiaza.

YOUNG, ALICE The first witch executed in America. She was hanged on May 6, 1647.

The Art of Dying
Kachelofen, ca. 1497
Leipzig

Z

ZAHORIS Spanish wizards capable of seeing through objects and discovering hidden items, often by virtue of a pact signed with the Devil.

ZALMOXIS Among the Getae, god of the dead.

ZAMBRI In medieval Christian legend, the opponent of Pope Sylvester I (314-335). Zambri killed a fierce bull by whispering in its ear the name of the Jewish god (the Devil). The Pope restored the bull to life with the name of Jesus, proving the superiority of Christianity over Judaism.

ZARATHUSTRA Founder of a religious system based on a dualism embracing an eternal conflict between good and evil. The reformer, who flourished in the sixth century A.D., is also known by the Greek name of Zoroaster. His teachings are explained in the sacred writings known as the Zend Avesta.

ZARATUS OF MEDIA Ancient Chaldean sorcerer.

ZAVEHE According to the Book of Enoch, one of the leaders of the rebellious angels who swore eternal allegiance to Samiaza.

ZAZEL According to the Book of Enoch, one of the leaders of the rebellious angels who swore eternal allegiance to Samiaza.

ZEBULON In medieval legend, a magician associated with the Vergil cycle. He appears as Abulon, the one who provides the love potion, in Beaumont and Fletcher's *The Custom of the Country* (1619 or 1622).

ZEDECHIAS An eighth-century Cabalist who is supposed to have caused regiments of sylphs to appear publicly and to invite men to join them in their kingdom. The sylphs put at the disposal of their guests airships and the aurora borealis.

ZEHUT Early form of the name of the Egyptian god Thoth.

ZELATOR The second rank or grade in the hierarchy leading in occult teachings to the sphere of God. Certain practices established for the Zelator, who occupies sephira 10, the sphere of the moon, resemble yoga.

ZEPHAR Grand duke of Hell. According to John Wier, he induces men to practice pederasty.

ZERVANISM A heretical sect known to the Greeks as early as the fourth century B.C., and later partially incorporated by nascent Mithraism. According to the Zervanite heresy, infinite time is the originating principle of existence. It is prior to the dual principles of good and evil.

ZITO (ZITEK) A famous sorcerer who performed incredible feats in Prague about the year 1400. Some of his exploits later were attributed to Faust.

ZLATA ULICKA See Street of Gold.

ZLITO Fourteenth-century sorcerer, attached to the court of King Wenceslaus of Bohemia.

ZODIAC A branch of the occult arts based on the study of the sky, the stars, the planets, and their relations to each other. The signs of the zodiac mark the twelve compartments of the heavens. They are Aries, Taurus, Gemini, Cancer, Leo, Virgo, Libra, Scorpio, Sagittarius, Capricorn, Aquarius, and Pisces. The word zodiac may derive from Greek words meaning 'wheel of life.'

ZOHAK In the Zend Avesta, the personification of evil in the shape of a serpent.

ZOHAR A compendium of Jewish Cabalistic lore introduced into Spain in the thirteenth century by Moses de Leon, who ascribed the book to Simeon ben Yohai, a second-century rabbi. It is reputed to be the oldest extant treatise on the Hebrew esoteric religious doctrines. It contains a complete theosophy, treating of God, the cosmogony and cosmology of the universe, and other matters such as the soul, sin, and redemption.

ZOMBI A corpse which is presumed to move and act as if it were alive. In vodan (voodoo) cults, a human whose soul has been possessed by another person through evil magic and whose body is at the disposal of the magician. In West African voodoo cults, the zombi was the deity of the python. In the West Indies, the zombi is the snake god in the voodoo rite, a supernatural power capable of entering and animating a corpse. Many inhabitants of the West Indies believe that the dead can be returned to life and made to work as zombies, or mindless, mechanical beings.

ZOMBISM A cult of the West Indies, imported from West Africa. The rites, performed by the practitioners of voodoo, are centered around the cult of the zombi, the supernatural power that can reanimate the dead.

ZOOLATRY The cult of animals. Also called theriolatry.

ZOSMIMOS OF PANOPOLIS A third-century alchemist and non-Christian Gnostic. He was probably an adherent of the Poimandres sect and a follower of Hermes. In his treatises, he relates a number of visions combining pagan and Christian elements. He is the author of an encyclopedia of alchemy.

ZOTZILHA CHIMALMAN In Maya religion, the god of light and darkness. He lives in a cave and struggles against Kinich Ahau, symbolizing the eternal conflict between day and night.

ZUG See Strappado.

ZULUS The Associated Press reported on March 30, 1964, that witch doctors continue to play an important role in the lives of the Zulus of South Africa. Though the *Abathakathi* or enchanters are a dying breed, the *Isangoma* or witch doctors are expanding their clientele and numbering whites among their patients. They are consulted on many occasions: childbirth, sickness, rainmaking, foretelling the future, banishing evil spirits. The Isangoma bases his diagnosis of an illness on the pattern formed by bones which are cast on the ground by the patient. The profession is determined by the spirits of the Isangoma's ancestors. If, on their advice, a man embraces the profession, he must live as a hermit for two years and undergo many ordeals.

During his apprenticeship he is initiated into the secrets of witchcraft. To become a bona fide witch doctor he must kill with his own hands a huge python, eat its raw flesh, and participate in ceremonies marked by ritual dances and extending over a forty-eight hour period. One of the oldest witch doctors of Johannesburg, Nkayipi Dumisani, insists that bones never deceive the one skilled in reading them. Others blame the patient who casts the bones in case a diagnosis is wrong.

ZURICH EXORCISTS In February, 1969, six persons were convicted of causing the death of Bernadette Hasler, a Swiss girl of seventeen whom they believed to be possessed. The jury found that would-be exorcists had beaten the girl so severely that she died on the night of May 14, 1966.

ZWIMBGANANA In African voodoo cults, a creature raised from the dead due to the evil work of a witch. Natives rely on a plant, the *mbanje,* for protection. After seeing a zwimbganana or a witch, they quickly set fire to the plant and inhale the fumes.

Angel and Devil Disputing for a Soul
Detail of Court Scene, 1493/4, by Derick Baegert

www.ingramcontent.com/pod-product-compliance
Lightning Source LLC
Chambersburg PA
CBHW032031150426
43194CB00006B/238